APOCALYPSE RECALLED

The Book of Revelation after Christendom

Harry O. Maier

Fortress Press
Minneapolis

Scripture is from the Revised Standard Version of the Bible, copyright © 1946, 1952,
1971 by the Division of Christian Education of the National Council of the Churches
of Christ in the USA. Used by permission.

Cover art: *Explosion* (1917) by George Grosz. Oil on composition board, 18 7/8 x 26
7/8 in. Gift of Mr. and Mrs. Irving Moskovitz. (780.63) Digital Photo © The Museum
of Modern Art/Licensed by SCALA/Art Resource, NY. ©Estate of George
Grosz/Licensed by VAGA, New York, NY. Used by permission.

Frontispiece:
Saint John the Evangelist on the Island of Patmos (c. 1618) by
Diego Velazquez (1599–1660), oil on canvas, 135.5 x 102.2 cm.
National Gallery, London. Used by permission.

Poem on page 207 excerpted from "They Have Threatened Us with Resurrection,"
by Julia Esquivel. From *Threatened with Resurrection,*
© 1982, 1994 Brethren Press, Elgin, Illinois. Used by permission.

Cover and interior design: Zan Ceeley

Library of Congress Cataloging-in-Publication Data

Maier, Harry O.
Apocalypse recalled: the Book of Revelation after Christendom / Harry O. Maier.
p. cm.
Includes bibliographical references and index.
ISBN 0-8006-3492-6
1. Bible. N.T. Revelation—Criticism, interpretation, etc. I. Title.
BS2825.2 .M335 2002
228'.06—dc21   2002072449

06   05   04   03   02   1   2   3   4   5   6   7   8   9   10

APOCALYPSE RECALLED

"Maier reads the Book of Revelation reading Maier. He lets its ancient witness to an anti-imperial Christianity reread Christian life in the current empire of globalization. In this adventurous return to an Apocalypse we never left, Maier captures the subversive excitement of the text. His own writing is lively with popular culture and personal anecdote, rich in its transdisciplinary scholarship, prophetic but never heavy-handed in its 'cruciform irony.'"

—CATHERINE KELLER
Professor of Theology, Drew University
Author of *Apocalypse Now and Then* and *The Face of the Deep*

For Faith, Kristoff, Stefan, and Lukas

and for Emil Maier (1904–1945?) in memoriam

Nah ist
Und Schwer zu fassen der Gott.
Wo aber Gefahr ist, wächst
Das Rettende auch.

—Friedrich Hölderlin, *Patmos*

Near
And difficult to grasp is God.
But where danger lies,
Deliverance also grows.

Contents

Preface

Of all the books of the Bible, the Book of Revelation is probably the one that most of us would rather live without. Its strange characters and symbolism, its violent sequences of blood and death and war, its threats of judgment and eternal damnation make of Revelation a horrifying, bewildering, and confusing text. If this were not off-putting enough, the invocations of Revelation for manipulative ends by wild-eyed television evangelists, Christian sects, and leaders of religious cults argue for its best being left to religious fanatics and the weak-minded. In mainstream churches, one rarely hears sermons on the Book of Revelation. In fact, one rarely hears from it at all: the Revised Common Lectionary—the list of Scripture readings appointed for Sunday worship in mainstream North American churches—includes Revelation a bare half-dozen times. The response of mainline Christians and their churches has been largely to ignore the Book of Revelation altogether, even to refuse to read it on principle. Some argue that its very presence in the Bible is immoral.

This leads to a peculiar paradox. For, although mainstream Christians are happy to ignore the Book of Revelation, no other biblical writing captures the popular secular imagination more than the Apocalypse. Television shows like *The X-Files* and movies like *The Matrix*, not to mention popular books like the best-selling *Left Behind* series by fundamentalist authors Tim LaHaye and Barry B. Jenkins (a fictional account of the end of the world as foretold in the Bible's last book), indicate the hold of Revelation on popular culture. Opinion polls indicate that the majority of North Americans believe that Revelation is a prediction of an inevitable calamitous end to human civilization. At least one American president, Ronald Reagan, believed that his was the last generation before Armageddon. An astute reader of shared religious sentiment, when governor of California he publicly invoked and praised the theological perspectives of Hal Lindsey's *Late Great Planet Earth* (a fundamentalist charting out of the end of history as allegedly predicted by Revelation and other biblical apocalypses), thus reinforcing the popularity of Revelation and fueling the endtime speculation for which it is so well known. While apocalypse speculation convinced Ronald Reagan that America was a nation set aside to be a light of political righteousness in a divinely appointed historical conflict against Communism, Revelation has also given birth to more troubled citizens. Ron Powers, in an article in the March 2002 *Atlantic Monthly*, tellingly entitled "The Apocalypse of Adolescence," reports that many North American teens spend a good deal of their time reading the Book of Revelation. More chillingly, he argues that the nihilism that leads otherwise well-adjusted upper-middle-class American children to perpetrate acts of extreme violence is inspired by a habitual reading of Revelation violence and destruction. Given the hold of Revelation on people as diverse as American presidents and teens who commit mass murder, as well as its prevalence in popular media, it is peculiar that Revelation should be so ignored in North American mainstream churches. From religious traditions that pride themselves on social relevance and critical thinking about culture one would expect the opposite.

It is the thesis of this book that the Book of Revelation is not only worth studying in depth but, more importantly, that it forms an indispensable resource for helping first-world Christians conceive of their place in the contemporary world and meditate on the role the church is to play in a modern secular society. This is so because from start to finish the Book of Revelation is a call to Christian discipleship. It crafts a sober appraisal of faithful religious identity when the state oversteps its bounds and encourages its citizens to idolatry. The Book of Revelation, most probably written near the end of the first century c.e., is preoccupied with a call to faithful witness to God in the face of the military dictatorship and tyranny of the Roman Empire. While historically it has fueled endtime speculation, it has also been a resource for critical appraisal of the state, the relationship of Christians to political culture, and the place of Christian witness in society. John challenged the origi-

nal audience of his Book of Revelation to think critically about their
political culture. In particular, he exhorted his audience to look carefully
at the economic order of the Roman Empire and the human and ecological misery it unleashed on the world as antithetical to the intentions of
God for humankind and creation. John demanded that his audience
reassess its political and economic allegiances and offer a pointed counterimperial witness in faithfulness to the victim of Roman imperial domination, the crucified Jesus of Nazareth.

I argue in the chapters that follow that this is as timely a message now
as it was then. For, like John's original audience, contemporary first-
world Christians are being encouraged toward idolatry. Daily we are
invited to worship at the altars of consumerism, to champion the expan-
sion of an empire of global capital, to seek security behind walls of military might, to pursue ideals of greed and selfishness at the cost of
environmental degradation and destruction. Like John's audience we
are increasingly faced with a choice—to be citizens who participate in
empire blithely uncritical or studiously unconscious of the suffering it
daily unleashes on the world, or to seek a more costly way in testimony
to an alternative construction of our social and planetary order. If there
were ever a biblical writing that urged a critical appraisal of society, Revelation is surely the one. If there were ever a time for Christians to think
critically about empire and its costs, it is now. Revelation is the book of
the hour.

It should be obvious by now that this is not a book that speculates
about the end of the world. Readers who want to know who the
Antichrist is or how America fits into the end of the world should look
elsewhere. To be sure, subsequent pages of this book imply a kind of
world-ending discipleship. That is to say, the book urges Christians to
live out an ending to greed and selfishness and to discover a new vision
of civic identity centered in the religious particularity of the Christian
story, one that interrupts and renounces the forms of violence, greed,
and despair that lessen us as human beings. The book encourages a
postliberal vision for a socially engaged religious identity in an irreli-
gious, secular, pluralistic society. In that sense the book urges an eschatological commitment—a commitment to living endings. But it does not
anticipate any inevitable ending to history other than that which must
surely come if present destructive courses of action are not ended or
significantly delimited. Thus, far from reading Revelation as though it

contained the headlines of tomorrow's newspapers, I rather insist on a reading centered in a Christian response to today's headlines.

In what follows I assume that the Book of Revelation is best interpreted as an expression of a genre of literature common in antiquity. What has in time become a book to map out an ending to history was not originally intended to be read in that way. I am assuming a broad consensus of academic biblical scholarship that John self-consciously chose the literary medium of an apocalypse to drive home the urgency of his exhortations and admonitions to his listeners. Revelation shares a set of literary properties with other Newer and Older Testament apocalypses and apocalyptic literature—most notably Mark 13, 1 Thess. 4:15—5:11, and the Book of Daniel—as well as several extracanonical Jewish and Christian apocalypses roughly contemporary with it. The features of this literature include numerical symbolism, otherworldly journeys, cosmic battles between God and God's enemies, visions, portraits of judgment and beatitude, angelic messengers, and a periodized notion of history that is interrupted by divine interventions. Whatever John's experiences on the island of Patmos, it is an inescapable observation that his Revelation bears a striking resemblance to other contemporary apocalypses. Consistent with that observation is the corollary that he quite possibly chose the literary form of an apocalypse in order to make his message more dramatic and urgent.

That message has usually been interpreted as one of comfort. In fact, it is often assumed that apocalypses generally are composed against a backdrop of human suffering and disappointed hope. On the more traditional account, apocalypses seek to overcome the despair associated with human suffering by an appeal to an imminent future in which God will intervene to vindicate the faith threatened by the harsh disconfirming experiences of sorrow and loss. While some ancient apocalyptic literature probably functioned to offer comfort and to shore up disappointed hope, ancient apocalypses were also written to warn the indolent of coming judgment, to critique political abuses of power, and to call for repentance in the face of imminent divine judgment. My reading of Revelation departs from the general scholarly consensus that Revelation was written as a means to comfort churches suffering religious persecution under the Roman Empire. What evidence exists for Roman imperial suppression of the ancient church indicates that persecution was relatively rare and sporadic. In what follows I argue that, while some of

John's audience may have been suffering imperial persecution, Revelation's overwhelming preoccupation is not to comfort the persecuted but to challenge Christians who are too enthusiastic supporters of the economic and military might of the Roman Empire. The problem the Apocalypse addresses is not too much persecution, but too little. As a means toward a hortatory end, John offers an apocalypse. That is, as the Greek cognate suggests, Revelation presents an "unveiling"—of empire, domination, military tyranny, and idolatry. As such, it is prophetic—not in the sense of a foretelling of the future, but as a form of *forthtelling* of a set of truths and realities hidden and obfuscated by Roman imperial propaganda. Revelation is an unveiling of political realities and a call to live a form of counterimperial religious resistance.

In what follows I argue that John uses all of the literary, theological, and political resources available to him to urge his audience not to be swept away by Roman imperial slogans promising peace and security, but to live a counterimperial identity in faithfulness to Jesus Christ. The majority of the chapters that follow seek to identify the hortatory strategies John used to drive his point home—a point that has an enduring relevance for anyone seeking to reflect critically on Christian discipleship in the face of forms of imperial domination, whether they be those of the Pax Romana, or of the Pax Americana. Thus, while the Apocalypse is usually interpreted as a series of theological snapshots of otherworldly realities, in what follows I offer a reading of Revelation rooted in this world. Indeed, one of the chief arguments of this book is that an otherworldly reading of John's Apocalypse is a fundamental misreading of Revelation. Preoccupied with a call to faithful witness, Revelation offers a portrait of this-worldly discipleship and Christian commitment. If it leaves the future to God, it invites consideration of a present filled with the sounds of faithful testimony to its counterimperial hero, Jesus.

When I first set out to write this book, I intended a sociopolitical charting of networks of patronage linking tradespeople and the imperial cult in first-century Asia Minor.[1] Books, however, have a way of taking on a life of their own, and this one quickly began to grow in unanticipated directions. At an early point of my research, Virginia Burrus—an unusually astute reader—noticed that my thinking about the Book of Revelation

bore an uncanny resemblance to things I had been telling her about growing up a son of German immigrants. At a key point she urged me to step
back from exegetical preoccupations to consider how my social location
was leading me to read Revelation as a series of exhortations centered in
questions of sociopolitical identity. The result was a fundamental reworking of my initial project and the attempt to wed exegesis with autobiography so as to come to a fresh reading of Revelation at once exegetical,
theological, and consciously political.

It was also the birth of a title—*Apocalypse Recalled: The Book of Revelation after Christendom*. "Apocalypse Recalled" expresses the temptation of the mainstream churches to "recall" the Apocalypse from the
shelf of Christian faith, as though it contained a manufacturer's defect—
a temptation I urge Christian readers to resist. More important, it
expresses a call to memory and the reminder that John's Revelation is
framed as a narrative reminiscence, which in the course of exegesis
prompts my own "memory work" as I recall my family's memories of
lived Apocalypse in 1945. The subtitle—"The Book of Revelation after
Christendom"—expresses the exegetical and theological task at the conclusion of modernity, when overarching and abiding appeals to be
thoughtful, humane, and ethical beings no longer exist or are swept away
in favor of appeals to be greedy, acquisitive, and inhumane. Recalling
Apocalypse after Christendom, I argue, furnishes Christians with the
warrants for and means of being ethically governed humans committed
to discovering in religion the resources necessary for more humane
forms of this-worldly living.

I have wondered more than once whether I am smart or shrewd
enough to write a book like this, and I am by no means convinced that I
have pulled it off. I have tried to offer a reading of the Apocalypse "from
this place," that is, a reading that repeatedly returns to context, social
location, and politics to inform what I hope are exegetical insights and
theological and political analysis.

Autobiography can be the last refuge of a scoundrel—narcissistic,
even solipsistic, and I am not certain that I have successfully avoided
these vices. Nevertheless, through an autobiographical exegesis, my
intent has been to show that, given the inescapable hold of the Book of
Revelation on our culture, we have no choice but to try to make sense of
it. How we do so will, I argue, always be inextricably tied to our own
autobiographies and sociopolitical locations. The chapters that follow

chart my own journey into the Apocalypse and how my family's experiences as German refugees in 1945 and their subsequent immigration to Canada have helped to shape me, for good or ill, to be a reader of the Book of Revelation and an interpreter of contemporary culture. The book may be read as an invitation to readers to consider the personal and societal forces that predispose them to interpret this perplexing and bewildering book and what effect those forces have in forming a particular kind of civic identity. Not all the topics that I discuss will have an immediate resonance with all readers—and some readers will notice glaring omissions: there is, for example, no extended discussion of gender and the Apocalypse. Autobiography, like exegesis, is selective. I have written about what I think I know, and I have chosen a judicious silence with respect to what I do not know. Hopefully there is enough here to prompt critical reflection on a variety of topics, not all of which are directly addressed in what follows.

I have been blessed with numerous colleagues and friends, without whose contributions, remarks, and personal encouragement this book would not have been possible. I owe an enormous debt to Karen VanderMeulen and Philip Harrison, who pored over earlier versions of my manuscript and saved me from glaring errors and stylistic infelicities. My thinking has been challenged and deepened through conversations with Anabaptist theologian and peace activist Anita Fast, a dear and trusted friend. Paul Quist was particularly helpful in revisions to chapter 2; David Ourisman helped to save chapter 3 from anachronism by inviting me to relate the Apocalypse to ancient literary theory outlined in Aristotle's *Poetics;* Chris Shultis and Scott Gould offered valuable feedback and insights for the conceptualization and revision of chapter 4. Wes Howard-Brook read an earlier draft and urged me toward a more politically focused autobiography. Lloyd Gaston and Daniel Boyarin have been encouraging readers. Special thanks go to Sallie McFague for her enthusiasm for my ideas and for urging me to seek a home for my manuscript at Fortress Press. Without Virginia Burrus's prompting and insight I would never have journeyed along the difficult way of Apocalypse recalled. Over the several years that have gone into conceiving and writing this book, my students at Vancouver School of Theology, through their excellent questions and exegetical insights, have contributed richly to my reading of Revelation. I am thankful for their patience with a professor struggling to find the words and categories to describe what I think the Apocalypse is finally about. In particular I am indebted to Rose-Hannah Gaskin, Douglas Scott, and Matthew Senf.

I am grateful for the financial support of the Alexander von Humboldt Foundation, which helped to fund a sabbatical year of study at Ruprecht-Karls-Universität Heidelberg; and to my faculty colleagues at Vancouver School of Theology who faithfully took up my share of administrative responsibilities during my absence. Professor Gerd Theissen was a most gracious host and mentor for my research project. Fellow New Testament Humboldtians Peter Balla and Pieter Craffert were spirited seminar colleagues who offered critical and insightful comments on early drafts of the chapters and who urged me to a more balanced set of perspectives. Vicky Balabanski helped me recognize fundamental flaws in my treatment of the Apocalypse as political parody. Frau Heike Goebel and Dr. Gabi Theekötter helped make my family's stay in Heidelberg pleasant and memorable. The Jakobus Gemeinde Bibelkreis, especially Christiane Schadewald and Jürgen Meier, gave me much spiritual support. Christiane recognized the trauma inherent in Apocalypse recalled and became a source of profound encouragement.

Most important, I am thankful to Faith for her love and affection. It is one thing to write a book about the Apocalypse, it is another thing to have to live with someone doing so. Without her patience and love in the latter, the former would never have been possible. My journeys through apocalyptic time and space too often left me an abstracted husband and father, an absence Faith has borne with magnanimity and grace. Finally, it is relatively easy to read and write and speculate, but to live the daily round faithfully, abundantly, and courageously is the mark of a human being fully alive. For Faith, who by her example daily invites me to do the same, I give praise.

1

Apocalypse Troubles

I miss more than one thing in this book [of Revelation], and this makes me hold it to be neither apostolic nor prophetic. . . . There is one sufficient reason for me not to think highly of it—Christ is not taught or known in it. . . . I stick to the books which give me Christ clearly and purely.

—Martin Luther, preface to Revelation
in his 1522 translation of the New Testament

A CRISIS OF INTERPRETATION

Wherever the Book of Revelation shows up, trouble is not far behind. It is a menace to public safety. The Christian Crusades, Savonarola's reform of the Florentine Republic, Radical Reformation movements to establish earthly theocracies of the Spirit, the discovery and colonization of the New World, the violent Christianization of First Nations peoples—these troubling episodes name only some better-known flashpoints ignited by the Apocalypse's arrival.[1] In the Reformation, competing apocalyptic theologies that were sparking trouble around Martin Luther, especially among the German peasants, so troubled the Reformer that he resisted including Revelation in the canon. John Calvin positively excluded it.[2] Yet Luther's editors knew better. Immersed in the currents of popular apocalyptic expectation,

they furnished his 1522 New Testament with twenty-one full-page illus-
trations to accompany the Book of Revelation, the only biblical book
accompanied by a complete pictorial commentary. Not that Luther was
immune to the lure of endtime speculation, as his repeated denuncia-
tions of the pope as Antichrist suggest.[3] Borrowing fire from popular
apocalyptic sentiment, the Reformer forged together differing political,
economic, and religious elements to trouble his time. But he knew his
was not the only endtime scenario in which to fit contemporary events.
Luther's criticism of Revelation in 1522 (cited in the epigraph above)
indicates how nervous he was about how some were using the Apocalypse to fan flames of discontent among German peasants. Later, in his
preface to his 1530 and 1546 translations of the New Testament, looking
back over the charred ruins of the Peasants' Revolt, he offers more irenic
observations concerning Revelation and its canonical status, saving his
scorn for alleged "Enthusiast" misreadings of John's visions.[4] Like theologians before him who similarly used the Apocalypse to trouble the
times, he knew people got burned playing with Revelation's fire.

A nuisance to theologians, the Apocalypse has also stirred up trouble
in politics. The desire for an earthly realization of Jerusalem the Golden
(Rev. 21:1—22:5) fired English and French revolutionaries. In the United
States it fanned the flame of the American Revolution, the abolition of
slavery, and faith in Manifest Destiny.[5] John of Patmos's millennial
visions have sparked the imagination of utopian political agendas of all
stripes. Witness William Blake:

> And was Jerusalem builded here,
> Among these dark Satanic mills?
>
> Bring me my bow of burning gold!
> Bring me my arrows of desire!
> Bring me my spear! O clouds unfold!
> Bring me my chariot of fire!
>
> I will not cease from mental fight,
> Nor shall my sword sleep in my hand,
> Till we have built Jerusalem
> In this our green and pleasant land.

The antidote to William Blake's "dark Satanic mills" has been prescribed in movements as diverse as the Social Gospel idealism of the nineteenth and twentieth centuries, the National Socialist Third Reich, the Marxist worker state, and the global extension of democratic capitalism.

In a new millennium, Revelation continues to sound tonalities of resistance and utopian or dystopic arrival: postmodernism, post-structuralism, the "end of history," the "end of Christendom," even "after Christendom" (making a public nuisance in the subtitle of this study). What, after all, is left of a "poetics of post-modernism," to borrow a phrase from Linda Hutcheon, without the edginess of an apocalyptic announcement of modernity's end?[6] Jacques Derrida reaches for Apocalypse when he titles a state-of-the-union account of his discipline "Of an Apocalyptic Tone Recently Adopted in Philosophy."[7] One would not be exaggerating too much in claiming that the chronicle of Western history reads like an Apocalypse's *Who's Who*. Wherever there is historical trouble (or troubled historians, philosophers, and theologians), scratch the surface and you are likely to find the Apocalypse.[8]

It would be simplistic to see the Book of Revelation as the sole driving force in each of these instances. It would be imprudent to ignore it. The stories we tell and their roles in helping configure ourselves as actors on a historical stage are indispensable for furnishing sensibility to our brief sum of months and years. Such stories are as important as the rise and fall of monarchs, the victories and defeats of battle, the advent of new technologies, and the modes of production and patterns of trade. The Apocalypse has offered fertile earth for cultivating tales to feed the imagination and to motivate the behaviors and goals of those historical characters inhabiting both the mainstream and more marginalized Western traditions. If television ratings and box-office successes are anything to go by, the Apocalypse's soil is far from depleted. A secular version of the Apocalypse finds itself played out in nightly airing of conspiracy-theory entertainment, like the television hit *The X-Files*, and at the cinema in such films as the *Terminator* series.

In the last months of the twentieth century, the hold on the popular imagination of dystopic conspiracy-theory-laced entertainment was unveiled in the box-office windfall (at press time, two sequels were in the works) of *The Matrix*. The film expresses the Apocalypse-styled secularity of a postmodern world. The movie's protagonist, Neo Anderson (literally, "New Son of Man"—the title borrowed from the Little Apocalypse of Mark 13), leads an all-out messianic assault against FBI-like agents who are in fact guardians of an elaborate computer program ("The Matrix"). The Matrix creates a virtual world in which Americans are fooled into believing the illusion that they live in a democratic republic. In fact, American citizens are victims of a technological totalitarianism, literally farmed to feed an all-consuming machine. *Apocalypse* here means, as its Greek root suggests, "unveiling": following an end-time apotheosis and Armageddon battle, Neo Anderson (*aka* "The Chosen One") brings "The Operating System" crashing down and inaugurates a new age, in which the lies are stripped from the truth of the human condition and political despotism.

This is the box-office stepchild of the Apocalypse. Clearly, its writers/producers, Larry and Andy Wachowski, believe they have a message to preach: the film was released on Easter Weekend, 1999. The film's title track, "Rock Is Dead," by anarchistic transvestite rocker Marilyn Manson, played during the credits and set the tone for leaving the cinema and for bringing Apocalypse to the streets in a challenge of contemporary "operating systems" that hold the world in thrall to their illusionary disguises.

In fact, the Wachowski brothers have been getting what they have been asking for—but it is not resurrection. All too tragically in modern secular society, life imitates art. The power of an apocalyptic lens in which nothing is ever what it seems found itself enfleshed in the real-time tragedies of the bombing of the Federal Building in Oklahoma City and in the suicides of the apocalypticist David Koresh and his Branch Davidians in Waco, Texas. *X-Files* creator Chris Carter claims that, judging from the fan mail he gets, his conspiracy-theory episodes are the most popular. John of Patmos is at large and he is making trouble: "Am I putting ideas into people's heads?" Carter wonders. "Other groups out there right now who've made big news are saying they don't trust the government. I don't want people to confuse what I'm saying with that political agenda. And it's weird—a lot of people contact me saying they are or were 'in the loop.' There's an enormous number of conspiracy theorists out there, and they're trying to get me to tell their story."[9] Oklahoma City bomber Timothy McVeigh believed he was "in the loop." Under oath he testified that the U.S. government had implanted an electronic device in his buttocks to enable constant surveillance.[10]

The testimony of a young man in trouble? Indeed, troubled by the Apocalypse. In a mass culture in which we are urged by omnipresent media broadcasts to play out roles and narratives furnished by scriptwriters and advertisers, bringing virtual television apocalyptic scenarios to the street is not a big step. The Oklahoma bombers and the Branch Davidians are only more sinister versions of "Apocalypse on the streets." In a recent study, Wes Howard-Brook and Anthony Gwyther document the Apocalypse's influence on social phenomena as varied as near-death experiences, apparitions of UFOs and of the Virgin Mary, astrological predictions, and New Age prophecy. In some instances the parallels are so striking that Howard-Brook and Gwyther can tabulate parallels between reports of apparitions and altered states of consciousness and the Apocalypse.[11] These are popular expressions of millennialist hopes shaped by a culture in which the New Testament offers foundational cultural scripts. "We are in apocalypse," notes Catherine Keller, insisting upon the hold of the last book of the Bible on our collective imagination and societal expectations.[12]

In such a cultural situation, the same text means different things to different people. The Apocalypse is notorious for its excesses both of woe (lakes of fire, rivers of blood, beasts gorged on the valleys of the dead, ecological tumults) and of bliss (the tearless Jerusalem of eternal praise). Its unwieldy surpluses yield a jarring conflict of interpretations. This is what Stephen O'Leary distinguishes as the comic and tragic frame of Apocalypse. Deploying these phrases to explore Revelation's extremes, he accounts for the way the same biblical book gives rise to mutually exclusive interpretations of culture and history. A comic reading offers an open-ended future in which emphasis is placed on today's ethical decision as making a difference to the unfolding of tomorrow's world. Here the promises of Revelation's happier texts invite readers to imagine a history lured toward a happy ending, realized through careful politics. The comic frame greets doomsayers with skepticism and delights when prophecy fails and pessimistic apocalyptic timetables are overturned. The tragic mode finds in the Apocalypse's texts of woe a miserable end to human history, determined from the outset by an irreversible divine plan or tragic societal flaw. In this tragic perspective, political platforms to engineer the good society are either naïve or deceptive. Inevitable disaster may, however, be staved off through taking up the urgent call to repent.[13] Either view, however good or bad things really are, uses the Apocalypse to frame human experience, molding it to conform to its construction of the world. O'Leary's analysis of the effects of the Apocalypse in culture, religious or secular, shows how the same Book of Revelation gives birth to the most pessimistic and optimistic of children. "About this book of Revelation," Luther commented in the preface to his 1522 New Testament, "I leave everyone free to hold their own ideas."

Maybe Luther was making a virtue of necessity, playing wise uncle to John of Patmos's unruly offspring, who seek neither his approval nor permission. You can ground a teenager, but it's hard to keep him or her from sneaking out at night. Luther's apparent belief, changing the metaphor slightly, that one could solve the troubles springing forth from the Apocalypse's rich earth by putting Revelation's canonical authority into cold storage was as naive as it was short-sighted. In the Christian West a text as culturally formative as the Apocalypse can hardly be weeded from the Bible, especially after it has entered mainstream popular culture. The most one can hope for is pest control. As they have done with the Psalter, the compilers of the church's lectionary cycles (the cycle of biblical passages read in the churches of the historic confessions during Christian worship) have carefully expunged the Apocalypse of passages offensive to their respectable church-going hearers. Outside of liturgical texts, the regular Sunday worshiper listening to appointed lessons Sunday by Sunday can expect to hear from the Book of Revelation less than half a dozen times in the course of a year. The abridged lectionary version offers a gutted Apocalypse, lacking the famous blood and violence of the complete text—the hallelujahs without the woes; the promises without the threats; the victories without the blood.[14] The mainstream North American church may be the only place where the Apocalypse does *not* make trouble! Such a close eye is kept on John, the miscreant nuisance from Patmos, that he has to behave himself or get kicked out of the church altogether. Thus the church, surely a place where the full spectrum of the human condition in all its bloodiness could be addressed, whitewashes the biblical text. Ironically, an institution centered in the bloody crucifixion of a criminal finds itself playing into what Canadian sociologist Ernest Becker astutely described as a cultural "denial of death," shielding its members from the more unseemly features, indeed the very fact, of their mortality and the terrors that go along with it.[15]

This leaves average churchgoers who encounter the uncensored Apocalypse, either through popular media or from other Christian groups, treating it with bemused incredulity, thinking that it belongs to horror-movie aficionados or literal-minded Christians seeking veiled allusions to the headlines of tomorrow's news. Or if they pick the book up to see what all the fuss is about they discover themselves so offended by its rivers of blood, lakes of burning fire, and promises of pestilence and death to God's enemies that they refuse to read it on principle. In either case, the continuing importance of the Book of Revelation in culture is ignored or underestimated. Or its potential for critiquing contemporary culture is ignored, adopted by a few marginal voices that find in the Apocalypse's narratives a challenge to the dreams of a secularized capitalist New Jerusalem.[16] A premise of this book is that the Apocalypse makes trouble too important to ignore, and not all of it is bad—especially for mainline churches traditionally aligned with the governing establishment. This book will have accomplished its purpose if only a little of Revelation's trouble is let loose on the church, and its theologians help the bemused, puzzled, and offended find a way to negotiate its blacklisted texts.

THE OPEN WORK

Today, if you are looking for Apocalypse-style trouble anywhere near the mainstream church, you have to go to the academy. Behind closed doors (for example, at the annual meetings of the Society of Biblical Literature), you can still discover John making trouble. There, academics of all persuasions and confessions gather to debate, contest, defend, attack, measure, explain, analyze, poke, and prod the textual incarnation of John's apocalyptic imagination. These scholars find Revelation difficult to summarize. David E. Aune's commentary on the Book of Revelation, the crowning achievement of a lifetime of scholarship, is three volumes and some 1,500 pages in length. And this work only sums up the thousands of books, articles, and unpublished papers at his command.[17] The span of Aune's colossus is testimony that everything about the Apocalypse is disputable—date, provenance, authorship, purpose, literary form, social setting, theological meaning—even whether the Apocalypse is "apocalyptic"!

More positively, a cornucopia of conflicting and often mutually exclusive opinion awaits anyone wishing to sample the results of scholarly investigation of Revelation. There are as many readings of Revelation as there are readers. Here is a taste of various competing readings. David Aune, for example, argues that the final text of Revelation cannot be properly understood unless one interprets it as the product of a series of theologically differing sources clumsily stitched together by a later editor.[18] No, argues David Barr, insisting on the big picture: "It is easy to miss the most important thing for understanding the Apocalypse: it is a narrative."[19] Whether it is stitched or seamless, others like Tina Pippin, reading Revelation for its ideology and treatment of women, discover in John's vision of a raped and cannibalized whore of Babylon (17:16) "a misogynist fantasy of the end of time."[20] Another feminist interpreter, Elisabeth Schüssler Fiorenza, responds that such a reading of Revelation's gendered heroes and villains literalizes and reifies Revelation's rhetorically coded uses of gender categories and thus "negates the possibility of readers' ethical decision and resistance insofar as it does not leave a rhetorical space. . . to read Revelation 'otherwise.'"[21]

Theologians of the two-thirds world focus on Revelation's comforting of the oppressed. Thus Alan Boesak insists that "those who do not know . . . suffering through oppression . . . shall have grave difficulty understanding this letter from Patmos."[22] Costa Rican author Pablo Richard claims that "Revelation arises in a time of persecution—and particularly amid situations of chaos, exclusion, and ongoing oppression."[23] Liberationist-minded first-world exegetes, like Adela Yarbro Collins, interpreting more psychologically, read Revelation's vanquishing of God's enemies "as part of a process for containing aggressive feelings," to help Christians harassed for their faith and thus doubting their election as God's people to cope with dangerously anti-Roman sentiments.[24] John Gager, in a similar argument, argues that John's apocalyptic myth of Rome's demise helped persecuted Christians "overcome unwelcome contradictions between hope and reality, between what ought to be and what is, between an ideal past or future and flawed present."[25] Others, like Leonard Thompson and David DeSilva, contest such readings, arguing instead that John's problem was not that there was too much persecution, but too little: "Certainly, the attempt link the Book of Revelation with upheaval and crisis is wrong-headed."[26] "It is not an attempt of John the Seer to console the churches. . . . The Apocalypse is a social challenge to the seven churches to maintain their liminal status against the mounting external pressures."[27] Christopher Rowland, identifying

John's liberationist challenge to an imperial order, argues that Revelation "criticizes a political economy geared to the satisfaction of the fortunate minority at the centre of trade. It encourages suspicion of institutions, of our motives and the ongoing questioning of the character and extent of our involvement. . . . It questions what is widely assumed to be reasonable and realistic by offering a different perspective on what we understand by rationality."[28] Ron Farmer exegetes Revelation as a process theologian and discovers in John's visions of a conquering slain lamb and of faithful testimony overthrowing evil the celebration of a new kind of power in the world, one that "is persuasive not coercive, influencing not controlling, relational not unilateral."[29] Or Richard Bauckham in a more Evangelical vein champions Revelation's liberating impulses as anticipating a new world order to which the church bears prophetic witness even while persecuted by the beast. "In this period the powers of evil will do all they can to suppress the church's witness, but their very success in putting Christians to death will be the opportunity for the truth of the church's witness to prove its power to convince and to convert the nations."[30]

Keeping a more suspicious eye on Revelation's use of Roman imperial motifs, still others, like Stephen Moore and Robert Royalty, question whether the Apocalypse offers any liberation. Revelation's narrative urges its audience not to get mad but to get even. John "counter[s] the magnificent imperial cult with the image of a yet more magnificent heavenly cult (the latter modelled on the former) . . . result[ing] in a fascinating (con)fusion of figures, the Roman emperor coalescing with the Jewish-Christian God." John's "hypermasculine deity" is an imperial tyrant in Yahweh's clothing, contributing to a cultural construction of male gender as destructive to men as it is dangerous for women.[31] Resistance "to dominant [Roman imperial] culture in the Apocalypse is not an attempt to redeem that culture but rather an attempt to replace it with a Christianized version of the same thing. . . . The text creates a new culture of power that mimics the dominant ideology; only the names and labels are changed."[32]

Another set of interpreters seeks new readings by bringing the insights of cross-cultural anthropology and sociology to their interpretations. Contesting that John's churches were facing danger from an antagonistic empire, Philip Esler writes that the Apocalypse is the record of a witch hunt. "Rome is not, in fact, a source of any great difficulty for the

Christian communities of Asia at this time. Rather it functions in the cycle of myth created in the work as a scapegoat for problems that are largely internal to the seven congregations." By urging them to rally behind opposition to a common enemy and to purge themselves of false teachers alleged to be the devil's minions (2:6, 14-15, 20-23), John achieves "a socially functional displacement of aggression from troublesome insiders to an outsider sorcery figure—Rome."[33] Continuing in the cross-cultural vein, Bruce Malina complains of scholars who read Revelation "'indoors' apart from actual astral scenarios, as a purely literary phenomenon imparting a set of ideas. . . . The prophet John has his initial, ecstatic vision while considering the vault of the sky," he says. "John's visions derived from experience generally unavailable to human perception in a culture such as ours." So Malina claims, "John is an astral prophet. . . . [H]is prophecy was rooted in reading the sky. . . . Such prophets read the sky by means of observations, sky visions, and sky trips."[34]

Whose interpretation, which exegesis? These scholarly opinions could be multiplied many times. They reflect the state of academic biblical study in general, in which competing exegetical methods (in the above examples, historical, redaction, narrative, feminist, rhetorical, ideological, sociological/anthropological, and post-structuralist criticism) result in differing interpretations—often on the basis of the *same* texts! A century ago—coincidentally a more imperial age—there was exegetical harmony concerning Revelation, orchestrated by the leading historical-critical exegetes of the day. Today's interpretive voices offer a dissonant polyphony reflecting a post-industrial culture in epistemological crisis. One observer sardonically describes the exegetical chaos of the academy "as a state of seemingly stable if not actually permanent anomie."[35] A less elegant writer might say that exegetical discipline is out the window. I imagine John, now as miscreant student, slouching at the back of the class and smirking. Maybe he blows a spitball when the teacher turns to scratch on the blackboard how best to interpret his Apocalypse. He loves trouble. Or maybe his smirk masks a scowl at those who, as a result of the rigorous application of method, continue to add to and subtract from his text, flagrantly disregarding his warnings at tampering with it (22:18-19). John would put biblical exegetes out of a job. To write a book on the Apocalypse at the end of Christendom is to flirt with disaster. You can end up getting consumed by the Apocalypse's fire. "Surely we're all damned!" observes Tina Pippin. "Every interpreter—we are all adding to and subtracting from the book as we interpret, as we write alternative midrashim on it, as we struggle with its hard message."[36]

The range of Apocalypse interpretation arises from John's composition of an open work. Umberto Eco borrows from aesthetic theory the phrase "the open work" to describe the way art yields varieties of interpretation. While at a physical level a work of art is traditionally complete unto itself and closed (a musical score, a text, a canvas), at the same time it constitutes "an *open* product on account of its susceptibility to countless different interpretations which do not impinge on its unadulterable specificity. Hence every work of art is both an *interpretation* and a *performance* of it, because in every reception the work takes on a fresh perspective." Attending to a work's openness contests limiting texts to a single meaning or interpretation. It urges "performers" of texts to pay attention to how they bring themselves to interpretation, the ways in which they "supply [their] own existential credentials, the sense conditioning which is peculiarly [their] own, a defined culture, a set of tastes, personal inclinations, and prejudices."[37] It invites autobiography, a relative newcomer to the stage of exegetical performance.[38] When applied to biblical texts, Eco's observations challenge exegetical methods that seek a text's single objectively true meaning. Attention to one's "existential credentials" demands that interpreters come to terms with their own political interests and cultural background(s) and how these are implicit in any exegesis, rendering one's exegesis specific to a particular time and culture. As Fernando Segovia and Mary Ann Tolbert insist, exegesis and interpretation are always from a particular place.[39]

Above I referred in passing to an epistemological crisis that gives rise to competing, often incommensurable, readings of Revelation. The Greek word *krisis*, from which the English "crisis" derives, means judgment. Attending to the exegetical performance of a text means noticing how one comes to one's interpretive judgments concerning a text, why one privileges one set of meanings over another, the reasons one gives for placing one set of texts in the foreground and others in the background. It involves observing the processes and influences that enable one to "make sense" of a work that yields a range of meanings. For Revelation only makes sense if there are readers to supply a sensibility to John's sounds and visions of the end of the world. The crisis of interpretation I am describing wrestles with John of Patmos and risks coming away limping, but better for the competition, even with a blessing. "Blessed are those who read aloud the words of the prophecy" (Rev. 1:3). Such a crisis enacts two judgments—one on the text and its possible meanings, the other on oneself and community. The latter seeks a troubling interpretive performance—what Roland Barthes calls the "text of bliss": "the text that discomforts . . . unsettles the reader's historical, cultural, psychological assumptions, the consistency of his tastes, values, memories, brings to a crisis his relation with language."[40] It means allowing oneself to be troubled by John of Patmos without deciding in advance just what kind of trouble he brings. In chapter 2, I explore exegetical attempts to restore rhyme and reason to the New Testament's most discomfiting writing and John's refusal to occupy contemporary exegetical straitjackets. I discuss how his Apocalypse seeks to unsettle. For now, let us imagine our ecclesially ignored and censured John as a thief in the night, whose unexpected arrival leaves the clues of his advent everywhere.

Taking It Personally

This study of John's Apocalypse attends to the way my own existential credentials, my "defined culture, . . . set of tastes, personal inclinations, and prejudices," result in an idiosyncratic exegetical performance of the Book of Revelation, and how John of Patmos continues to break into my first-world context. In what follows I keep an eye on my social, political, and cultural position in order to engage in a two-way conversation with Revelation.[41] I note how that position leads me to be a particular kind of interpreter of Revelation, and the ways that Revelation shapes the cultural definition of my tastes, inclinations, and prejudices. In other words, I seek to understand the ways I read Revelation and how Revelation reads me. Such a two-way conversation is at work, most often unconsciously, in the interpretation of any text, but especially in a text as culturally formative as the Apocalypse. Here I want to bring that conversation to consciousness. My social location and set of autobiographical credentials are not yours; this study invites readers to identify their own cultural location, to understand the ways in which they both read and are read by Revelation. My interest, however, is not only to observe and record. Attending to such a two-way conversation of text and interpreter creates possibilities for cross-examination and critique.

The critical voice of Revelation is often muted by interpreters who read the Apocalypse as a word of comfort to those suffering persecution. I am not among them. My interest is in Revelation's word of challenge to a sleeping and culturally assimilated church. A little later I will describe what it would be to read Revelation "as a Laodicean," that is for its words of warning rather than of promise. Again, the critique is two-way; if text challenges context, context cross-examines text. Wedding sociopolitical critique with autobiographical exegesis, I explore the enduring relevance for good and for ill of Revelation. The marriage results in a difficult if not downright troubled love-hate relationship of text and interpreter. Such is the trouble John of Patmos brings. There is no reason to suppose he is going to make an exception here.

The place from which I read Revelation is that of a second-generation western Canadian; more particularly, that place brought into focus by my German family's memories of expulsion from Eastern Europe after World War II and emigration to Canada in 1950. In spite of the unease of my Lutheran tradition with the Book of Revelation, the Apocalypse furnished my family and its German immigrant community a means to make sense of and to express the loss of World War II, as well as to construct a new cultural identity as Canadian immigrants. All of this, in turn, shaped me to be an idiosyncratic reader of the Apocalypse.

In the winter of 1945 the world ended for ethnic Germans living in Eastern Europe. As the German army retreated before the Soviet advance, Eastern Europeans who had been terrorized and brutalized by their Nazi occupiers exacted revenge on the ethnic Germans whose ancestors had settled where they lived centuries before. By 1950, some fifteen million ethnic Germans had either fled or been expelled from Eastern Europe. Two and one-half million civilian Germans either died or went missing in the "ethnic cleansing" of Soviet-occupied Europe in the years immediately following World War II.[42]

My mother was twelve years old when on January 18, 1945, she and her mother, brother, and grandparents were given twenty-four-hours notice to load their possessions and evacuate their tiny village of Chodziez near the Warthe River in central western Poland.[43] The refusal of the Nazi regime to acknowledge the collapse of the eastern front and to accept the reports that the war was being lost translated into a complete lack of preparation for evacuating German civilian populations from the advance of the Soviet army. Only days before my mother's family was given the order to evacuate, German men, too old to fight on the eastern front, were busy digging anti-tank ditches to slow the Soviet advance. In evacuating, my mother's family joined a line of refugees that stretched westward as far as the eye could see. Independent descriptions confirm their accounts of this as a train of chaos, despair, death, and misery as people fled in panic for their lives. Less than two weeks later, the advancing Soviets intercepted the westward stream and, after pillaging the possessions of trapped refugees, ordered them to return to their villages.[44] My mother's family, after being stripped of all their possessions except for the clothes they wore and carefully concealed money, turned around and walked home. Here women and girls were raped, and men were beaten and murdered. Through propaganda and firsthand experience of the brutality of SS "occupation" detachments in Eastern Europe, occupying Soviet soldiers were convinced that civilian Germans were little more than dangerous animals to be tortured and liquidated. The family now stayed here, strangers in their own village, their property expropriated and handed over to Poles. Their new masters ordered the returning women to refill all those anti-tank ditches dug a fortnight earlier. My grandmother worked in a Soviet military camp as a virtual slave, suffering horrors she was never able to describe but which hung over her like a cloud of despair until her death. In December 1945, a carefully hatched plan resulted in my mother's family escaping occupied Poland for Soviet-occupied Germany.

Meantime, as my mother's family were fleeing their village of Chodziez, at 4 P.M. on January 19, 1945, ethnic Germans in Komorowo, near Konin, were also escaping the Soviet advance. Among them were my father, his older sister, toddler brother, mother, and grandmother. The Soviet army rolled into my father's farm less than twenty-four hours later. A week later, on January 24, my father's family too were captured by Soviet forces, robbed at gunpoint, and ordered to return home. My father was sixteen, the "man" of the house: his father had perished on the eastern front in 1944. In the preceding months he had ignored the whispered urging from retreating German troops to flee for his life, laughing at the suggestion that Germany was going to lose the war. Upon returning to his local village, he was loaded onto a boxcar with all the other German males of his vicinity, and deported to work as a slave laborer at a factory in Charkov in present-day Ukraine. There he stayed for seven months, at the end of which he was the bare shadow of a human being, louse-ridden, diseased, and in an advanced stage of starvation. Small for his age, he was able to lie about his age and, with all the prisoners under sixteen, he returned to Soviet-occupied Germany, working in Berlin for two years. Less lucky ones were to remain in prison until released a few years later, while others, never permitted to leave, were resettled in Siberia, where most of them perished. It was not until 1949 that my father found and rejoined the surviving members of his family.

Remembering Apocalypse: the winter of 1945, when humankind lay in ruins and the world exacted its revenge. John's Revelation continues to give voice to the recollections of these traumatic events. In my family, whether at home or among relatives, conversation inevitably returns to that winter of 1945 and adopts the darkest of apocalyptic categories. They borrow language from Revelation's symbolism of evil (violent millennial programs, divine punishment, cursing God, monstrous armies, persecutions, disease, starvation, bodies, rivers of blood) to speak their memories.

Without the language of the Apocalypse their trauma would have remained mute. A recent study treats the apocalypse genre as a paradoxical speaking after the end of the world. James Berger argues that the ability to narrate the end is what carries peoples and cultures through the traumas that annihilate personal and collective identities. Trauma becomes both cataclysm and revelation—an ending and an unveiling, both of which become the resources for storying and for stubbornly surviving. "Until the end of the world . . . we tell stories." [45] After it we do so as well, or we suffer the consequences. In two recent books, Ursula Hegi explores German silence concerning the horrors of World War II. In *Tearing the Silence*, Hegi offers biographical sketches of German American émigrés born shortly after 1945 and observes that, for most, talk of the war was taboo.[46] A phantom past haunts her interviewees, leaving them paralyzed in the present. She explores this silence in her bestselling *Stones from the River*, the story of a German village from World War I until the 1960s. The story's narrator, a dwarf, is the only one willing to talk about history after the war, her diminutive stature symbolic of her ability to see beyond the illusions of prosperous post–World War II

Germany; the majority of other characters just want to forget. One of
Hegi's messages is that until one stops trying to forget, there can be no
healing.

My family's experience, however, was different. Sometimes it seemed
that all we ever talked about was the war and its associated tragedies. Perhaps these refugees from the east, with their bone-deep knowledge of
what it was to be an alien and a stranger, were cherishing what they had
been able to carry into exile to preserve their distinct character: memory
and story, and nothing else but their bare lives. Maurice Halbwachs's
studies in memory as a social act argue that collective memories of the
past are inextricably tied to the social contexts and physical localities in
which we construct our mores, values, and ideals; commemoration and
place are always a whole.[47] My family, together with its Eastern European,
German Canadian community, became living proof of Halbwachs's
thesis. Now aliens in another dominant culture—English-speaking
Canada—traumatic memory was a resource for storying and thereby pre-
serving cultural identity.

Revelation furnished traumatic memory with language. It also
scripted a cultural performance for new immigrants. Revelation's stories
of material and political reward for faithfulness amid adversity (Rev. 2:9,
11; 7:9, 14-17; 11:12, 18; 19:7-8, 12-14; 21:10-21) translated into material
success as my family built a new life in western Canada. Theirs was the
earthly realization of a promised heavenly paradise. Thanks to the work
of Lutheran humanitarian relief agencies, which resettled millions of displaced Germans all over the world, my parents' families arrived in
Canada in 1950. They eventually settled in Edmonton, Alberta, where
my mother and father met, and were married in 1953. Together with
Ukrainians, Russians, Jews, Japanese, and Chinese who came to Canada
before World War II, German immigrants transformed the country's two
colonizing cultures of Britain and France into a multicultural mosaic.[48]
All brought their ethnic heritages with them. As in Eastern Europe, ethnic Germans built German Lutheran churches, cultural centers, and language schools. Across the country, German-speaking neighborhoods
sprang up. I was baptized in a German Lutheran Church and did not
learn to speak English until I was a young boy. As a child growing up in
Calgary, I would chafe under the yoke of a German ethnic heritage, having to forego Saturday-morning television and Friday-night sleepovers
to join oddly dressed children learning German at the "Shangri-La Ger-

man Canadian Club." For good reason—even after forty years in Canada—my grandparents could barely speak English.

In 1950, just as Canada was giving up its grand narratives of Britain and France in order to accommodate itself to the technological imperium to the south, these refugees arrived on Canada's shore, and carried their powerful stories west. At a time when western Canada was still largely rural, requiring skilled labor and technical know-how, these Eastern Europeans were the people of the hour. They helped develop the resources to power a growing American empire. More pointedly, Revelation's happy ending provided the narrative template for finding a satisfying conclusion to an unhappy past. Later, in chapters 3 and 4, I return to the cultural desire for a satisfying conclusion by investigating Revelation's central hortatory strategy for winning allegiance to its ethical injunctions—persuading its readers that they are continually watched by God. The post-Apocalypse speech in German Canadian communities similarly rendered its listeners visible, resulting in assimilation to the ideals of the dominant culture. To achieve its ends, John's Revelation deploys some of the unruliest Greek grammar in the New Testament and thereby marks a countercultural Christian identity contesting the ordered syntax of Roman imperial rhetorical culture. Similarly, even as there was pressure to assimilate, the broken English-German speech of ethnic Germans symbolized resistance to the colonizing values of anglophone Canada. Memory of Apocalypse 1945 housed in improper grammar created an opening for ironizing and parodying an anglophone Canadian culture, which, in the postwar period, having fallen under the spell of Pax Americana's promises of military security and economic prosperity, was busy transforming itself into a client state. Chapter 6 explores Revelation's uses of irony and parody to champion resistance to empire, and the way its parody and irony may help Christian communities feel less at home in the American Rome.

LIFE AMID THE RUINS

Postapocalyptic stories of expulsion and immigration, of revenge and building a paradise: if I am "in Apocalypse" (Catherine Keller), this is how I got there. When I come to the Apocalypse as biblical exegete, such stories furnish me with, as Eco said, "the sense conditioning which is peculiarly my own, a defined culture, a set of tastes, personal inclinations, and prejudices." A goal of the following study is to encourage readers to reflect on the means of their own arrival, and the sense conditionings, inclinations, and prejudices they bring with them. For Catherine Keller, the Apocalypse in which most of us find ourselves is dominated by the future tense—an inevitable unhappy ending to humankind's story (O'Leary's "tragic mode"). But my journey into Apocalypse has been led neither by dread nor hope, but by memory. It was remembering Apocalypse that got me there; I was raised overhearing the paradoxes of post-Apocalypse speech. Growing up, the postapocalyptic reminiscences of the ruins of January 1945 textured the Canadian peace and prosperity I saw all around me, especially as I grew into the realization that my material comfort was bought at the price of a continuing social and environmental apocalypse, at home and abroad. If postapocalyptic speech functioned to assimilate us into the dominant culture, it also marked social difference and became a resource for cross-examining an empire-loving contemporary culture and for seeing the ruins masked by the shiny façades of first-world success.

The narrative voice of John's Revelation is similarly postapocalyptic and cross-examining. The Apocalypse is a retrospective narrative. John stands at the end of his Apocalypse looking back. He frames his tale in the past tense: "I was on the island of Patmos. . . . I heard . . . I turned . . . I saw . . ." (Rev. 1:9, 10, 12). The audience hearing the Apocalypse is brought up-to-date through its performance, carried through time to where John the faithful narrator stands at the end (22:8), where present-tense narration dominates (vv. 11-21). Retrospection allows John to slow his narration down or to speed it up, to leap forward or back. He holds the whole of time in his hands and entangles his audience in a play of hours and years, weeks and months, framing it in stories told from their ending. Later, in chapter 5, we see how John's sense of an ending allows him to offer a tensely narrated story, juggling, circuslike, past, present, and future in death-defying apocalyptic acts. John's "games with time" work against turning Revelation into a tale of inevitable ending (tragic or comic) and offer a reappraisal of what listeners are doing "in the meantime." John's *post*-millennial voice, speaking *after* the chaos and bliss, offers the possibility of what Frank Kermode calls "a special kind of middle."[49]

John remembers endings: Antipas, the martyr from Sardis (Rev. 2:13); the reigns of tyrannical Roman emperors (17:9-10); Moses and Elijah (11:4-12); Ezekiel (10:9-10); Older Testament stories of liberation (for example, 15:3; 18:4). Most important, John recalls the fate of Jesus of Nazareth. So centrally does the death of Jesus figure in the Apocalypse that Jacques Ellul could interpret the entire Book of Revelation as a kind of extended midrash on Golgotha and the consequences for human existence of Jesus' historic ministry, death, and resurrection.[50] Perhaps more than any other contemporary exegete, Ellul rightly insists on the degree to which the Apocalypse looks back in time as much as forward.[51] In fact, a precondition of its forward-looking perspective is precisely that it casts its eye backward.

This not to say that the Apocalypse is a trip down memory lane. John's narrative is not nostalgic. It is a form of *anamnesis,* or recollection. That is, in recalling, such narratives make the past present. For John, the death of Jesus is of course a past historical event. But its reality is present; its effects are now. The author admonishes his audience to live into a *present* story. This is most evident in John's repeated modulations from past- into present-tense narration: "*Now* the salvation and the power and the kingdom of our God and the authority of his Christ have come. . . !" (Rev. 12:10); "behold *he is coming!*" (1:7); "Grace and peace from the one who was, who is, and who *is coming*"; "Behold *he is coming!*" (1:4, 7—present participles); "these are they who have come out of the great tribulation. . . . Therefore they *are* before the throne of God . . . " (7:14-15); "I looked, and lo, on Mount Zion stood the Lamb. . . . and they *sing* a new song before the throne. . . . It is these who have not defiled themselves with women for they *are* chaste; it is these who *follow* the Lamb wherever he *goes*; . . . they *are* spotless" (14:1, 3, 4, 5). Even the reference of Rev. 1:9 to John's sharing the "tribulation and the kingdom and the patient endurance," usually cited to situate the Apocalypse in a historical time of Roman persecution, is as cogently read as a marking out a present that John insists all those "in Jesus" share.[52] Living into this present means living into Jesus' death.

This wedding of past and present tenses turns the Apocalypse into a subversive piece of memory-work. Like the Passover Seder, in which the Passover meal, through food and family dialogue, both recalls and makes present the exodus liberation of the children of Israel from bondage in Egypt, so the Apocalypse deploys memory to re-create the present through recollection. Anamnesis invests the present with renewed significance. Anamnesis belongs to what Bruce Malina describes as a Mediterranean pre-industrial understanding of time, in which the present is never dissociated from the past; the present carries the past, expressing and thereby conserving it.[53] So also the Apocalypse, a product of a pre-industrial Mediterranean culture, insists upon an inscription of the past in the present.

In Revelation, anamnesis repoliticizes the present imperial moment. As we shall see below, comfort for those oppressed by empire is only half of Revelation's story. The rest is a word of challenge to listeners living too comfortably amid the economic benefits of the Roman order. To make that challenge, John certainly looks ahead. He also looks back. Gerd Theissen, reflecting on the politics of memory in Scripture, coins the phrase "contra-present memory" to explore the Bible's uses of historical narrative.[54] That phrase aptly describes John's wedding of apocalyptic visions with his recollections of the death of Jesus and his faithful testimony unto death. Such a marriage of images is contra-present; it is also contra-imperial. Revelation opens up a present, contrary to the present lived out in the grand Roman imperial narratives that frame the world in which the Apocalypse's characters play out their roles.

The Apocalypse belongs to a sociopolitical world in which memory was paramount. A central feature of cities in the Roman Empire, such as those of the seven churches John addresses (Rev. 2:1—3:22), was creating monuments to history. They gloried in a hallowed past preserved in inscriptions on their public buildings, recorded in the charters of their innumerable associations, and sanctified on the funerary monuments that lined avenues leading into urban centers. Celebrating offices held and patronage enacted, such inscriptions promoted, usually through formulaic repetition, civic ideologies. The Roman Empire appropriated these civic traditions, their gods, and their festivals, and "rewired" them to power its own political ends. The emperor cult in Asia Minor was a refurbishing of Hellenistic practices to serve the occupying interests of Roman social and economic domination.[55] The Apocalypse offers a conflict of memories in contrasting the death and exaltation of Jesus, the victim of imperial domination, with the apotheoses of dead and not-so-dead Roman emperors. For John, memory of the political execution by crucifixion of Jesus, as well as of the martyr Antipas, functions politically to unmask the cruel reality of Roman imperial domination. John deploys an edgy hermeneutics of suspicion on the much-touted imperial propaganda of the Pax Romana and its claims of divine blessing. He seeks instead to remind those Christian listeners who support the imperial economic order too enthusiastically of the blood and tears on which the Roman Empire is built. He seeks to convince his listeners that the grand buildings and avenues of their pro-imperial cities are façades that hide the ruined lives on which the Roman Empire was built. As we see in the final chapter, John's anamnesis is a parodying of imperial might and honor and an ironical destabilizing of hierarchical notions of power, whether on earth or in heaven. John offers contra-present memory for living life amid the ruins.

Remembering Apocalypse, if painful, is salutary—for John's listeners cozying up to empire, for those who live the ripple-effects of trauma, for a mainstream church that would just as soon forget the final book of the Bible. Even as it challenged listeners in the Roman Empire, Revelation's contra-present memory offers a striking challenge to a first-world church at home in the American Rome. Its anamnesis is an edgy riposte to the contemporary love of amnesia. Amid the ruins, whether those concealed by the political rhetoric of an ancient empire or the ones hidden in the glowing promises of contemporary economic globalization, John's Apocalypse is healthy reminder. This is especially because, like John's first-century listeners, most of us would rather forget.

NIETZSCHE'S COWS

Remember when you could remember? A century ago, Friedrich Nietzsche began his essay "On the Uses and Abuses of History" by envying a field of cows happily grazing and fertilizing, wholly oblivious to history. He sought to challenge a culture staggering under the weight of history. For Nietzsche, forgetfulness required a heroic act of will, necessary to throw off a monumentalizing past that made citizens slaves to Christian pieties and virtue, and to live courageously in the present, free at last from dehumanizing historical ideologies, antiquarian triviality, and the paralysis of a critical historical science.[56] Are we not enviable like Nietzsche's cows? Memory and history seem a thing of the past. If once only Nietzschean heroes could forget, today it requires a heroic act of will to remember anything. Computer memories, databases, instantly accessible information on the World Wide Web—surely these make memory redundant. As Plato well knew, the first casualty of recording technology is memory.[57] If the medium is the message, to borrow Marshall McLuhan's famous phrase, then what message is to be gleaned from the sound bite, the rapid-fire music-video imagery, twenty-four-hour news coverage, information at a click of a mouse? Is the message that there is no longer a need to remember? That memory is a species of culture endangered, if not extinct?[58] Now people who can remember are guests of talk-show hosts, prodigies who entertain us with their computerlike recall of lists of trivial information. They are would-be infomercial millionaires promising wealth beyond imagining to forgetful businesspeople who may still, while quantities last, realize the financial benefits of mnemonics through memory-course tapes and videos. Do such entrepreneurs not have something we need? Or maybe, like Charlie in the film *Rain Man,* those with powerful facilities of recall unnerve us. An autistic savant, Charlie can instantly recall numbers, series of items, and amounts. As the film unfolds, we see him become the disquieting reminder to his younger brother, who is living off a thin veneer of good looks and charm, that he is a con-man.

Modern artist Anselm Kiefer expresses the cultural loss of memory in his ironical execution of an archive of books whose pages are made from lead retrieved from the roof of Cologne Cathedral, and on which he has fastened items from and photos of nature. Kiefer in parody calls his "Zweistromland: Doppelregal mit Bleibüchern" ("Two-River Country: Double Book Case with Lead Books") a work in progress. Just as modern media render disposable the leaden moveable type of the printing press, so increasingly is the natural world becoming redundant. Kiefer recycles both lead and nature into an archive comprised of massive lead books too heavy to take off the shelf and read, and thus useless for a posterity populated by amnesiacs. We can have all we need of nature in photographs, even possess it in brighter and bolder form, as Sallie McFague insightfully observes, in the *National Geographic* world of super-model Mother Nature, the glossy, touched-up object of male delight. The book, like nature and memory, belongs to a redundant cultural past, or to the world of make-believe.[59]

Remember when memory formed an indispensable backdrop for public exchange—the Berlin Wall, the Prague Spring, Vietnam, Nicaragua, the civil war in El Salvador? These sites necessitated memory; indeed, they made forgetfulness dangerous. Can you remember when citizenship required one not to forget why there was a nuclear arsenal, why democracy had to keep an eye out? Can you remember when you could not forget? How quickly we have become Nietzsche's cows. The Berlin Wall is now a museum piece. A section of it stands like a relic of a bygone past, in Bonn in the National Museum of German History since 1945. Another remains in Berlin, preserved *in situ* as a concrete surface for contemporary art. Today the anarchistic slogans that decorate it belong to an antiquated past and form the backdrop for a quick tourist photo. Finally, we can forget! The once-communist East is now democratic—like us. Why bother remembering? The statues of Stalin and Lenin are on the junk heap. In Berlin, street vendors purvey Soviet uniforms on streets where the uniformed once kept close watches. There have been free elections. Half the former East-bloc countries are joining the European Union, proof "we won" the Cold War, evidence of our natural superiority.

Francis Fukuyama heralds this as the advent of "the end of history," brought to you by the victory of capitalism over communism. Sure, he admits, the sheer boredom of consumerism, and hence the advent of Nietzsche's "last man"—the modern citizen consumed with triviality, a slave to the mediocrity of creature comforts—threatens this new world order. [60] So there will always be the temptation to return to "the first men" of bloody history, if for no other reason than to interrupt our lives of interminable consumerist boredom. Fukuyama, however, remains optimistic. [61] The end of history: would not remembering get in the way of Fukuyama's bravado? Memory triggers bad memories, leading in turn to uncomfortable questions. Why then the need for the Strategic Defense Initiative, the American refusal to sign onto the Comprehensive Test Ban Treaty on nuclear weapons, its abandonment of the Anti-Ballistic Missile Treaty, its refusal to enforce the 1972 Biological and Toxic Weapons Convention banning germ warfare? Why the increasing gap between rich and poor? Why rampant unemployment in Eastern Europe? Why growing racism, genocide, and resurgent nationalisms? Why are anti-globalization protesters denied the right to assemble, walled off, pepper-sprayed, arrested without cause, murdered in the street? Why September 11? Better to forget, to forget it all, to roll over and fall back asleep, to medicate oneself out of edginess, or, better still, in fulfillment of the Nietzschean prophecy, to go shopping. The collapse of the Soviet Union has delivered all the future we wanted; technology furnishes us with the rest. Writing in 1994, Jean Baudrillard wondered if there could ever be a year 2000 because of the speed of news events, the bombardment of media messages steadily eroding any significant sense in which one might say that there are "events" worth dating.

These societies, these generations which no longer expect anything from some future "coming," and have less and less confidence in history, which dig in behind their futuristic technologies, behind their stores of information and inside the beehive networks of communication where time is at last wiped out by pure circulation, will perhaps never reawaken. But they do not know that. The year 2000 will not perhaps take place. But they do not know that. [62]

If there are no longer events, only the endless circulation of consumer goods, Baudrillard argued, there is no movement toward the future. There can only be a present filled with the reporting of passing moments and fashions whose very recording trivializes them into yesterday's news. But, inflecting Baudrillard, I am now wondering if there was ever really a 1945, a 1962, or a 1968. What happened in 1989? If there is memory today, it takes the form of nostalgia—MTV bricolage culled from across the centuries, a kind of history by free association: Elton John in a Mozart costume and wig, singing good-bye to Norma Jean. In my home city, Vancouver, the central public library is a building in the round reminiscent of the Roman Colosseum. It is a beautiful building of glass and stone that nevertheless leaves one with the unsettling feeling that people who read books belong in antiquity, or that the social function of reading is circuslike entertainment. [63] In Greek mythology, the muse of history, Clio, is Mnemosyne's (Memory's) child—offspring of her coupling with Zeus, the king of the gods. If there is no memory, the story teaches us, there is no history, and we breathe from a disenchanted atmosphere emptied of the divine.

Life after God is how Vancouver author Douglas Coupland stylizes the contemporary West. [64] Its protagonists are dazzled consumers who talk in sound bites, lead lives in imitation of what they see on television, endure dead-end jobs in the service industry, or pour the best years of their lives and talents into information-technology jobs in pursuit of becoming millionaires. The closest they get to memory is nostalgia—for the time when there was "God," when there was something or someone or some reason to be ethical, when, in fact, there was something worth remembering. They at once resent and envy their parents for being able to believe.

Coupland's fiction expresses what others have been describing philosophically for some time. Jean-François Lyotard characterizes the modern world as living out a crisis brought on by the collapse of ideologies—large-scale frames of meaning such as Marxism, fascism, democratic liberalism, social democracy, and Christianity. For Lyotard, "the postmodern condition" is that there are no traditional metanarratives or big stories or mythologies with which to shape the collective imagination of modern technological society. The postmodern is a world of fragmentation. Such fragmentation, he argues, is in the service of ever more specialized modes of capitalist production.[65] Lyotard's partner in cultural criticism, Theodor Adorno, similarly describes the culture of late capitalism as one in which the abolition of memory is a matter of economic necessity. He warns of the specter of a citizenry without memory, smiling wryly at Weberian theorists who relegate tradition to an outmoded feudal past on its way toward the "rational" bureaucracy of the bourgeoisie. "This means no less than that the advancing bourgeois society liquidates Memory, Time, Recollection as irrational leftovers of the past."[66] Modern bureaucratic functioning and memory or tradition are mortal enemies in the modern state, for tradition may at any moment cross-examine a purely instrumental means of capitalist manipulation of the world's goods.

Frederic Jameson together with Jean Baudrillard has similarly assessed the culture of postmodernism as a reflection of late-capitalist image production. Jameson portrays modern consumers as living in a virtual-reality hall of mirrors, enacting roles produced by Hollywood directors for mass consumption. We experience historical amnesia because there is no need to remember anything in order to be a consumer, except perhaps only what we saw last night on television or in the cinema.[67] Baudrillard names this the *simulacrum*, the production of self as copy of the original with no need to be able to tell the difference. Late capitalism, according to Baudrillard, is Disneyland (or Hollywood) on the streets, "the order of the hyperreal and of simulation. It is no longer a question of a false representation of reality (ideology), but of concealing the fact that the real is no longer real." Disneyland exists "to make us believe that the rest is real, when in fact all of Los Angeles and the America surrounding it are no longer real." It is "a perfect model of all entangled orders of simulation."[68]

"Life after God"; this is the end of Christendom, the end of the world as we know it, and we are supposed to feel fine. The "end of Christendom" as a phrase usually designates the triumph of the secular over a Christian world order, and declining church membership. It can also be used as shorthand for the end of all official ideologies and the skepticism that greets belief in anything in a modern secular world other than the pursuit of wealth. The "end of Christendom" names more than a parochial reality. It describes the social world challenging any person who wants to take seriously the abiding value of tradition and ethics in the modern world, who wants to be more than a grazing and fertilizing consumer. The end of Christendom signifies a secular, allegedly narrative-free world well summarized by Stanley Hauerwas when he describes secularity as the "story we learn when we learn that we have no story."[69] Here the Christian narrative falls victim to secularity, as do all those narratives secular society once adopted on its way toward technology and empire: Marxism, socialism, liberal democracy, and so on. We no longer have need of these hypotheses, relics of a time when, like eighteenth-century appeals to God to account for aberrations in the orbits of planets, they were invoked to account for economic realities.

For those still interested in the church, a corollary of this argument is that the Social Gospel Movement, that ecclesial desire for a better society through strategic allegiance with government and the support of secular democracy, and (in Canada) the creation of a social democracy, must now be seen as a fossil of a bygone era of Christendom.[70] The grim truth of the relevance of religion to modern secular society is well attested by the memorial services organized, respectively, by the Canadian and American governments to mourn the victims of the September 11 terrorist attack on the World Trade Center. The Canadian government opted for a wholly secular memorial on Parliament Hill, remarkably—given the role that religious belief played in the attacks—without any reference to God or religion. By contrast, the American service at the Washington National Cathedral was an extravaganza of patriotic civil religion—as much an assurance that America remained an untarnished righteous nation of God's elect, and the victims in the attack were her holy martyrs, as a mourning of senseless violence. In either case—by ignoring religion or using it expediently for political ends—

religion in secular society, except on the most private of terms (and then only, as Alexis de Tocqueville observed, as a means of promoting the virtues of industry and prudence indispensable to a capitalist state), remains irrelevant to the public governance of daily affairs and is permitted no role in critiquing it.[71]

If this is not enough to give Social Gospelers pause, that the days are long past when, in the governance of the nation-state, prime ministers and presidents look to or take seriously the insights and critiques of church officials, then sobering second thoughts should come with recognition that the form of government with which the church traditionally allied itself is either extinct or on the endangered species list.[72] With the advent of a global economy, both Canadians and Americans are increasingly discovering themselves to be taxpayers first and citizens a distant second. Thus, it is not an enduring notion of a *civitas* or *res publica*—city-state or republic—which shapes our common life, but the *fiscus*—the state treasury. To quote Robert Bellah, the citizen has been consumed by "economic man."[73]

Christians who still believe that the gospel has as much to do with life before death as after it, and that Christianity has a public role to play in contemporary society, will need to think in completely different categories about the relationship of Christ and culture. The traditional ally of the Social Gospel, the social-democratic state, is on its deathbed, in the process of being euthanized by the pressures of economic globalization. If the church is looking for transformation, it will need to find new allies—perhaps watchdog nongovernmental organizations powerful enough to convince transnational corporations to pursue just employment and environmentally friendly practices.[74] Later I agree with John Howard Yoder that the fatal flaw in Christian liberalism is the notion that "the fundamental responsibility of the church for society is to manage it."[75] This is the manifesto outlined by H. Richard Niebuhr in his tellingly uncritical assessment of the relation of Christ to culture as one of "Christ transforming culture."[76]

In contrast to Niebuhr, borrowing trouble from John of Patmos, I argue that the task of the sidelined Christian church in Western secular society is not to transform or manage culture but to trouble it. At the end of Christendom the Christian church exists to insist on the troubling story of the cross, and to form this-worldly believers who contribute to and enrich secular pluralistic society through lives of spirited public witness to the God incarnate in Jesus of Nazareth, who reveals a way of being human on terms other than the insatiable desire for more, military domination, and national security. This, I argue, is the God John's Apocalypse reveals—even, paradoxically, in its most militaristic and triumphalist episodes. For John, the cross as instrument of Roman execution reveals political despotism and the ruin covered up by an imperial façade of peace and prosperity. From the perspective of the cross, imperial successes are seen from a new vantage point. The cross insists on a hermeneutic of suspicion, a truly critical reading of our most important ideas. The Apocalypse urges a contemporary first-world church living amid the peace and prosperity of contemporary empire to continue this cross-elevated suspicion. Even as Revelation discovers life and power in a way of witness to its unlikely counterimperial hero, Jesus the slain Lamb of God, so does it trouble the contemporary church into asking where it finds life.

Reading Revelation calls for the church to confess the disinvestment of divine power in the self-emptying of Jesus of Nazareth on the cross and God's act in raising him from the dead. It urges a life immersed in what I will later call "costly testimony"—a contra-present witness to God's self-revelation in a powerless slain lamb. The Book of Revelation urges its audience to believe that in the life of the slain lamb what opens before us is a gift of and call to a strikingly new way of being human. This gift of being human puts believers on a collision course with competing invitations to becoming human, in particular those that result in environmental waste and human degradation in return for the material promise of an insatiable consumer culture. In place of an invitation to conspicuous consumption, Revelation urges conspicuous generosity. The vocation of this way of being human is to express the lavish self-giving of God in the most routine features of everyday life and ethical decision making even if (especially if!) that brings it into direct conflict with pungent religious discourse from the public sphere. For such a vocation is troubling to the secular world's normal way of doing business. On such terms will Christians discover the virtues necessary for what Mark Kingwell calls "the good citizen," namely, the communal formation of individuals equipped "to make sense of themselves, as citizens, within the larger demands of life itself."[77] A communal Christian formation, one among many in a pluralistic culture, will be publicly recognizable by its particularly religious speech, the specific theologically informed warrants it adduces for being ethical, and the consistency of the characteristically religious narratives to which it appeals in setting out the goals of a Christian ethical life.

My diagnosis of our cultural condition is that the Book of Revelation is indispensable to mainstream first-world churches of the historic confessions struggling to come to terms with their institutional mortality. Indeed, it may be the most important book of the Bible for this task. Too often muzzled by the strict separation of church and state, consigning religion to the private recesses of the human heart, North American Christians have for too long been silent and willing participants in a consumer culture that degrades us all. John urges us to be troublemakers by teaching us the power of public confession of belief. I later insist, with Martin Luther, that the church must be a *Mundhaus,* a "mouthhouse," or house of proclamation ringing with confession of the gospel of God's action in the life, death, and resurrection of Jesus Christ. If the churches are looking for transformation, here they will find it. Only then will we find the courage to envision new ways of being in society and face the fact that we no longer inhabit the halls of privilege. More seriously still, such courage may lead us to repentance for the idolatrous misapprehension that we could ever have comfortably sat in halls of economic pragmatism even as they brought us into direct contradiction with our gospel identity of God's lavish expenditure for the world. Such reorientation will require us to seek forgiveness for transforming the theology of the cross into a social triumphalism. The Book of Revelation's demand is to learn to be more marginalized, edgier disciples leading lives of costly testimony.

In the final chapter I return to the place of a post-Christendom church within a secular society "after God" and consider what it might mean to bring apocalyptic-style trouble to culture from the margins. But for Revelation to become these things, for it to become a book unmuzzled and worth remembering to read in the once-mainstream, now-sidelined church, it must be heard and read afresh. Most often interpreted as a book of comfort to the persecuted, it must be listened to as a letter of challenge to the culturally comfortable and ecclesially indolent. Amid the ruins of Christendom, Revelation—the full and bloody version—is the book of the hour.

READING AS A LAODICEAN

You say, I am rich, I have prospered, and I need nothing; not knowing that you are wretched, pitiable, poor, blind, and naked. Therefore I counsel you to buy from me gold refined by fire, that you may be rich, and white garments to clothe you and to keep the shame of your nakedness from being seen, and salve to anoint your eyes, that you may see.

—Rev. 3:17-18

Reading as a Laodicean means, in the first place, to try to see the Apocalypse's world with eyes other than those of a Philadelphian (Rev. 3:7-13). It requires some corrective lenses to counteract the exegetical myopia of traditional readings of the Apocalypse. More than any biblical text, the Book of Revelation has been accounted for by reference to the need for comfort in the face of disappointed eschatological expectation brought on by Roman imperial persecution. Hence, the reigning scholarly paradigm for accounting for the Apocalypse is that it was composed as a response to overcome "cognitive dissonance." This is a phrase sociologists use to account for the origins of apocalypticism, a social phenomenon which arises when groups convinced of their elect status are faced with the disconfirming evidence of persecution or rejection, and so overcome their disappointed expectations by appeal to a future vindication of belief through coming divine punishment of enemies. To see the Apocalypse through Philadelphian eyes is to see it as a strategy for overcoming the cognitive dissonance of persecution by appeal to a coming judgment and vindication.[78] Such a belief supports Alan Boesak's insistence that "those who do not know . . . suffering through oppression . . . shall have grave difficulty understanding this letter from Patmos."[79] The power of this lens is magnified when the text is read in situations of political oppression and suffering. Read against such a social backdrop, the Apocalypse offers powerful counterpolitics. For those on the receiving end of oppression and abuse, the Apocalypse is indeed a comforting text, for the Apocalypse anticipates the vindication of martyrs' faith, and celebrates a preferential option for the poor. "I know your tribulation and your poverty (but you are rich)" begins the message to the Smyrnaeans. "Be faithful unto death and I will give you the crown of life" (2:9, 10).

Comfort, however, is only one side of Revelation's story. Of John's seven letters to the churches of Asia Minor (Rev. 2:1—3:22), only half are comforting. The rest bring messages of warning and challenge, messages particularly challenging when the social backdrop is one in which listeners are the beneficiaries instead of the victims of empire. More traditional historical-critical readings of the Apocalypse mine the seven messages to the seven churches in order to cash in their symbolic values for the hard currency of historical referentiality.[80] Too often ignored is how their arrangement serves a persuasive end and offers a hermeneutical orientation to the chapters that follow.[81] A careful look at the sequence of the seven "letters" to the seven churches reveals a rhythmic alteration of blame and praise, inscribing ambiguity, literally, into the Apocalypse from its outset and setting the tone for what follows from chapter 4 onward. Censure and approval follow one another in an alternating order as one completes what forms John's first cycle of seven (anticipating the sevens to come), becoming ever more contrasting as one progresses from the first to the last message. The result is a hortatory architecture that is best recognized when sketched out in table form.

Table 1. The Hortatory Architecture of the Seven Letters
to the Seven Churches

1. Ephesus (2:1-7) praise (vv. 2-3) criticism (vv. 4-5) praise (v. 6)		5. Sardis (3:1-6) criticism (vv. 1-3) praise (v. 4)
2. Smyrna (2:8-11) praise (v. 9)	4. Thyatira (2:18-29) praise (v. 19) criticism (vv. 20-23) praise (v. 24)	6. Philadelphia (3:7-13) praise (vv. 8, 10)
3. Pergamum (2:12-17) praise (v. 13) criticism (vv. 14-15)		7. Laodicea (3:14-22) criticism (vv. 15-18)

The table shows how the seven messages can be divided into two sets of three, with the fourth address, to the Thyatirans (2:18-29), occupying a rhetorically significant middle position. Thus, in the first message (2:1-7), John first praises (vv. 2-3), then criticizes (vv. 4-6), and finally praises (v. 6) the Ephesian church. The second message, to the Smyrnaeans (2:8-11), contains unqualified comfort (v. 9) in the face of imminent harassment. In the third message (2:12-17) John returns to criticism, now of the church at Pergamum, again with reference first to a more faithful past (v. 13) giving way to present faithlessness (vv. 14-16).

Passing over the Thyatiran message (2:18-29) for a moment, we come to a second set of three "letters," to Sardis (3:1-6), Philadelphia (3:7-13), and Laodicea (3:14-22). The same pattern of criticism/praise/criticism appears. In the case of censure, however, the tone has become brusquer. In the message to Sardis, lengthy criticism (vv. 1-3) is only slightly diluted by a brief reference to "a few names in Sardis" (3:4). The letter to the Laodiceans, the numerically significant *seventh* message occupying the rhetorically significant last position of the seven letters, greets that church with pure criticism (3:15-18). With respect to praise, the Philadelphian church, unlike the church at Smyrna which is about to suffer imprisonment (2:10), has *already* endured (3:8, 10). Thus, the second set of three letters recalls the first three, but in an intensified way.

The fourth message, to the Thyatirans (2:18-29), is the longest of the seven. It furnishes the most detail concerning the state of a church, is the most polemical, and is placed, like the letter to the Laodiceans, in a rhetorically significant spot of the seven messages, directly in the middle. Here again John sends a mixed message: after a brief word of praise (v. 19), the majority of the message offers censure (vv. 20-23). Here John offers the most detail concerning an enemy, a female prophet, rhetorically caricatured as the Older Testament anti-hero Jezebel (v. 20). "Jezebel" (coincidentally like the Nicolaitans and the similarly rhetorically named Balaam of 2:14, 15; cf. v. 6) leads community members "to practice immorality and to eat food sacrificed to idols" (v. 20). She was given time to repent but refused and thus sealed her fate. The same fate awaits her "children" (vv. 22-23) unless they repent. Not all is bad, however, in Thyatira. The second half of the letter offers promise to those who have resisted her teaching (vv. 24-28).

Thus, two sets of three, with increasing intensity of criticism, praise, and criticism, flank a significantly longer and detailed letter of criticism

and praise. One discovers in these letters both reference to coming persecution and to lack of it, division and concord, insecurity and safety. Of
course, one can read the evidence as a Philadelphian. Such a reading
accepts John's own point of view; with what other church could it be
better said that it "shares" with John "in Jesus the tribulation and the
kingdom and the patient endurance" (1:9) if not the church at Philadelphia? On the other hand, it stretches the exegetical imagination to see
how the Laodiceans enjoy the same status, even though they are equally
addressed as doing so. This represents the opposite extreme to the
Philadelphian reality. And it makes a difference whether one reads the
Apocalypse as a Laodicean or a Philadelphian. Reading as Laodicean
means to place oneself in danger and to discover oneself in trouble. In
succeeding chapters I will be paying attention to how the Apocalypse
plays to both audiences—Philadelphian and Laodicean—and how the
modulations of its opening seven messages continue as the Apocalypse
unfolds.

A compelling social backdrop for understanding John's criticisms of `
the seven churches has been offered by Leonard Thompson and Paul
DeSilva.[82] Both read Revelation as the call of a feisty prophet to resist
behaviors that compromised Christian identity. They argue that what
vexed the prophet John was the willingness of certain Asia Minor
churches to engage in pagan activities indicated polemically in the con-
demnation of "eating food offered to idols and practicing immorality"
(Rev. 2:14, 20). John levels this criticism against relatively wealthy Christians invested in the economic life of the Roman Empire, most probably
through trade. John is taking a hard line in a community-dividing dispute not unlike what one can find represented in 1 Corinthians 8–10, in
which Paul criticizes "the strong" who eat idol food (1 Cor. 8:10-13;
10:14-30).

Thompson in particular builds on Gerd Theissen's groundbreaking
social-historical analysis of the Corinthian dispute, in which Theissen
argued that the consumption of idol food (i.e., meat) was status-specific
behavior in which the wealthier of Paul's community's were more
inclined to participate.[83] Given the ancient world's inextricable connection between religion and economics, the latter customarily conducted
in the context of pagan ritual in order to secure divine blessing, the
debate in Corinth was no academic one. Since Paul's mission depended
on the patronage of wealthier members to furnish homes and material

resources, preservation of his patrons' economic livelihood was of practical importance. Paul's "don't ask/ don't tell" strategy, outlined in 1 Cor. 10:23-30, permitted wealthier members to participate in the dinner life of their social equals, to the degree that their participation took place "behind closed doors" in the relative privacy of guild halls and pagans' private homes. Paul offers a compromise permitting wealthier members to preserve their economic interests and so protects the financial foundation for his churches.

For Thompson and DeSilva this represents precisely the kind of position promoted and accepted in some of the seven churches (i.e., by those represented by the rhetorical titles Balaam, the Nicolaitans, and Jezebel), and rejected by the prophet John and his followers.[84] Unlike Paul, however, John insists upon a non-accommodating stance with respect to *all* pagan festivities. To drive the point home, Thompson argues, he adopted the literary form of an apocalypse, whose chief property was, as a matter of literary form, to depict a world in crisis. But John's churches were not, in fact, in crisis, and that was the problem—not too much persecution, rather too little. John attempted to prompt a crisis rather than describe one. Through the literary form of an apocalypse, John offered a kind of "deviant knowledge" highly critical of the Roman Empire, designed to harden the social boundaries eroded by alleged community-compromising actions. In John's estimation, the Roman Empire, far from being the benign preserver of the public good favored by the pagan gods and celebrated in Asia Minor's city-state cults, was a luxury-loving, violently tyrannical empire governed by Satan.

John's message was a bitter pill for his audiences to swallow: late-first-century Asia Minor was the place to be for a merchant wanting to become prosperous and enjoy the benefits of the Roman Empire. The evidence of Paul's letters and references to the Asia Minor churches in the Book of Acts indicate that John's audience was most probably constituted by relatively well-to-do merchants who would have found in "Jezebel's" teaching a very welcome message indeed. John's hard line would bring the church into direct conflict with the dominant pagan culture surrounding it. Obviously John's position found little support among the rank and file, and arguably it was not "Jezebel," or her analogues ("Balaam," "the Nicolaitans"), who were initiating schism, but John and his supporters. DeSilva argues that John was keenly prophetic: John saw those who accepted his non-accommodating position placing themselves on a crash course with the Roman Empire, ending in persecution. More focused studies of the relations among the imperial cult, pro-imperial religion, economic patronage, and trade patterns in Asia Minor in the period generally associated with the Apocalypse support this social reading of Revelation.[85]

Revelation is not, however, only a window into the social world forming its backdrop. John's configuration of his sociohistorical situation through the apocalypse genre results in the literary creation of a world in its own right. The world of the text re-creates the world behind the text and seeks to persuade readers to come and occupy it. In a recent monograph, Robert M. Royalty studies John's rhetorical treatments of wealth as a means toward persuasion. His study takes up Elisabeth Schüssler Fiorenza's insistence that exegesis attend to "the rhetorical strategy of Revelation" and its "rhetorical situation."[86] Royalty argues that John's depiction of his backdrop must be read in the light of other ancient social narratives competing for hearers' allegiance. "Revelation is a highly rhetorical text that tries to *do* something; it is, in fact, performative rather than referential language."[87] Royalty hears echoing throughout the Apocalypse the jingle-jangle of money. John continually turns to the language of wealth and riches to describe the state of the seven churches and to explore social identities that listeners are to pursue or reject. The Book of Revelation is money-talk.[88]

The Laodiceans boast of their riches and security, but they are poor; only from God can they purchase "gold refined by fire" and so "be rich" (Rev. 3:17-18). On the other hand, Jesus knows the "poverty" of the Smyrnaeans, but still they are "rich" (2:9). The Philadelphians wear a "crown" (3:11). All the churches are symbolized with seven golden lampstands (1:20). The white garments clothing the faithful at Sardis (3:4-5) copy the costly clothing of the "one like a son of man, clothed with a long robe and with a golden girdle round his breast" (1:13). The imagery associated with the seven churches sets the stage for the more sustained deployment of wealth imagery in the vision of the heavenly throne room of Revelation 4-5. John likens the one seated on the throne to jewels (4:3-4); the twenty-four elders wear white garments and golden crowns (4:4-5, 10); they, together with the four living creatures of 4:6-8, hold golden bowls of incense (5:8). They and thousands others proclaim that the slain Lamb is worthy to receive, among other things, "wealth" (5:12). Later, John continues using economic language, when he sees the martyrs vested with the son of man's more luxurious costume (7:13). The righteous deeds of the saints are "fine linen" (19:8); the church is a bride bedecked in fine linen and bright costume (19:8); Jerusalem is a golden city adorned (21:2) with the jewels and gold described in 21:10-21. Into the city the kings of the earth bring their wealth (21:24), echoing the hymn of praise of 5:12. All of this language belongs to a long, Older Testament tradition symbolizing God, divine election, and the rewards of faithfulness with metaphors of wealth.

Likewise, John couches wickedness and divine punishment in economic terms hallowed in Scripture. Babylon is a luxuriating whore (17:4-6); punishment takes the form of the loss of wealth (18:9-19); there is no buying or trading without allegiance to the Beast (13:17); pagan murderers of the two witnesses celebrate their death by exchanging gifts (11:10). This repeated attention to wealth helps us recognize how important the Laodicean letter is in the series of seven messages: it at once summarizes what is at stake in the earlier letters and prepares the way for what follows. Here one discovers the elements of the Apocalypse's grammar of reward and punishment. Royalty notes insightfully how the language of wealth belongs to a world in which socially determining categories center on patronage, honor, and shame. In this world, honor is won by reward by a patron (in this case the patron deity, the resurrected Jesus Christ, the speaker in the seven messages), and shame is a public exposure and loss of dignity. The Laodiceans think they are wealthy, but they are poor; they need to purchase (that is to be honored with costly) white garments, or risk the shame of having their nakedness exposed (3:17-18). The reversal echoes the paradoxical Smyrnaean identity—poor but rich because faithful. This elemental grammar sets the framework for a kind of apocalyptic syntax of what in the course of our discussion we will name "costly testimony." Costly testimony refers both to the call of the Apocalypse to witness to the patron deity, Jesus, and also to its meritorious reward. Further it sums up the reversals that are to come as the Apocalypse unfolds—the rich will become poor, the faithful poor will become rich through the price of testimony.

A weakness of Royalty's fine analysis of the Apocalypse's rhetorical strategies of persuasion lies in its failure to explore the way John's rhetoric of wealth plays itself out in the stories that comprise the Apocalypse. To read as a Laodicean is, with Royalty, to notice the prevalence of Revelation's money-talk; it is also to attend to the ways John develops his heroes and villains, and to how John's apocalyptic stories result in "a symbolic transformation of the world."[89] Focusing on narrative strategies of persuasion traces Revelation's coding of the world through the play of words and symbols. Such a reading looks for the development of metaphors and the unfolding life of stories. It takes note of the characters who appear and reappear in slightly changed personas, the conflicts they meet, and their fate. The Apocalypse is a developing narrative (or, better, set of narratives).

Edith McEwan Humphrey in recent studies has given sustained attention to the transformation of female characters in a series of narratives, from distress to reward; and she notes how the church in Revelation, personified as a woman/bride, similarly undergoes a profound metamorphosis.[90] Humphrey's focus remains on the personified church. A Laodicean focus shifts the attention to Jezebel and her sympathizers and the ways in which John uses negative economic personifications to achieve another transformation, not from distress to reward, but from reward to punishment. John develops a twin story as the Apocalypse unfolds from its hermeneutically orienting seven letters, thus presenting his audience with what Barbara Rossing aptly calls "the choice between two cities"—Babylon and Jerusalem—and the rhetorically charged characters associated with each of them.[91] On the one side, he returns in varying profiles to characterizations of the praiseworthy Smyrnaeans and Philadelphians (2:8-11; 3:7-13), who in due course are personified as a bride/heavenly city adorned for her groom, Jesus (21:2, 9). On the other side, he pillories the adulteress Jezebel (2:20-23), who becomes in turn the whore of Babylon (17:1-6). Both experience unanticipated reversals of fortune. The result is a textual world that introduces to the economic expectations of John's hearers an unanticipated semantics, resignifying the lives of John's listeners, urging those too invested in the Roman imperial order to revisit their priorities and allegiances. The Laodiceans who boast that they are rich, prosperous, and in need of nothing discover by the end of Revelation's apocalyptic tales that they are pitiable, poor, blind, and naked (3:17). That promised narrative reversal, like the others in the seven letters, alerts the person who enters John's textual world that nothing is as it appears.

To read the Apocalypse as a contemporary Laodicean is also to begin to see that things are not as they appear. It is to read the Apocalypse as a revelation, not of what is to come but of present structures of domination and tyranny—as a revelation of empire and one's place within it. With Daniel Berrigan it is to realize that "those who dwell in Babylon do not know they are there" ("For you say you are . . . not knowing that you are"—Rev. 3:17),[92] and to be challenged with sobering identifications. Here my own reading diverges significantly from Royalty's. Royalty argues the Apocalypse with its metaphors of impoverished idolaters and the wealthy faithful merely replaces one plutocracy (that of the Roman emperor and his minions) with another (that of God and his slaves in the golden Jerusalem). Summing up, Royalty states, "For those who oppose this ideology, the text offers judgement without justice; crisis without catharsis."[93] For Royalty the Apocalypse's streets of heaven are just those of Rome with a different name. If he is correct, then the final book of the Bible inscribes in the canon a theological defense of the very domination liberationist interpreters like Pablo Richard and Alan Boesak claim Revelation overturns and rejects. Royalty's resistance to the Apocalypse gets intensified when wedded with Stephen Moore's appraisal that Revelation offers little more than rule by another Domitian who goes by the name of Yahweh.

My own response, again, is to read as a Laodicean. For where is a first-world white male of privilege to find himself described in the Apocalypse if not in this seventh message—rich, not needing anything, neither hot nor cold, but lukewarm—the typical citizen of a reigning order that keeps the majority of the planet's inhabitants in servitude to furnish me with my comforts? Who if not me needs persuasion that I am naked, blind, pitiable, and wretched, I who walk down golden-lit streets in my expensive clothing with the jingle-jangle of money in my pocket, window shopping as recreation beneath jewel-colored neon lights urging me to buy? Who if not me should be frightened when there is a knock at the door—maybe a thief to steal my riches or even my life away? Who if not I should be offended at the suggestion that a stranger should invite himself over to eat in *my* house, challenge me with shortsightedness, and invite me to a new economy of scale? Who if not I needs salve for my eyes and to be rescued at last "from single vision and Newton's sleep"?[94] And who should tell me, seduced as I am by the beauty of my weapons, that there is another way to conquer and be conquered?

To read as a Laodicean means to look into John's open heaven in the fear that Royalty and Moore are finally wrong in their insistence that, at the end, the Apocalypse's reversal is just more of the same old damned stuff dressed up in different clothing. In the final chapter I turn to a more detailed analysis of the Book of Revelation's reversals and discover whether a Laodicean such as myself can expect from the Bible's last book a misogynist's eternal capitalist paradise or something more costly still. Remembering apocalypse will accompany the way.

2

I, John

Madness has ceased to be—at the limits of the world, of man and
death—an eschatological figure; the darkness has dispersed on
which the eyes of madness were fixed and out of which the forms of
the impossible were born. Oblivion falls upon the world navigated
by the free slaves of the Ship of Fools. Madness will no longer proceed from a point within the world to a point beyond, on its strange
voyage; it will never again be that fugitive and absolute limit.
Behold it moored now, now made fast among things and men.
Retained and maintained. No longer a ship but a hospital.

—Michel Foucault, *Madness and Civilization*

John's Banishment . . . obviously must have been a traumatic
experience.

—Adela Yarbro Collins, *Crisis and Catharsis*

A STRANGE CASE

"I, John . . . was on the island called Patmos on account of the word of
God and the testimony of Jesus. I was in the Spirit on the Lord's day,
and I heard behind me a loud voice like a trumpet saying, 'Write
what you see in a book. . . .'"

40

A simple enough introduction, yet what mysteries lie concealed beneath. This John not only hears voices; he *sees* them (Rev. 1:12). His tone poems are impossibly sketched at the boundary of hearing and of sight: the seven golden lampstands; the son of man with hair white as white wool, white as snow, eyes like flaming fire, feet of burnished bronze, and a voice like the sound of many waters; white, red, black, and pale horsemen; the seven-eyed lamb; the sun-clothed woman, crowned with seven stars and the moon at her feet; the warrior mounted on a white horse, robed in bloodied dress; virgin bride and saints; whore on a scarlet-clad beast drunk with blood; the sea of glass; seven bowls of the wrath of God; beasts on land and sea; angels, frogs, and locusts; the sub-altern saints; the city of God alight without sun or moon. And eyes, everywhere eyes, peering out in front, behind, beside. How well did William Blake capture the bizarre vision of the throne room of Revelation 4–5 when he depicted it with eyes suspended in midair, arranged all about. What are we to make of this strangely sighted man? Whence these visions and why such a tale? With the nineteenth-century poet, William Bowles, we may well wonder.

> And who, in this sad place, was this Old Man?
> Who in this island, (where robber scowl'd)
> Exil'd, and destitute, was this old man,—
> Old, but so reverenc'd, the murd'rer pass'd
> His rocky dwelling, and bade peace to it?[1]

Most of John's career, speaking now with reference to the Apocalypse's history of interpretation, has been occupied in exile. Lately he has been showing up in the clinic. Let us first consider John the prisoner. His sojourn at Patmos marks only one chapter of a lengthy ecclesiastical career cobbled together by Christian tradition from Newer Testament writings and the early Christian testimony, collected most notably by the fourth-century church historian Eusebius (*Eccl. hist.* 3.18-24).[2] Iconographic representations most often depict him as imprisoned in exile. In medieval iconography he is typically an overlarge body squeezed onto a tiny Patmos, as in the case of the illuminated twelfth-century *Estense Apocalypse*, as though a celebration of Revelation's unruly excesses. In manuscript illuminations, the book's setting and apocalyptic visions dominate. They depict John, of course, but often alongside or in the background of vision portraits. This is the case, for example, in the manuscript miniatures of the West-Flemish Apocalypse (ca. 1400 C.E.), in which the artist crowds Patmos with apocalyptic visions that dwarf John in his wilderness exile. In these and dozens of other representations like them, John and his visions remain out of doors, in the untamed wilderness, at large.[3]

Later portraits offer better perspective, but again John remains very much the outdoorsy island man. The Renaissance portrait of Hans Memling (1430/40–1494), "Saint John the Evangelist on Patmos," portrays John in calm isolation on his lonely rock, with pen poised to record the visions his heavenward-fixed eyes receive. In the painting of the same title by Hans Burgkmair (1473–1531), John is again outdoors, this time surrounded by exotic trees and tropical birds, a foretaste perhaps of the restored paradise to come. The Patmos landscape of Hieronymous Bosch offers a cameo appearance of a fantastic creature, borrowed from "The Garden of Earthly Delights," to stand at John's feet, the sign that nothing here is what it seems. Mystic calm gives way to terror in Titian's depiction of circa 1560. Hands thrust heavenward as a late-breaking vision scatters storm clouds and cracks the sky in two; John stands impossibly oblique, a marionette with his left hip twisted and right leg distended in hideous foreshortening. Perspective and movement conspire to express what is foreign, troubling, other. Albrecht Dürer's woodcuts of 1498/1511, like those of Lukas Cranach the Elder for Luther's 1534 translation of the Newer Testament, similarly infuse representations of the Apocalypse with movement and energy. Again impossibilities reign as John's descriptions are translated into bizarre images. Even so, Dürer and Cranach, like Titian, insist on placing John in the island-wild of Patmos.

In these representations and countless others like them, John is oxymoronically the banished man at large, untamed like Burgkmair's exotic trees, playful like Bosch's miscreant demon, too big for the tiny Patmos that holds him. They challenge the reasonable and the everyday with a surplus that spills over Patmos's geography with fecund excess. Dürer's woodcuts make the eye roam across Patmos of the Apocalypse, teach it a new grammar of seeing, question reason, cross-examine sensibility. These artists' translations into a pictorial medium create irreducibly absurd representations, and so challenge any mastery through exegesis or interpretation. Their question is not what we will make of John, but what he will make of us.

Albrecht Dürer,
Apocalypse: St. John up in clouds, surrounded by 24 elders

Diego Velazquez's *St. John on the Island of Patmos* marks an end and signals an arrival (see frontispiece). It is prophetic. It foreshadows a later diagnosis of Apocalypse, makes of John a strange case, anticipates a therapy, and iconographically inaugurates a new exegesis that will eventually strip Patmos of its earlier excess, cut John down to size, and tame wild Patmos. We will need to wait almost four hundred years before John can challenge us again with madness, when in the wake of the disappointments of the twentieth century painters will return to wild Patmos and its strange resident to express the madness lurking within modern reason.[4] Painted in 1618, *Saint John on the Island of Patmos* coincides precisely with what Michel Foucault names "the great confinement" of the mad of the seventeenth century in prisons, a confinement that later gave birth to the asylum, the clinic, and the hospital and their therapies.[5] Before this time, Foucault notes, the mad freely roamed the countryside—like John, people at large—inhabiting a kind of liminal space at the margins of European cities or towns. Or, especially in northern Europe from the Renaissance onward, banished from the "reasonable" society of townspeople and city dwellers, they were assigned to the unreason of the sea, and sailed about in literal "ships of fools." In these borderland spaces (water from classical antiquity onward was always associated with the mantic, with the primordial, with chaos) they played an important social function of contesting accepted notions of reason and sociability, of exposing the madness masked in reasoned social convention and custom.

During the first quarter of the seventeenth century, the mad began to be confined in newly established "hospitals." Originally these were not places of healing as the contemporary use of the term implies. Rather they were places to hold, contain, and police the large numbers of beggars and disenfranchised that swelled city populations as a result of the religious wars of the sixteenth and seventeenth centuries. In such *hôpitaux generaux,* or "houses of correction," as they were named in France and England, European monarchies, the bourgeoisie, and the church could regulate the members of these populations. No longer free to roam the edgy spaces of city boundaries and country, or to sail with troupes of the similarly insane and outcast, the mad now began to be housed in these new institutions. Here in turn they eventually came to be treated. Stripped of a prophetic social role, they were now to be rehabilitated, brought "back to reason," to a recovered, rationally ordered sovereignty over the self. The troublemakers of reason were now considered themselves to be troubled and so became cases to be cured, subjects to be treated.

It is to this period of confinement that Velazquez's depiction of St. John belongs. With it we are invited into a new landscape, not of Patmos, but of John's mind. Like other similarly religious works he painted early in the seventeenth century, the artist takes traditional religious themes but treats them in a new way, placing the religious element in the background and focusing instead on the religious personality in question. In these paintings he sets out deliberately to confuse the viewer, relishing in Baroque insertion of pictures within pictures and shifting perspectives of light. Where religious imagery appears, Velazquez plays with representation. Sometimes such imagery looks as though it could be only a mirror reflection of something outside the painting; or it can seem to be suspended between viewer and subject, as though it were perhaps an hallucination or the object of the central figure's imagination. In these paintings Velazquez introduces ambiguities of perspective. Their effect is to create the possibility of psychological explorations. They reflect a time when madness was being rewired into a new social circuitry powering the increasingly centralized authority of European states.

Velazquez's depiction of St. John on Patmos confuses. At first glance, it looks to be a familiar treatment of a religious theme. There are echoes of inherited iconographic commonplaces: dark clouds over a distant landscape; a suspended revelation; the author writing what he sees; an eagle. But a closer look reveals that Velazquez has introduced ambiguities. To begin with, as we look on the portrait we discover that we are not quite certain where we are. John at first glance appears to be out of doors. To the left, behind him, is the Patmos landscape, suggesting that this initial impression is correct. Yet a pile of books, a robe, and a mat at his feet seem to indicate an indoor setting. Does the canvas mark out a section of an indoor cell? Or is it the opening of a cave?

More ambiguous still, in the upper-left-hand corner of the painting, toward the rear, suspended in midair over the distant water, a heavenly figure brings a revelation amid parted clouds. It appears at once close, in the foreground of the painting, and far, in its background. John is looking up—but is it to see or remember? and, for that matter, is the depiction of Patmos in the distance real, a memory, or could it be a vision? The painting at once offers all three possibilities but refuses to settle on any one of them.

Velazquez arranges all these possibilities around the figure seated at the center of the painting: the apocalyptic seer dressed in a resplendent white gown. This is the obvious object of Velazquez's interest—not the content of the final book of the Newer Testament, but its author. The viewer's eyes fall first upon the seer. The artist trains our eyes to gaze upon this rugged mulatto figure—all the features of the painting point to him. John's deep brown eyes, his sensual, parted lips, his slightly inclined head, his thick brown hair, the quill over the book lying open on his lap, captured at the instant John is about to write—all suggest a depth waiting to be explored. The artist invites us to attend to John's face, his posture, his clothing, to pay attention to his gaze fixed heavenward, the way he holds his quill in one hand and his book in the other. In so doing he introduces us to a new topography. It is not a geographic, or even an apocalyptic landscape we are to consider, but rather a mental one. The question of where we are becomes moot as we attend to him. Even the vision returns us to John. Its sole reason for being in the painting is to provide the source of light to illumine John's face and figure. It otherwise has no role to play; one may even think it was a last-minute addition. The painting foreshadows what in the mature artist will develop into Velazquez's development of the baroque—playfulness with iconography by foregrounding the seemingly unimportant as a focus of natural interest and bathing his subject with various perspectives of light. Here, whether the seer is remembering or hallucinating, dreaming up or dreaming of, all the elements of this painting urge us to return to him.

Velazquez's interest is in the mind of an author. What he strikingly creates is the possibility of an apocalyptic psychology, opened in the midst of the canvas that marks a wholly ambiguous opening—cave, and cell. A room with a view, not of Patmos or even of a vision, but of John: this cave/cell suggests an open space. It is an opening for what emerged in the seventeenth century—a space for observation, for diagnosis, and, in the end, for hypotheses to account for such strange visions.

Velazquez's cave/cell, as we will see in a moment, can quickly be adapted into a clinic. Once John was free to roam Patmos, free to disturb us with bizarre images, but lately we have begun to ask ourselves whether he was disturbed. Once, we found ourselves *alongside* him, as indeed in earlier representations he stood alongside and was dominated by the pictures that presented themselves to him. We saw what he saw; heard what he heard. We stood before his visions, in front of his text to witness them with him. His visions gave us eyes to see the world and ears to hear it—what I describe in a later chapter as a grammar for seeing and understanding. But in this later depiction John stands between his visions and us. To know their truth we must first enter an interior landscape, master John, determine his motivations, and record his history. Who is this one who sits unconscious of the fact that we are watching him? What claims does he make for this vision illuminating him? That it is memory, or hallucination? If we once found him arresting, now we wonder if he should have been arrested.

This author responsible for the final pages of the Newer Testament, who prophesied a cosmos-destroying violence, was he not just a little unhinged? D. H. Lawrence certainly thought so.

> John of Patmos must have been a strange Jew: violent, full of the Hebrew books of the Old Testament, but also full of all kinds of pagan knowledge, anything that would contribute to his passion, his unbearable passion, for the Second Advent, the utter smiting of the Romans with the great sword of Christ, the trampling of mankind in the winepress of God's anger till blood mounted to the bridles of the horses, the triumph of the rider on a white horse, greater than any Persian king: then the rule of Martyrs for one thousand years: and then oh then the destruction of the entire universe, and the last Judgement. "Come, Lord Jesus, Come"![6]

To Lawrence, "He was a shameless power-worshipping pagan Jew, gnashing his teeth over the postponement of his grand destiny" (84). His book is "repellent . . . because it resounds with the dangerous snarl of the *frustrated, suppressed* collective self, the frustrated power-spirit in man, vengeful" (Lawrence's emphasis; 73). The work "of a second-rate mind" that "appeals intensely to second-rate minds in every country and every century" (66), it is "what some psychologists would call the revelation of a thwarted 'superiority' goal, and a consequent inferiority complex" (73).

Lucky for John and for us that we have him where we need him. The cave/cell/clinic offers up the author to a nonreciprocal clinical gaze, opens him to investigation, like T. S. Eliot's patient "etherised upon a table." It permits us to compare, measure, classify, diagnose, prescribe, heal. Here John's work can be classified according the diagnostic inventories of seasoned apocalypse experts (Apocalypse Type 1Ib—"Otherworldly Journeys with Cosmic and/or Political Eschatology).[7] All along John will remain completely oblivious to the fact that his thoughts and imagination are being scrutinized, explained, understood even better than he himself understood them. We can return him, without his even knowing it, to some semblance of reason; we can rehabilitate him, justify his place in the canon, or justify removing him, read him or not read him with a clear conscience. We can learn from his mistakes, learn how to overcome apocalyptic urges toward violence, to make wiser and more reasonable choices. Along the way he can give us moral instruction, bring us face to face with our desires and fantasies, their role and function, and so create the possibility of mastering ourselves.

Velazquez marks a new arrival. We can dispense with Patmos. Gone forever is the overlarge John of the illuminated manuscript, squeezed into a tiny Patmos. Gone are fantastic trees, the bizarre postures, the miscreant demons. Gone are the impossible woodcuts. There is a new perspective. John is cut down to size. He can even return from canonical and lectionary exile. Medicated with exegesis he can walk the streets of Ephesus again as a safe and rational citizen. We can find a way toward a reasonable account of John in the cave/prison cell that in only a short while will double as a hospital room.

FROM CELL TO CLINIC

To convert Velazquez's cave/prison cell into the examination room of a clinic or psychiatrist's office requires only a little rearranging. The essential elements are already there. Required only is a language to translate what one sees into a set of symptoms and a diagnosis, the visible into a disease. Carl Jung in many ways picks up where Velazquez leaves off, and it is to Jung that I now turn to set the stage for some remarkable exegetical experiments and some ingenious attempts to rehabilitate our wild-eyed seer.[8]

The Apocalypse is of course a likely candidate for Jungian psychological interpretation. It contains all the necessary ingredients: archetypal performances by virgins, whores, and brides; the play of stark opposites—Christ and Antichrist, Lamb and Beast, Heaven and Hell—dystopic violence interrupted with visions of utopia; entire symbol sets of numbers and colors; astronomical figures; and so on. But perhaps most important of all is the biography furnished John by the tradition. He is at once apostle of love, the author of the Fourth Gospel and the Johannine Epistles, and apocalypticist of hatred and violence. This is a nut Jung cannot help but crack. He knows that the identification of the author of the Apocalypse with that of the Fourth Gospel, not to mention the Epistles, is contested. But in the end it is a hypothesis he cannot dispense with. Here he finds the perfect patient to diagnose and to give his prescription for a return to healthy society.

John provides an intriguing case. "I have seen many compensating dreams by believing Christians who deceived themselves about their real psychic constitution and imagined that they were in a different condition from what they were in reality. But I have seen nothing that even remotely resembles the brutal impact with which the opposites collide in John's visions, except in the case of severe psychosis."[9] Though "he runs the risk of a dissociation" (435), "let us be psychologically correct" (449), "John gives us no grounds for such a diagnosis"; he was "not necessarily . . . an unbalanced psychopath" (450). The "psychological findings" (449) of Jung's exegesis reveal a more profound truth.

> The "revelation" was experienced by an early Christian who, as a leading light of the community, presumably had to live an exemplary life and demonstrate to his flock the Christian virtues of true faith, humility, patience, devotion, selfless love, and denial of all worldly desires. In the long run this can become too much, even for the most righteous. Irritability, bad moods, and outbursts of affect are the classic symptoms of chronic virtuousness. (449)

John, the apostle of love, found he was trapped in what Jung calls "enantiodromia" (444), the battle of opposites contained in the conscious and the unconscious life. John of course could have no way of knowing that his revelation was in fact the projection of his unconscious life. Nor, evidently, would Jung have known this, except that John's unconscious lets the *complexio oppositorum* (the complex of opposites) be "slipped out" in the oxymoronic symbol of the "wrathful lamb" (439). From this "slip" a whole profile rushes forth.

> In all this [i.e., John's vision of the wrath of the lamb and the opening of the book with seven seals] I see less a metaphysical mystery than the outburst of long pent-up negative feelings such as can frequently be observed in people who strive for perfection. We can take it as certain that the author of the epistles of John made every effort to practise what he preached to his fellow Christians. For this purpose he had to shut out all negative feelings, and, thanks to a helpful lack of self-reflection, he was able to forget them. But though they disappeared from the conscious level they continued to rankle beneath the surface, and in the course of time spun an elaborate web of resentments and vengeful thoughts which then burst upon consciousness in the form of a revelation. From this there grew up a terrifying picture that blatantly contradicts all ideas of Christian humility, tolerance, love of your neighbour and your enemies, and makes nonsense of a loving father in heaven and rescuer of mankind. A veritable orgy of hatred, wrath, vindictiveness, and blind destructive fury that revels in fantastic images of terror breaks out and with blood and fire overwhelms a world which Christ had just endeavoured to restore to the original state of innocent and loving communion with God. (438)

John's "torrent of negative feelings seems inexhaustible." They reveal "an unusual tension between conscious and unconscious" (444), that "he was seized by a collective, archetypal process, and he must therefore be explained first and foremost in that light" (443).

Indeed not only explained, but classified, diagnosed, and finally understood better than John could have understood himself. We are squarely in the clinician's chamber. Here Velazquez's and the doctor's gaze meet and commingle in the open space of the cell/examination room. Jung translates a text into signs and symptoms, and thence into pathology. "The clinical gaze has the paradoxical ability to *hear a language* as soon as it *perceives a spectacle*," writes Michel Foucault, describing the birth of classical clinical medicine at the end of the eighteenth century, not so long after John found himself incarcerated in Velazquez's Spanish prison.[10] "To describe is to follow the ordering of the manifestations, but it is also to follow the intelligible sequence of their genesis; it is also to learn to see, because it means giving the key of a language that masters the visible."[11] In an earlier age madness was irreducible and, together with disease and sickness, contained an inexhaustible surplus of meaning. In the classical clinic the naming of symptom as disease exhausted both madness and sickness of their surplus and, by classifying symptoms, contained and left the illusion of controlling them, a fiction that continues to this day.

It is natural to expect that such a complex case as John of Patmos should engender some disagreement in the case room. Jung's diagnosis is only one of a series. C. A. Meier considers Jung's reconstructed biography of the frustrated apostle of love too far-fetched and not consistent with the assured results of historical-critical exegesis. John can more simply be accounted for as the typical product of an introverted intuitive personality unable to distinguish accurately between a rich inner life and the exterior world, which forms the backdrop for visions erupting from a troubled unconscious. John's visions were experienced as objective reality, but in fact they were nothing but products of his inwardly directed self. With therapy John could have come to a full understanding of these visions and have won a renewed and integrated personality.[12]

In a similar, though Freudian, vein, Béla Grunberger treats the Apocalypse as the projection of deep-seated anxiety. The vision of the total destruction of the world, replaced with the heavenly Jerusalem, is, unbeknownst to its author, evidence of a disappointed narcissism. The Oedipal loss of privileged relationship with the Mother is recovered through aggressive fantasies against an idealized enemy (the Father) and is restored in the bliss of the heavenly Jerusalem into which that enemy is refused entry.[13]

The Parisian psychoanalyst Janine Chasseguet-Smirgel agrees that the apocalypse reflects a recovery of the narcissistic child, but detects in the apocalyptic drama far darker tones. Apocalypse is the product of perversion. With his banishment from the heavenly Jerusalem of anything impure and adulterous (Rev. 21:27; 22:15), John reveals a narcissistic compensation of the Superego for the forbidden Oedipal desire of the Unconscious for the Mother.[14] The Warrior/Superego (Rev. 19:11-21) conquers the Dragon/Beast/Penis, vanquishes the Whore of Babylon/Perversion of the Id, and wins the favor of the Wilderness Woman/Mother (12:1-6, 13-17), through virtue/the sublimated erotic, as Bride (21:1-8).

In contrast to these theories of a disintegrated personality, Eugen Drewermann, insisting on a Jungian reinscription of archetypal theory, interprets the Apocalypse as the recovery of integration through apoca-lyptic vision. Through John's visions, the psychic instability caused by the suffering and persecution of the early church was overcome by the bursting forth of archetypal symbols from the collective unconscious. They gave John courage to face the future, and hope in the face of his finitude.[15]

In all of these readings the text is treated straightforwardly as a win-dow into the psychic life of its author. Visions and voices are sympto-matic of deeper drives, and desires or archetypes evidently presumed to be universal. With the psychoanalytical exegesis of Harmut Raguse we arrive at a new level of sophistication. Raguse weds psychoanalysis with reader-response criticism and historical-critical exegesis to plumb the psychic depths of a recovered literary creature. Our apocalyptic subject slips off the psychiatrist's couch to let the text's implied author and nar-rator take his place. Psychological observation is now restricted to the alleged author standing behind the narrator telling the story, the wizard pulling the strings behind the stage of apocalyptic narration.

An author by any name, however, can be equally as schizoid. Raguse diagnoses the implied author as suffering from a depressive condition expressed through a paranoid-schizoid relationship with the world.[16] The implied author projects himself into the disguise of the narrator. Like a virtuoso ventriloquist he throws his voice into the cartoon actors of the plot. He refracts himself in the arrangement of the story. He thereby wins a "second self" to resolve the Oedipal conflict symbolized in the competition with the dragon over the mother of Revelation 12. Oedipal anxiety is overcome by the end of narrative, where Lamb and bride are wedded (21:1-2, 9)—symbolizing, now with a Lacanian modu-lation, the recovery of the phallus. Childhood narcissism is recovered, again, as with the authors listed above, in the exclusive domain of the heavenly Jerusalem.[17]

The clinical and the exegetical gaze thus commingled uncover a spec-tacle and, by means of a robust "allegory of reading,"[18] inscribe it within a classificatory language. John of Patmos finds himself imprisoned not in Velazquez's cave/cell, but locked in an Oedipal desire for the phallus with no way to get out except through fantasy.

Though the schools of interpretation are not always as clear (or con-sistent) as in the psychoanalytic treatments listed above, John's fantasies and/or their social role have been the occupation of biblical scholars of the Apocalypse in recent years. Some scholars write of the attainment of millennial bliss through myth. The disappointment of the millenarian hopes of the first Christian generation as a result of the persecution of Domitian gave rise to a therapeutic myth of the heavenly Jerusalem. In its hearing, for a fleeting moment, present fears and dangers dissolved in an ephemeral experience of the future mediated through apocalyptic narrative.[19] Some interpret the Apocalypse as a means of managing aggressive feelings: John fashioned his narrative to lead his hearers through a dramaturgical process of catharsis. Hearing John's tale played a social-psychological role in the purging of negative feelings against Rome engendered by persecution, by displacing them onto idealized enemies (the Beast, the Whore of Babylon, Jezebel), or turning them inward against the self to be expressed in poverty, chastity, and obedience.[20] For others, the Apocalypse represents gender politics in the form of an unconscious male fantasy about death and desire bred by political repression and eschatological disappointment—patriarchy at once drooling for virgin bride and fantasizing over scarlet-clad whore. John played his "phallocentric" self out in his violent tale of the end of the world. He achieved a catharsis of hostile feelings only by insisting on *male* archetypes of war and destruction directed against a fetishized feminine object of contempt, all at the expense of an alleged (and essentialized) *women's* way of knowing.[21] And finally, to end our whirlwind tour of the exegetical hospital ward, there is John's "rod of iron" (Rev. 2:27; 19:15) peeking out between the lines of the Apocalypse and the Lord Jesus who "comes again." Such language represents a means of making a man via "a textual unconscious," through insisting on masculine domination of the female.[22]

AGAINST INTERPRETATION

I am arguing that I see the Apocalypse in terms of plurality rather than unity. . . . [T]here is a 'playful pluralism' at work in the act of reading this biblical text. The desire for unity and cohesion is a natural one. . . . But I again want to push against the boundaries of interpretation. I want to play with the theory that this text is an open text. I want to play with a deconstructive reading.

—Tina Pippin, *Death and Desire:
The Rhetoric of Gender in the Apocalypse of John*

Tina Pippin's sentiment would no doubt be shared by all the interpreters listed above. Indeed, Harmut Raguse champions his psychoanalytic historical-critical interpretation of the implied author of the Apocalypse as dialogical—a psychoanalytical conversation, a Freudian encounter with apocalyptic tradition.[23] Still I want to ask, to what degree is a text a plurality, and how much room for playfulness, or indeed dialogical encounter, is left when it has been accounted for by reference to social/psychological theories alleged to be universally operative, a kind of natural law, in every gathering or individual? What space is there for a plurality of interpretation when a text is presumed to be a kind of Manichaean battlefield of the unconscious between male and female archetypes that are operative everywhere? And what possibility is there to "push against the boundaries of interpretation" once a text is subjected to overpowering interpretive theories—in this case the psychological theory that is asymptomatic of the desire for the phallus? What happens when a text is interpreted as an ideologically inscribed means of overcoming a "lack," the playing out of deep-seated anxieties lodged in an author's childhood, or, more mysteriously, in the never-never land of a "textual unconscious"? Do such readings treat the Apocalypse as "an open work," or do they simply open it in order to slam it shut once again, its meaning, its intentions, its effects wholly secure? Is this not evidence more of allegory, or the recoding of a text within another system of signification, than of a conversation? And do not such allegories, as Susan Sontag argues, imply a degree of dissatisfaction with the text or even contempt for it?[24]

Conversation implies, following Hans-Georg Gadamer, a to-and-fro movement between partners, the possibility of *being read* by a text as much as reading it.[25] To interpret is to be made sense of as much as to bring sense, to be caught up in a dynamic "fusion of horizons" as interpreter and interpreted greet and mutually inform one another.[26] It is to acknowledge one's place within a history of effects, including one's interpretive methods, and to give up the privileged position of ahistorical dispassionate observation or suspicious ideology critique that paradoxically inscribes its own theories of meaning in the very act of deconstruction.

With Gadamer, I hope for such a two-way conversation, of text and interpreter, a dynamic to and fro. I want the text to read me as much as I read the text. This means that I must give up any unassailable position as analyst or critic of ideology, to see that even as John is on a horizon so am I, including the ideological convictions and methods I bring to the text. "Interpretation must itself be evaluated, within a historical view of human consciousness," writes Susan Sontag, reflecting what may be described as a Gadamerian desire for conversation with a text.[27]

For Sontag, and for me, this does not mean, of course, that there can be readings without interpretation. I am not appealing for a naive traditionalism, and even less the gentle Romantic classicism of Gadamer, the Heidelberg gentleman, whose soothing landscape greets the new millennium untarnished by the bloodiest century in recorded history.[28] The appeal, rather, is for a way of reading that permits the text to stand as other without an attempt to translate it into overpowering hermeneutical categories. I am here describing what Paul Ricoeur names "a second naïveté," a reading not ignorant of, or worse unconcerned with, ideological considerations arising from any interpretation of the text, but playful enough not to be straitjacketed (along with John, the patient from Patmos) into a monocular assessment determined from the outset.[29]

MAKING IT PERSONAL

"When a well-told tale engages us, it not only occupies our time, it occupies us. We are colonised, occupied by a foreign imaginary world, and we can never be the same again."[30] John's is a gripping tale. "I, John, your brother heard . . ." (Rev. 1:9-10); "I John am he who heard and saw these things" (22:8). "I heard," "I saw": this is the Apocalypse's refrain. The rhetorical power of the use of the first person in the Book of Revelation can hardly be overemphasized. First-person narrative draws us into the story line of the Apocalypse by inviting us to witness with John what he saw. John's eyes become our eyes and his ears our ears. We are caught up not only in what he sees and hears, but also in the time he inhabits. Sometimes John makes the visions more vivid by exchanging the past for the present tense, as in 13:12-14, where he describes the actions of the beast of the earth in present tense, or in 15:3-4, where we overhear the hymn of those who conquered the beast through martyrdom even as they sing it. This first-century equivalent to "on-the-scene reporting" adds a sense of urgency and vividness to the text. "Behold, he is coming with the clouds; every eye will see him, even those who pierced him; and on his account all the tribes of the earth will wail on account of him. Even so. Amen" (1:7). John here is present, tensely, somewhere between what was, is, and will be, impossibly inhabiting present and future at once, and thereby offering his audience the gift of time travel. By the end of the story, when John cries, "Amen, come Lord Jesus!" we have already had a sense of that coming in John's strategic use of the present tense funneled through his first-person perspective. "I saw"; "I heard": in fact, we find ourselves with John looking back on what has happened, a glimpse back to the future.

John does not only invite us to see and hear with him. He also wants us to experience with him. Unlike other Jewish and Christian, as indeed pagan, apocalyptic literature, the Newer Testament Apocalypse is not pseudonymous. More usually, writers of ancient apocalypses adopted pseudonyms of famous heroes or mythic characters to receive their revelations (Adam, Enoch, Moses, Daniel, the mantic Sybil, the apocalyptic Tiresias of Sophocles' *Oedipus Rex,* the ancient Seer of Er of Plato's *Republic,* and so on). Such pseudonyms added an inviolable stature to apocalyptic narratives, and enabled them to be presented as though they were in accordance with the legendary, time-honored tradition of the teachings and events of a sacred past. It was as though what was revealed was not anything new (innovation in ethics and religion was generally, as in other tradition-centered cultures, frowned upon in ancient society), just kept secret from the foundation of time (hence the apocalypses of Adam and of Enoch) or, until revealed, hidden from all but the wise (for example, Daniel—Dan. 5:13-16; 6:3).

Some scholars, noting this pattern, argue that perhaps "John" is a pseudonym of an esteemed hero of an alleged "Johannine circle."[31] But in pseudonymous apocalyptic literature the impersonation of an esteemed legendary or mythical character has the effect, alongside winning an impressive pedigree for the revelatory message, of distancing the narrator from the audience and singling out his/her otherness from it. John, however, draws close to his hearers. "I John, your brother, who share with you in Jesus the tribulation and the kingdom and the patient endurance," John writes while invoking familial language of belonging (also powerful in the tradition-oriented societies of the ancient Occident) and an idealized solidarity in suffering with his listeners. John does not want to undertake the apocalyptic journey by himself; he wants to take his audience with him.

John draws us into his perspective affectively as well as cognitively. His emotions loom large in the Apocalypse. After Mark's Jesus, John of Patmos is the moodiest character in the Newer Testament. We learn, for example, of his emotional reactions to the things he saw. "I fell at his feet as though dead," John reports (1:17) when describing his vision of the "one like a son of man" (1:12-16). We see him "weeping much" that none is worthy to open the scroll with the seven seals (5:4). He "marvels greatly" at the vision of a woman sitting on a scarlet beast (17:6-7). All of this again draws us closer to him, as does his miscalculated worship of the angel represented as the angel of revelation at the end of the book (19:10; 22:8-9). This story calls on us not only to see and hear with John, but also to identify with him emotionally. In the first century and in ancient Greco-Roman society generally, instilling a sense of identification with a person giving a speech, called *pathos* by ancient teachers of rhetoric or the art of persuasion, was an important step toward winning over an audience to one's point of view.[32] In Asia Minor, whence comes our text, the style of rhetoric was particularly hot-blooded, noted (disparagingly by its more sanguine Roman critics) for its mood swings, sudden shifts in tense and grammar, and abrupt stylistic changes—all of which characterizes the Apocalypse.[33]

John does all he can to compel us to see things as he does. Pathos is only a preliminary step in audience participation. The nurturing of empathy serves to win an audience over to a particular point of view. John does not only want us to "weep much" with him at the unopened scroll. He also wants us to affirm his dilemma, namely "that no one was found worthy to open the scroll or look into it" (5:4), and to rejoice in its solution (5:5). His visions do not stand open to any interpretation. Always on hand to interpret what he sees for us, John gives us what he considers as the correct understanding.[34] Sometimes his on-site commentary is at the very surface of the story. The best-known example is the number of the Beast (666). After describing the oppressive actions of the Beast, which form the content of a vision (13:11-16), John steps in to comment in a kind of dramatic aside. "This calls for wisdom: let the one who has understanding reckon the number of the beast, for it is a human number, its number is six hundred and sixty-six " (v. 18). We see here John's interpretation, but perhaps more importantly an ingenious strategy of drawing the audience into participation with his vision and of cementing John's trustworthiness into place. For John does not actually *say* who this person is (as indeed two thousand years of false identifica-tions testify), but in calling upon someone with wisdom to identify its number John at once communicates that *he* of course is wise, as is his comprehending audience.[35]

John the impresario also appears when he interrupts apocalyptic per-formances with offstage narrative commentary. He may claim to be over-come with emotion at what he is seeing, but he never loses his head. He retains a firm hold on the drama and insists on his leading role by keep-ing us abreast of the action, or even keeping us from the full knowledge of things (10:4). Always the trustworthy apocalyptic guide, John punctu-ates the narrative sequence of events with editorial markers. For exam-ple, he numerates the three woes prophesied at 8:13 (9:12; 11:14; the third woe is performed instead of marked in chapter 18), and he interprets visions as calls for endurance (13:10; 14:12) or understanding (17:9). By offering explanations to account for the waves of violence that crash through the narrative (for example, 9:20) he assures his audience that the earth-shattering violence revealed to him has direction and purpose. It is easy to forget that what John *claims* to be doing in the Apocalypse is sim-ply reading off the contents of a scroll (5:1-2) or two (10:8-11), and that he is merely its faithful mouthpiece. But these examples show that John is doing more than reciting what he reads.

Other commentary is more deeply embedded in the narrative, most often in relative clauses, and again shows how much John retains control over the content of the Apocalypse. Usually taking the form of short phrases embedded in the midst or at the end of sentences describing a vision, both their presence and their importance in shaping the expecta-tions and understanding of the audience easily slips by unacknowl-edged.[36] In John's vision of the heavenly throne room, for example, he writes, "I saw a Lamb standing, as though it had been slain, with seven horns and with seven eyes," and then concludes, "which are the seven spirits of God sent out into all the earth" (5:6b-d). Here John tightly interweaves vision and interpretation. Strictly speaking, the vision is part of the revelation. But John has positioned his description so that it easily presents itself as belonging to the revelation also.[37] This is a playful ambi-guity, but it has a powerful effect. When this ambiguity is multiplied throughout the narrative, the audience, by subtle degrees, is brought around to a new way of seeing and understanding. In fact, just by read-ing the book we have no choice but to see and hear things the way John chooses to tell them; we become "colonized," to borrow the metaphor from Wayne Booth quoted above.

John achieves a similar result through the use of simile and metaphor. He renders exotic visions imaginable by likening them to or representing them as more familiar objects. In the opening vision, for example, John sees in the midst of seven lampstands one "like a son of man." He goes on to describe him through simile: he has hair "white as wool, white as snow," eyes "like a flame of fire," feet "like burnished bronze, refined as in a furnace," a voice "like the sound of many waters," and a face "like the sun shining in full strength." In the concluding vision John uses metaphor to present the water flowing through the heavenly Jerusalem as "the river of the water of life, flowing from the throne of God and of the Lamb, through the middle of the street of the city" (22:1-2a). These examples could be multiplied many times over, for simile and metaphor make of the Apocalypse a revelation. It has sometimes been suggested that John lets his visions speak for themselves and that he otherwise gets out of the way of their telling. But as these examples show, John is very much the narrator in control even where he appears only to be reporting. Again, it is not clear where revelation ends and interpretation begins.

As with the use of relative clauses, the use of simile, adjective, and metaphor trains us to see what John sees in a particular way. Simile and metaphor draw us into the text and bring the exotic together with the commonplace, allowing us to experience them uniquely. Their use makes us ever more dependent upon John, for simile and metaphor are always irreducible. To say something is *like* something is also to indicate that it is *unlike* it, and to identify one thing in terms of another (a river as "the water of life") means in some sense to obliterate the identity of either. Albrecht Dürer's woodcuts of the Apocalypse illustrate this well, for his painstakingly detailed representations of apocalyptic visions only serve, through visual clarification, to render them incomprehensible, thus exposing the slippage between referents. The effect of John's continued deployment of simile and metaphor is to keep us engaged as his audience and to make us dependent on his clarifications—clarifications which simultaneously function as further mystification and thus keep us listening and reading to win fuller insight.

John borrows most of his similes and metaphors from the Older Testament (in fact, there is little in the Apocalypse that does not in one form or another already appear in Hebrew Scriptures). This infuses John's descriptions with an inviolable character—a kind of apocalyptic wrapping of them in the flag—and links them with the legendary sacred narratives and heroes of a revered history. To describe, for example, the character standing in the midst of the seven lampstands as "one like a son of man" is, through a simple twist of phrase, to merge a vision (or is it an interpretation?) with time-honored prophetic traditions, especially Ezekiel (34:2ff.; 37:3ff.; 38:2ff.), the apocalyptic representations of Daniel (7:13; 8:15-17; 10:5,18), and a powerful christological current within the primitive Christian tradition (Mark 13:26; Matt. 8:20; Mark 2:27-28; compare 1 Thess. 1:10). In fact, the Apocalypse scripts virtuoso performances of Older Testament themes, characters, and events. In the Bible only the Book of Daniel can compete with John's dizzying intertextuality, and John trumps Daniel by adapting the motifs the earlier apocalypticist developed to fit John's own purposes.

Interpretive sleight of hand occurs again where John practices ventriloquism. Ancient Greek had no quotation marks, and contemporary translations with their set-off quotations represent the educated guesses of expert translators. In some cases these are relatively straightforward (for example, Rev. 19:1-8). To many instances, however, John introduces playful ambiguity. Eugene Boring illustrates this well in his attempt to discern, identify, and tabulate the various voices in the Apocalypse.[38] He identifies no less than twenty-eight kinds of narrative voice in Revelation, ranging from straightforward commentary by John (13:10c, 18) to the narrative report of the seven thunders of Rev. 10:3b. Perhaps the most instructive feature of his tabulation is that it shows the degree to which narrative voices are doubled in Revelation. Often Boring is unable clearly to demarcate where John is speaking, where a character is talking, or where both seem to be speaking together.[39]

The classic example, bane of all red-letter Bible editors (red depicting words spoken by Jesus), as indeed anyone who wants to furnish the Greek with quotation marks, is Rev. 22:10-18. Depending on which red-letter Bible one reads, different words are highlighted. Clearly Jesus is speaking in verses 6-7, 12, 16, and 20. But how are we to represent the blessing at verses 14-15, the invocation of the Spirit and the Bride of verse 17, and the warning of verses 18-19? Are these the words of John or of Jesus? In some versions the verses (or differing parts of them) are in red, in others not. Again, the ambiguity is instructive. For like the other literary characteristics listed above, John here is cleverly embedding himself in the Revelation he describes. Such a doubling of voices brings John and Jesus in close proximity. Indeed, is not the entire Apocalypse already framed by such an ambiguity ("The revelation of Jesus Christ, which God gave him [John] . . . [1:1])? Whose words in the end does the entire book claim to represent? And how much more compelling is the warning of verses 18-19 if they are the words of Jesus? Thus not only is the book stamped with a seal that can never be broken, but, implicitly, so are John's interpretations. Here John peeks out from behind the robes of Jesus to perform one final persuasive tour de force. Who would dare to see things *other* than the way John/Jesus does?

To enter into the narrative world of the Apocalypse is to lend our eyes and ears to John. After all, we only see and hear what he wants us to. We may be dissatisfied with this. We may want to translate his narrative into another system of signification. We may suspect his motives, engage him in cross-examination, convince ourselves that we *mirabile dictu* have discovered *the* key to break his apocalyptic code. Still, John does not easily give up control. For the time that we read/hear the Apocalypse is the time that, wittingly or not, we *become* John and thus find ourselves tangled up in his strange, apocalyptic configuration of the world.[40]

For audiences convinced of the reasonableness of a Roman military order whose economic prosperity was bought at the price of incalculable human suffering, John the troublemaker from Patmos unsettles reason and asks his audience to reconsider what counts for sanity. But what is it he wants us to see? To what end does he exert this control? What kinds of performances does John outline in this story? It is into John's apocalyptic theater that we now go.

Remembering Apocalypse

My earliest memories are in German. I did not learn to speak English until I was five. My most vivid memories are situated around our kitchen table, pushed up against a turquoise wall and covered with a yellow plastic tablecloth. There, usually every Sunday morning, during the one meal that we would gather to eat together as a family (for otherwise my father was working), we would, ritually, even liturgically, rehearse the past. The abundance of the family feast became the occasion for gathering the collective memories of apocalypse-styled deprivation, tragedy, and loss. As though the food itself triggered the memories of apocalyptic horsemen and the sounds and sights of war, famine, pestilence, and death.

Sunday was the time to offer sacred anamnesis. The table became the site to collect and represent time, to inscribe in space an enduring notion of place and story. Prompted by the questions of a curious boy, who was, as I recall now, beginning to play war with imagined enemies, my family would describe the world around them. Thus was I schooled in apocalypse. Having been refugees only nine years before I was born, my parents maintained apocalypse as a coefficient in their lives—its products shaping my life in ways , even today, of which I am scarcely aware.

My earliest memories are of fire. I knew before I was five that the Canadian citizens of the town where we lived had burned down the German Lutheran church during the Second World War and had forbidden worship in German. I heard about the terror and horror of exploding bombs, of how the earth shakes and the sky screams during an air raid. I learned stories of murder and starvation, of disease and torture, of revenge against the losers of a war. When these stories were told they were always presented as endings: the end of families, the end of communities, and the end of a culture, the end of youth. My parents were only teenagers when they experienced these things. Yet these things were told as though they had only happened yesterday.

Apocalypse gave me eyes to see the world. The memories are couched in the categories of the Book of Revelation. Hitler first as Messiah, then as Antichrist; a loaf of bread sold for a month's wages; block upon ruined city block, rubble as far as the eye could see, where once merchants and traders had made their fortunes; the wilderness pursuit of women and children by evil soldiers. The play of binary oppositions, of Pole and Russian against German, life against death, good against evil, light against darkness. And then, of course, the promise of a new land, safety, a new life, and the possibility of prosperity and safety in Canada. The happy ending, but one that could not forget its terrible beginning, and what it now meant to say that you were German. Early on I learned the fragility of safety and the possibilities of darkness.

I would, I now remember, sneak out of my crib at night, and tiptoe down the hall, just to see if my mother and father were still in their bed. For my young world was populated by soldiers who could come knocking in the middle of the night and steal you away into unspeakable darkness.

It may be that I can refuse to read the Apocalypse. What I know is that I could not keep it from reading me. In the process of being read I was urged to become a faithful actor on utopia's stage, Canada—the refuge from tragedy and death. Apocalypses told and remembered, however, were not intended for passive consumption. Both John's Apocalypse and the remembrance of my family's demanded audience participation, to become characters in a drama with God as audience and director, where one suspects the reasonable and commonsense as a peculiar form of insanity.

So it is, script in hand, that we now step onto Apocalypse's stage, to see how Revelation tries to convince us, its audience, that we are always being seen, and to enact a peculiar form of theatricality. The curtain is about to rise. Let us hasten to discover what kinds of actors Revelation urges us to be.

3

Seeing Things

EYEING JOHN

The Book of Revelation is a text filled with eyes. John sees God's throne, and around it "four living creatures, full of eyes in front/all around and behind/within" (Rev. 4:6, 8). He beholds Jesus who possesses "eyes . . . like a flame of fire" (1:14; 2:18; 19:12). Jesus is the lamb with seven eyes "which are the seven spirits of God sent out into all the earth" (5:6). Roaming the earth, these spirits not only look in every direction, they size it up and take stock of it. Each of the messages to the seven churches begins with an examination: "I know your works (2:2, 9, 19; 3:1, 8, 15); "I know where you live" (2:13). There is no escaping their scrutiny. "And all the churches shall know that I am he who searches mind and heart, and I will give to each of you as your works deserve" (2:23). In the world of the Apocalypse one is either seen or threatened with exposure. "Therefore I counsel you [Laodiceans] to buy from me gold refined by fire, that you may be rich, and white garments to clothe you and to keep the shame of your nakedness from being seen" (3:18). Jesus is the apocalyptic *paparazzo* with camera ready to expose the unsuspecting in their most compromising situations: "Lo, I am coming like a thief! Blessed are those awake, keeping their garments that they may not go naked and be seen exposed" (16:15). He promises forthcoming performances by characters dressed in outrageous costume: the harlot "arrayed in purple and scarlet, and bedecked with gold and jewels and pearls" (17:4); "the ten horns that you saw, they and the beast will hate the harlot; they will make her desolate and naked, and devour her flesh and burn her up with fire . . ." (17:16).

The Apocalypse is a visual feast. Long after the last curtain call and the echo of the cry for an encore, apocalyptic performance dies away; it is a sense of being watched that lingers. Perhaps one awakens in the middle of the night with the strange feeling that eyes are fixed upon oneself and that there can no longer be any secrets, or on the way to work the next day one steals a glance over one's shoulder for fear of being followed.

The threat of being seen is a powerful means of assuring obedience and shaping adherence. In the eighteenth century, Jeremy Bentham urged a reform of the contemporary prison system which until then was centered on corporeal punishment. He insisted instead on the rehabilitation of prisoners through a new form of prison architecture that he named the *panopticon*. Instead of being physically punished, prisoners would be rendered visible. Bentham's design arranges prisoners' cells around and opening out to a central watchtower where a guard is able to see each cell without himself being subject to detection. Prisoners, knowing that at any moment they may meet the guard's gaze, must keep watch over themselves. In this model it is no longer physical force, but visibility, that coerces. Being seen regulates. It insists that the prisoner behold himself even as the guard beholds him, and, in seeing himself, to consider his crimes, dispositions, and behaviors. Punishment gives way to a disciplining power of observation.[1]

One wonders if Bentham had been reading ancient Jewish and Christian apocalyptic literature when he conceived of the panopticon. A leitmotiv that runs through this tradition is the notion that because creation is visible to God's all-seeing eye, no sin can escape divine notice.[2] To enter the panopticism of early Christian apocalyptic literature is to find oneself in a world in which the divine eye perceives "the most elementary particle" and records "the most passing phenomenon."[3]

This sense of being seen drew from and strengthened an already powerful social current in ancient society. The Roman Empire has been aptly described anthropologically as an honor-shame culture. If, in the modern first world, people compete for financial power, in antiquity people competed for status. One either won it through birth (in which case status was conferred) or achieved it through patronage (in which case it was won), or reinforced the former by means of the latter (the reverse movement from won to conferred status was difficult if not impossible). It was, in other words, a world in which to enjoy social power (status) one either had to be *seen* to be someone, or at least *seem* to be acting like someone. This is attested in the most general and detailed features of Roman society, from the conspicuously placed inscriptions on public monuments, celebrating their erection by patrons, to the precisely calibrated ethical instructions of its moral philosophers on how to dress, walk, eat and talk. The ancient Greek maxim "better to be than to seem" addresses itself to the importance placed on appearance in this social world.[4] It was a visual culture. Thus, when the Apocalypse threatened its listeners with nakedness (3:17-18), it of course echoed a favored biblical metaphor for divine punishment (e.g., Ezek. 16:37-39; 23; Lam. 1:8; Hosea 2:3, 9; Nahum 3:5), but seen from a social-anthropological perspective it was drawing on visibility's coercive power in Greco-Roman culture.

What we may call a panoptic sensibility was not peculiar to the New Testament Apocalypse, nor was its potential for winning obedience to ethical demands a secret. Christian friends deployed it to great effect. Pagan foes decried it as a disingenuous tactic to scare the unwitting into subservience.

Another apocalypse from the same era provides a fascinating contrast with the Book of Revelation. *The Shepherd of Hermas* was apparently addressed to a fairly prosperous Christian community in Rome roughly contemporary with John's Revelation. In the passages from *Hermas* that follow, we hear a tone different from John's, and yet it may be Revelation's closest analogue, both in terms of a concern with the abuse of wealth and the pursuit of economic well-being, as well as the efficient deployment of panopticism.[5]

The work's protagonist, Hermas, a former slave or freedperson and once-prosperous businessperson, receives a series of apocalyptic visions and commandments to deliver to the Roman church. Rambling, moralizing allegorical explanations of visions comprise the majority of the work, through which Hermas learns that all is not well with his community. Bishops, elders, and other leaders, he discovers, love money and their business interests more than the church.[6] They are "double-minded," the *Shepherd*'s favorite term of reprobation. In other words, they are divided between allegiance to the church and to society, between the desire for obedience and ethical purity and social prestige and its attendant vices. On account of this situation, and unless it changes, Hermas learns from his apocalyptic guide, persecution is coming. He sees a ravenous beast approaching with fire to consume the church:

> Go then and tell the Lord's elect ones of his great deeds, and tell them that this beast is a type of the great persecution which is to come. If then you [plural] are prepared beforehand and repent with all your heart towards the Lord, you will be able to escape it, if your heart be made pure and blameless, and you serve the Lord blamelessly for the rest of the days of your life. . . . Believe on the Lord, you who are double-minded, that he can do all things, and turns his wrath away from you, and sends scourges on you who are double-minded. Woe to those who hear these words and disobey; it were better for them not to have been born. (*Vis.* 4.2.5, 6)[7]

To his horror, Hermas goes on to learn not only that punishment is coming to the church, but that he and the church are being watched. He discovers that God knows his thoughts, sees into his domestic affairs, and records his virtues and vices. The work opens with Hermas recalling the sight of his erstwhile master, Rhoda, bathing naked and his helping her out of the water. "When I saw her beauty I reflected in my heart and said, 'I should be happy if I had a wife of such beauty and character.' This was my only thought, and no other, no, not one" (*Vis.* 1.1.2). But now it is Hermas who is exposed. Praying one day to confess his sins (1.1.3), Hermas beholds an open heaven and then goes on to describe the encounter:

> I saw that woman whom I had desired (*epethumēsa*) greeting me out of the Heaven and saying, "Hail, Hermas." And I looked at her, and said to her, "Lady (*kyria*), what are you doing here?" and she answered me: "I was taken up to accuse you of your sins before the Lord." I said to her: "Are you now accusing me?" "No," she said, "but listen to the word which I am going to say to you. God . . . is angry with you because you sinned against me." I answered and said to her: "Did I sin against you? In what place, or when did I speak an evil word to you? Did I not always look upon you as a goddess? Did I not always

respect you as a sister? Why do you charge me falsely, Lady, with these wicked and impure things?" She laughed and said to me: "The desire of wickedness came up in your heart. Or do you not think that it is an evil deed for a righteous man if an evil desire come up in his heart? Yes, it is a sin," said she, "and a great one. For the righteous man has righteous designs. . . . But they who have evil designs in their hearts bring upon themselves death and captivity, especially those who obtain this world for themselves and glory in their wealth, and do not lay hold of the good things which are to come. Their hearts will repent yet have they no hope, but they have abandoned themselves and their life. But pray to God, and He shall heal the sins of yourself and of all your house and of all the saints." (*Vis.* 1.1.4–9)

Rhoda scrutinizes Hermas and finds him wanting. Hermas, Rhoda's client, fails to win from his social superior the honor only she can lend him. Instead he finds himself shamed.

The honor-shame code is more thoroughly applied as the story unfolds. Hermas later learns that God similarly has criticisms of Hermas's household. He receives a vision of "the angel of punishment" (*Sim.* 6.3.2–3) sent to discipline those "who have wandered away from God, and walked in the lusts and deceits of this world" (6.3.3). Hermas's household is among these sinners. "Your sins are many," Hermas's apocalyptic guide informs him,

but not so great as that you should be handed over to this angel; but your family (*ho oikos*) has done great iniquity and sin, and the glorious angel has become enraged at their deeds, and for this reason he commanded you to be afflicted for some time, that they also may repent and purify themselves from every lust of this world. When, therefore, they repent, and have been purified, then the angel of punishment will depart from you. (*Sim.* 7.2)

Hermas's troubles represent a public shaming of the patron deity.

Hermas can, however, through obedience, turn things around. In the concluding vision, a long allegorical exposition, the Shepherd (Jesus) builds a tower (the church) of various stones (types of Christians). Hermas meets virgins and women with long black hair (representing virtues and vices, respectively). Now, in a reversal of the opening vision in which Hermas had lusted after Rhoda, he learns that he is to sleep with the virgins.

> "You shall sleep with us," said they, "as a brother and not as a husband, for you are our brother and for the future we are going to live with you for we love you greatly." But I was ashamed to live with them. And she who seemed to be the first of them began to kiss and embrace me, and the others seeing her embracing me began to kiss me themselves, and to lead me round the tower, and to play with me. I, too, had, as it were, become young again, and began to play with them myself, for some were dancing, others were gavotting, others were singing, and I walked in silence with them round the tower, and was merry with them. But when evening came I wished to go home but they did not let me go, but kept me, and I stayed the night with them and slept by the tower. For the maidens spread their tunics on the ground, and they made me lie down in the midst of them, and they did nothing else but pray, and I also prayed with them unceasingly and not less than they, and the maidens rejoiced when I was praying thus, and I stayed there until the morrow until the second hour with the maidens. (*Sim.* 9.11.2–7)

The divine panopticon has rehabilitated Hermas. Once he had insisted on his purity, only to be disclosed burning with desire. Now, amid the overheated eroticism of his final vision, Hermas remains cool as a cucumber. Playing, dancing, embracing, kissing, sleeping with the virgins, Hermas has undergone a transformation from the vice of double-mindedness (the author's favorite depiction of sinfulness) to singleness of heart. In the narrative he in fact personifies his wider audience (indicated, in the quotation from *Similitude* 7 cited above, for example, in the change from second to third person). As the apocalypse unfolds his character becomes an ideal, undergoing the reversal its wider audience must replicate—away from too much concern with economic success toward penitent self-knowledge.[8] Having fallen under the gaze of God's all-penetrating eye, Hermas, at the story's conclusion, has learned how to govern his household, what kind of character to nurture, and what failings to correct. In terms of the honor-shame and status-competing code of the day, Hermas, by having fallen so favorably under God's eye at the end of the story, wins a status loaned from his patron, the Shepherd. *The Shepherd of Hermas* offers discovery and reversal, twin themes to which we will return in due course as these are central to the hortatory strategy of the Apocalypse. But first let us hear a word from the critics.

Pagan detractors of early Christianity suspected that this notion of the omniobservant God was a ruse to control the faithful. Late in the second century, the Christian apologist Minucius Felix imagined a fictional debate between Octavius, a Christian, and his pagan opponent, Caecilius. As they stroll on the beach of Ostia near Rome, Caecilius rehearses stock complaints against Christians, charging that their Eucharists are cannibalistic feasts and that their agape or love feasts are orgies. He goes on to complain about their omniscient God, who

> searches diligently into the ways and deeds of all people, yea even their words and hidden thoughts, hurrying to and fro, everywhere present at once; they make him out to be a troublesome, restless being, who has a hand in everything that is done, is shamelessly curious, interlopes at every turn, and can neither attend to particulars because he is distracted with the whole, nor to the whole because he is engaged with particulars.[9]

The voyeuristic God leaves Caecilius smiling wryly. Minucius Felix is, however, too much the apologist to leave Caecilius feeling smug for long. His Christian defender, Octavius, valiantly makes the weaker case stronger by meeting him halfway and then spinning the detraction more positively: "God, the author of all things and examining watchman (*speculator*) of all, present in darkness and present in that other darkness of our thoughts! Not only do we act under his eye, but with him, I almost say, we have our life" (32.9).

The roughly contemporary Justin Martyr, another Christian apologist and himself evidently aware of something like the pagan criticism, turns the argument around even more ingeniously—by appealing to the shrewd politics of an idealized surveillant state. Christians, Justin argues, are precisely the kind of citizens the emperor wants. Consider, he argues, what kind of obedience and social order would be assured were the emperor's eyes able to register the minutest behaviors of every citizen. If people only knew that they could never escape divine detection, he insists, "they would not choose wickedness even for a little, knowing that they go to the everlasting punishment of fire. They would by all means restrain themselves, and adorn themselves with virtue, that they might obtain the good gifts of God, and escape punishments."[10] The church achieves what the empire struggles to gain, only more efficiently and thoroughly.

Caecilius groans, "[Christians] threaten the whole world and the universe and its stars with destruction by fire. . . . Under this delusion they promise themselves as virtuous, a life of never-ending bliss after death; to all others, as evildoers, everlasting punishment" (*Oct.* 11.1, 5). Just so, Octavius agrees. In fact, he says, Caecilius has just made the case for Christian virtue for him!

It is possible that in all of this, friends and foes alike were thinking of the Apocalypse. John urges precisely this kind of conclusion when he exhorts the seven churches with the disciplining gaze of Jesus: "I am he who searches mind and heart, and I will give to each of you as your works deserve" (Rev. 2:23).

John utilizes similar strategies to create his own version of the panoptic. Like Hermas's, his apocalyptic telling of the end of the world is filled with stories of discovery and reversal. And he would have approved of the apologetic uses of the motif described above. The biblical Apocalypse insists on an ethical reform centered in the perception of divine sight. Indeed, Caecilius's "shamelessly curious" Christian God would have been at home in John's heavenly Jerusalem. What, after all, is this place where the glory of God is the light, where there is no longer night (21:23; 22:5), if not a space for rendering the unseen visible, a city where universal surveillance is perfected? Is the city of God a utopia or is it a reformatory?[11]

GOD'S SPECTACLE

Minucius Felix offers a temperate debate between a Christian and pagan friend at a seaside resort. Caecilius's paganism is always anemic, as vulnerable to and brittle before Octavius's robust defense as the shells he no doubt crushed underfoot as they walked along the beach. Indeed, so

persuaded is Caecilius by Octavius's defense that, at the conclusion of
the debate, he repents and embraces the Christian faith (40). It is an idealized apologetic performance, as gentle and studied as it is reasonable
and persuasive. It is intriguing, in this regard, that it is the pagan who
brings up apocalypse and not the Christian. Octavius never loses a step.
Always quick on the uptake in the debate with Caecilius, he not only
grants the point that the Christian God sees and registers all. He goes on
to conclude that since this must be so, virtue-loving Christians are a "fair
spectacle (*pulchrum spectaculum*) for God to see" (*Octavius* 37.1). They
respond to the threat of apocalypse by offering God pleasing performances. Caecilius only needs to join the show.

Minucius Felix's indicative is fragile. In another's hands it erodes into
an imperative. No longer on a seashore, or engaged in gentle debate with
a not-too-swift pagan, the late-second-century apologist, Tertullian of
Carthage, casts aside moderate Roman conversation concerning the
invocation of the end of the world and writes with the moralizing heat of
apocalyptic fire. "Doubtless," Gibbon remarks concerning Tertullian,
"there were many among the primitive Christians of a temper more suit-
able to the meekness and charity of their profession."[12] Tertullian lacks
Minucius Felix's patience with pagan criticisms of Christian faith. In his
many moral treatises (the larger portion of his extant *oeuvre*), as one
might expect, the concern is with more practical matters than gaining
points on abstract philosophical and moral problems that pagan
philosophers were having with Christian faith. Here Tertullian (even the
less shrill, pre-Montanist one) rarely flinches from full-scale invective
against the alleged capitulation of his apparently more easygoing
Carthaginian church to Greco-Roman culture. Minucius Felix nudges
Christian faith up the social ladder of status by staging the relatively
high-flying Caecilius and Octavius in sophisticated philosophical and
moral debate as nuanced as the elegant, modulating Ciceronian Latin
phrases of his text. If he tips his hat to Roman sensibilities, Tertullian
(master of Latin style and rhetoric that he is) could not care less.
Octavius embarrassedly gets to apocalypse only after the pagan brings it
up; Tertullian is quick to dive into the final chapters of the Bible's last
book, scented as they are with fire and brimstone, to drive his point
home. In his treatise *De Spectaculis* (On the shows), a pre-Montanist
Tertullian censures members of his Christian community for attending
the circus and, in doing so, he uncovers and then develops more fully a

feature of apocalypse to which Minucius Felix alludes.[13] Again, Tertullian's use of Apocalypse, and apocalyptic eschatology generally, helps to uncover a more neglected feature of the hortatory strategies of the Apocalypse's panopticism.

Tertullian hates the idea that Christians should be found at the circus, the favorite entertainment of people in the Roman world. Instead of attending spectacles, Tertullian warns, Christians should remember that they are performers in a show, the spectacle at which God has a front-row seat. He commands Christians to avoid the fraud, murder, deception, idolatry, and adultery luridly played out on the pagan stage, all of which God already sees and is angered by both on and off the stage. Instead, they should offer God a more upbeat performance:

> What greater pleasure is there . . . than to find yourself tramping underfoot the gods of the Gentiles, expelling demons, effecting cures, seeking revelations, living to God? These are the pleasures, the spectacles of the Christians, holy, eternal, and free. Here find your games of the circus.[14]

A little later he offers an apocalyptic inflection of his theme: in the last judgment, once again, there will be a show, one final performance for the immoral actors of the stage:

> There will be the tragic actors to be heard, more vocal in their own tragedy; and the players to be seen, lither of limb by far in the fire; and then the charioteer to watch, red all over in the wheel of flame; and, next, the athletes to gaze upon, not in their gymnasiums but hurled in the fire. (30.5)

He advises Christians to imagine themselves playing an alternative role in the spectacle of the Lord's return.

> But what a spectacle is that fast-approaching advent of our Lord . . . ! What the glory of the rising saints! What the kingdom of the just thereafter! What the city New Jerusalem! . . . How vast the spectacle that day, and how wide! What sight shall wake my wonder, what my laughter, my joy and exultation. . . . Such sight, such exultation. . . . And that all these, in

some sort are ours, pictured through faith in the imagination of the spirit. (30.1, 3)

Tertullian thus not only urges avoidance of the circus. In the light of forthcoming apocalypse, he scripts Christian roles to play.

The Book of Revelation knows a hortatory strategy at least as shrill as Tertullian's, but equally as inviting as Minucius Felix's. In his panopticon, John does not leave his audience to contend with God's scrutiny on their own. Like Tertullian, he offers his audience roles to pursue or avoid in the drama of the end of the world. With Minucius Felix, he shows the way toward becoming a "fair spectacle" for God to see. John treats his listeners to performances of damnation and salvation. He stages larger-than-life characters dressed in costumes rummaged from the clothes closet of biblical tradition—the scarlet-clad woman on the beast already mentioned (2 Kings 9:30; Isa. 3:18-23; Jer. 4:30; Ezek. 23:40) and the white-robed martyrs (Rev. 7:1-14; Dan. 11:35; 12:10). The audience overhears these characters sounding their dismay or joy, woe and jubilation as visions unfold (for example, Rev. 18:10, 14, 16-17, 19; 19:1-3, 5, 6-8). John invites his audience to side for or against these characters, to be moved by their performances, to be persuaded of his message, and to pursue his goals.

As with Tertullian, in the drama of the Apocalypse the line between stage and audience, between observer and observed, is fluid. The audience watches; it also discovers that it is a part of the show. John counsels the Laodiceans, for example, "to buy . . . white garments" (3:18). The faithful of Sardis learn that "they shall walk with me [Jesus] in white, for they are worthy. The one who conquers shall be clad thus in white garments . . ." (3:4-5). In the visions that follow the listeners will learn how to act out their parts, and some will discover themselves dressed in disturbing costume, or worse, in the costume that is no costume at all—nakedness (3:17, 18). In the songs and laments of these visions, in the responses to calamity and persecution, John's listeners discover idealized stories that provide scripts for performing in a Christian social world. Whether shrilly or gently, to discover oneself the unwitting performer in an apocalyptic show is to become convinced of a panoptic sensibility, and to coach oneself to play the part.

PERFORMING APOCALYPSE

The Apocalypse treats us to tales of discovery and reversal. John's audience sees itself performing apocalypse. Barbara Freedman in her study of Shakespearean comedy coins the term *theatricality* to describe this simultaneous process of seeing and being seen. For Freedman, *theatricality* denotes the state of affairs when "a person is aware that she is seen, reflects that awareness, and so deflects our look. . . . Theatricality evokes an uncanny sense that the given to be seen has the power both to position us and to displace us."[15] Freedman builds on the legacy of the social psychologist Erving Goffman as well as the psychoanalytical philosophy of Jacques Lacan in her study of theatricality. In his classic study, *The Presentation of Self in Everyday Life*, Goffman describes the function of roles in shaping behaviors and self-understanding.

> It is probably no mere historical accident that the word *person*, in its first meaning, is a mask. It is rather a recognition of the fact that everyone is always and everywhere more or less consciously playing a role. . . . It is in these roles that we know each other; it is in these roles that we know ourselves. In a sense, and in so far as this mask represents the conception we have formed of ourselves—the role we are striving to live up to—this mask is our truer self, the self we would like to be. In the end, our conception of our role becomes second nature and an integral part of our personality. We come into the world as individuals, achieve character, and become persons.[16]

Goffman's study may be read as a psychological unpacking of the truism that "life is a stage." We are actors engaged in performances that are formed by social expectations and that take place on more or less public stages.

For Freedman, however, this assessment requires the further insight, borrowed from the psychoanalytical theory of Jacques Lacan, that the images and roles we live out are reflections of a fantastic symbolic construction of the unconscious. Theatricality implies the presence of a gaze—an unconscious orientation to reality by means of which we appear to ourselves and we make sense of the world. "In our relation to things, in so far as this relation is constituted by the way of vision, and

ordered in the figures of representation, something slips, passes, is transmitted, from stage to stage, and is always to some degree eluded in it—
that is what we call the gaze." [17] "In the scopic relation, the object on
which depends the phantasy from which the subject is suspended in an
essential vacillation is the gaze." [18]

"Something slips, passes," "an essential vacillation": this is what
Freedman intends, in her definition above, by her reference to theatricality as "an uncanny sense." "If the eye is that which sees, the gaze is
that which elides the eye and shows us how we are caught out by our
own look—displaced in the act of spectatorship." [19] Theatricality leaves
us suspended in representation. As in a horror film, in which one has to
keep reminding oneself that what one is seeing is only a movie, one nevertheless finds oneself reflected in the actions and reactions of its actors.
The viewer is paradoxically on stage and in the audience, seer and seen.
Theatricality furnishes a relation to the world and implies a scopic relation to it.

Freedman uses these insights to understand the way that representation functions in Shakespearean comedy and tragedy and shows how its
strategies symptomize the preoccupations of Elizabethan and other
Renaissance societies concerning newly recovered classical ideals of
representation. [20] She does not intend to import anachronistic notions of
the unconscious, characteristic of the modern era, into an earlier period,
but rather to use Lacan's notion of the gaze as an analogue to earlier
strategies of representation. Lacan's explorations of optics and distortion offered him insights into the construction of the self as distorting
performance before an (invisible) audience. Similarly, Freedman argues,
the Renaissance discovery of perspective and the disciplined use of distortion to create the illusion of reality in portraiture gave rise to theatrical
explorations in portraying the relation of reality to representation.
Cross-dressing characters, plays within plays, mistaken identities—all of
which nevertheless function on stage to unveil the real in the very act of
disguise—were some of the ways the Elizabethan stage explored the way
perspective and representation construct reality even as they distort it.

Freedman shows how both Lacanian psychoanalysis and Renaissance theater are unique responses to the cultural legacy of visuality and
what it means to be rendered visible. These explorations of theatricality
are instructive for the study of apocalyptic tradition as well. [21] It is worth
recalling that Shakespearean comedy and tragedy with their stratagems

of hidden identities and actors playing actors (playing actors), as well as role reversals, draw from the traditions of the ancient stage and literature. Aristotle's *De poetica* (*Poetics*) is the canonical expression of the importance and function of these devices. A *vade mecum* for the basic elements of fiction, Aristotle's work summarized the ideals of fictional representation of the classical and Hellenistic periods, and set the standard for literary culture until our day. It is itself symptomatic of the visual honor-shame culture its prescriptions help to construct.

Good plots, Aristotle observes (privileging the eye), contain discovery and reversal.[22] Discovery and reversal attend the wily Odysseus on his long journeys and the apocalypse-like ending of his homecoming. They fuel the plots of ancient tragedy (Aristotle cites *Oedipus Rex* as his preeminent example of successful plot) and comedy. In the Latin comedy of Plautus, Terence, and Seneca, in which characters pretending to be something they are not trigger unpredictable burlesque, it is Aristotle's discovery, reversal, and interest in representation (*mimesis*) that remain constant.[23] These characteristics remain constant in ancient satire. Petronius in his *Satyricon*, for example, a sendup on the upward mobility of a newly created service elite that benefited from civil stewardship of the imperial household, presents Trimalchio, the upstart freedperson, as playing at being the Roman aristocrat. Moreover, he knows he is playing at it, as do the guests who witness Trimalchio's luridly misbegotten displays of conspicuous consumption.[24] Similarly, Lucian's treatises on flim-flam Cynic philosophers draw their humor from the recognition shared by Cynic character and reader that the philosopher is only an actor playing at being a philosopher, and that his patron is his unwitting dupe.[25]

Again, in so-called Greek novels, literature contemporary with the Apocalypse and for popular consumption by more or less middle-class audiences, plots turn on masquerade and revelation as heroes and heroines undertake long voyages.[26] Early Christian literature, in particular the apocryphal *Acts* of the apostles and the so-called *Clementine Recognitions*, draw upon this genre as apostles and disciples undertake long journeys during which discovered disguises and reversals hold the reader's interest in the heroic examples of Christian protagonists.[27]

In all of these examples, the elements of discovery and reversal reflect Greco-Roman antiquity's visual culture, in which representation played a central role in shaping its ethos and worldview. Of course, John did not have to reach for his Sophocles, much less Homer, to find the model for his own tale of discovery and reversal, nor did he need to read Aristotle to gain an understanding of these devices. He had the Older Testament, a treasure trove of classic stories of discovery and reversal, from which to draw. His Apocalypse, with its sixes and sevens, its roller-coaster reversals of characters clothed with glory, then stripping naked, its sword-mouthed warrior, destruction of mercantile cities, and Jerusalem apotheosis is far closer to the Hebrew Bible than anything Greek. Still one wonders if his Greek listeners, centered as they were in the heartland of a would-be imperial culture, could follow his virtuoso performances of the biblical tradition (for they challenge the abilities of even the most adept modern commentators, equipped as they are with concordances and software Bibles). For those listeners, one suspects, the tradition of Aristotle was closer at hand; tales of discovery and the reversals of the Greek stage, including that most apocalypse-like of shamed heroes, Oedipus, must have furnished some analogy to help make sense of John's Apocalypse. The Book of Revelation with its veilings and unveilings, its maskings and reversals, belongs to a hybrid culture, and one has to keep on the lookout for all of its strains to appreciate the genesis of John's adventuresome tale.

The Apocalypse, then, is a journey of discovery. Traveling with John, under God's watchful eye, one sees oneself in the larger-than-life performances of Revelation's characters. John positions us before unfolding events, and simultaneously displaces us by transforming us into mythologized form. As Edith Humphrey has shown, the Book of Revelation offers readers and listeners idealized stories of reversal with which to identify. She limits her discussion to "Lady" Zion personified as a female figure in select apocalypses (in Revelation, the congregation of God as persecuted mother [chap. 12] and then vindicated Bride [chap. 21]), but the insight can be applied more generally, and not only positively.[28] For example, John borrows a recurring Older Testament literary trope in which the modulating careers of heroes and villains are accompanied by changes in dress to represent more negative transformations.[29]

The Laodiceans, for example, are also promised a transformation from their present confidence in wealth toward nakedness (3:18), a punishment played out by that other Lady of the Apocalypse, the whore of Babylon (17:16). All this is foreshadowed by John's prophecy against Jezebel in 2:22, as I hope to show. Placed and displaced, entertained by promises of reversals, the reader in Revelation experiences a kind of vertigo, making us ever more dependent on John's interpretations, his point of view, and his staging of events and characters. The Laodicean example is only the last in a series of promised discovery and reversal. Between the opening address of the framing epistolary greeting of 1:4 and the final words of the seventh message to Laodicea (3:22), there are nearly twenty promised or threatened reversals of fortune, a topsy-turvy hortatory romp that foreshadows the creation-shattering reversals and discoveries to come.[30]

John's first-person Apocalypse, as I suggested in the previous chapter, makes his story personal. His eyewitness report is a powerful means of colonizing the audience to adopt his point of view. John's repetitive "then I saw," "then I heard" demand that one see through John's lens, or hear with his ears. John captures his audience in a new visual code. John's roving eye, recording all that it sees, enlarges notions of what is worth looking at. John teaches a grammar, a new way of seeing.[31] Beholding John's visions, the audience learns what to pursue and avoid. It discovers itself unveiled ("I know your works"; "I know where you live") and then re-veiled in the costume of forthcoming woe and bliss. The fantastic imaginary of John's apocalyptic stage reproduces his audience in what, borrowing a phrase from Martin Jay, we may call a "scopic regime."[32] John's sweeping historical and visual vistas offer a new relation to the world. Seen from the throne room, in which the script of the Apocalypse is opened and read (Rev. 5:1-5; 6:1; etc.), the churches are first positioned, then displaced. John's bird's-eye view offers churches fresh if disturbing perspective. With world-turning reversals of fortune, John's theatrical strategies entice them to see themselves as they could be. It lures them into contempt for what they are.

Let us take a closer look at these strategies and at the modulating performances of John's apocalyptic characters. The Apocalypse offers scripts for a self aware that it is on stage. In the Book of Revelation one encounters contemptible profiles and those worthy of emulation. These characters offer staged shows of the end. As characters take their part in various scenes, they lift before their audience a series of roles to play and actors with whom to sympathize or to reject. In visions of beatitude and torment, one sees alternative endings played out. A hortatory strategy of the Apocalypse is to convince its audience that when it beholds these endings it is witnessing itself. Staged in apocalyptic narratives,

Revelation positions or reveals the members of John's audience as they really are, and displaces, or masks, them, dressing them up as mythical larger-than-life characters, or casting them in legendary narrative (for example, the exodus: Rev. 18:4-5; 16:3-16; the Babylonian captivity: 17:5; creation: 21:1—22:5). John himself gets in on the action when he presents himself as a kind of Ezekiel *redivivus*, eating the scroll of prophecy (Rev. 10:9; Ezek. 3:1-3). Through parodies of social interactions, his hearers discover themselves distorted in a play of mirrors, as a series of more or less grotesque actors interact and enact what John reveals as the truth about his listeners and his hopes for them.

The so-called seven letters (Rev. 1:4—3:22), whose number links them from the outset with the seven cycles of visions to follow, offer thumbnail sketches of apocalyptic characters who, in one way or another, will be discovered, in revamped form, later in the narrative, and who will enact world-ending reversals of fortune. Preeminent among these is Jesus, the Apocalypse's most deft master of disguise and greatest agent of reversal. Garbed in apocalyptic costume (1:12-16; 2:1, 12, 18; 19:11-16), he promises breathtaking performances of woe and triumph, riding on stage (still dressed up) near the end of the story to bring the curtain (or the city) down (19:11-16; 21:1ff.). As the Apocalypse cycles to its ending, he keeps his word that every eye will see his coming and that those who pierced him wail (*koptesthai*—1:7); that the faithful will be robed in white (3:4); that he will rule the nations with a rod of iron (2:27); and that a new Jerusalem will descend (3:12). John will show kings wailing (*koptesthai*—the only other appearance of this verb in Revelation) at the destruction of Babylon (18:9). John will steal a glimpse at the end of the story to share his picture of ultimate reversal in the revelation of the white-robed faithful "who have come out of the great tribulation" (7:9-14). He will see Jesus come with his rod of iron (19:15), the resurrection and judgment of the dead (20:11-15), as well as the descent of the New Jerusalem (21:1—22:5).

Here again we encounter discovery and reversal, those basic elements of plot that Aristotle describes. When well-deployed, Aristotle states, discovery and reversal "will arouse either pity or fear" as they conspire "to bring about the happy or unhappy ending."[33] The Apocalypse is the ultimate surprise ending. As the story unfolds toward the unhappiest of happy endings, we encounter both emotions—pity for the lamenting kings, merchants, and shippers mourning the passing of their prosperity

(18:9-19), and fear at the punishment awaiting them and their associates for their idolatry and immorality (20:7-10). Whatever the source-critical questions surrounding the construction of this text, it is such discovery and reversal that knits what would otherwise be a patchwork of apocalyptic motifs into a complexly woven whole.[34]

John's depictions of the false prophet Jezebel (2:20) and of Balaam and the Nicolaitans (2:6, 14-15) represent the most sustained performances in the Apocalypse and add support to studies that treat the Apocalypse as a literary unity.[35] Their names are legendary. Jezebel in the Hebrew Bible personifies wickedness. The wife of the corrupt king Ahab (1 Kings 16:29-31), she leads the northern Israelites to worship Canaanite fertility deities (1 Kings 18:19). The archenemy of Elijah, she is the persecutor of prophets (1 Kings 18:4; 19:1-3) and a murderer (1 Kings 21). She wears her corruption by painting her eyes and adorning her hair and, thus charged with "harlotries and sorceries" (2 Kings 9:22), she is murdered and eaten by dogs (2 Kings 9:30-37; 1 Kings 21:23). Balaam, and by extension the so-called Nicolaitans (probably a Greek wordplay on the Hebrew name: "one who conquers/wears out the people"),[36] has a slightly less colorful but nevertheless prominent career. In one strand of the legends associated with Balaam, he is a false prophet responsible for the apostasy of the Israelites at Peor and thus is murdered by them (Num. 31:8, 16). Elsewhere he attempts, without success, to curse Israel (Deut. 23:4; Josh. 24:10; Neh. 13:2).

These characters in the seven messages are cartoonlike and most probably are not to be interpreted as the names of literal historical figures contemporary with John. Their presence functions, among other things, to link John's messages with sacred traditions and to give his prophetic pronouncements an inviolable quality. John's invocations of the characters look both forward and backward, at once foreshadowing reversals to come, and linking succeeding visions with the basic outlines of the Older Testament's prophetic traditions. He charges Balaam (or the Nicolaitans) and Jezebel with practicing immorality and consuming food offered to idols (*proneusai; phagein eidōlothuta;* Rev. 2:14, 20c, 22— fornication and idolatry are the stock complaints of sacred prophetic tradition).

John promises them and their supporters tribulation and destruction unless they repent (Rev. 2:16, 22-23). Later, at the annunciation of the descent of the New Jerusalem (21:8-9; cf. 21:27) and in the epistolary close of the Apocalypse (22:15), the terms *pornoi* ("sexually impure persons") and *eidōlolatrai* ("idolaters") appear again, first to describe the punishment of these malefactors and then to prohibit their entry into the heavenly Jerusalem. These two vices receive further attention in the visions contained between John's epistolary opening and closing, especially in chapters 17–18.

In John's visions, immorality and idolatry become the distinguishing characteristics of God's enemies doomed for destruction (Rev. 9:20-21; 14:8; 17:2; 18:3, 9; 19:2). Such recurring allusions unify the Apocalypse. Appearing near its beginning, they provide a hermeneutical orientation that anticipates subsequent visions (especially Babylon's destruction—chaps. 17–18) and bind the seven messages to the Revelation's ending.

John's insistence in chapter 2 on his enemies' sins of immorality and idolatry does more, however, than provide textual stitching. He praises or admonishes the churches depending on their allegiance to these figures (2:6, 14, 20-29). John's statements prepare the audience, who might otherwise sympathize with the figures these characters represent—and who can therefore recognize itself in these charges—to encounter in the descriptions of the actions, behaviors, and fate of these alleged evildoers a warning of destruction. Discoveries give way to stories of reversal. If, earlier in the narrative, Christians who are guilty of these charges wear the larger-than-life mythical garb of biblical antiheroes, later they will encounter those like themselves playing out roles in a spectacular cosmic drama and so discover themselves implicated in scenes of corruption and judgment. This audience, once entangled in John's representation, discovers that its leaders share characteristics and motivations identical with those that later visions attribute to God's enemies. Seeing itself displaced in the roles scripted for it in the seven letters, John's audience will discover the fate of those who are God's enemies, whose interests differ little from those John associates with the names Balaam, the Nicolaitans, and Jezebel. These characters' destiny instills fear as hearers begin to realize that it is hearing tales about itself. The biggest surprise for John's audience is that the alleged saint ("the woman Jezebel, *who calls herself a prophet*"—2:20) is God's enemy. The world comes crashing down. After John's pronouncement anything is possible, even the creation of a new heaven and earth.

Outside the seven letters, characters that John depicts rhetorically as guilty of idolatry and immorality appear at significant turning points.

They first appear in Rev. 9:20-21. These verses are significant, for they mark a brief *conclusio* to the revelation of the contents of the scroll with the seven seals that had begun in Rev. 5:1. The seventh seal broken and its contents revealed, 9:20-22 summarizes the effects of the action thus far, underscoring the obdurate wickedness of those who had escaped the plagues outlined in the blowing of the seven trumpets of 8:2—9:19:

> The rest of humankind, who were not killed by these plagues, did not repent of the works of their hands nor give up worshiping demons and idols of gold and silver and bronze and stone and wood, which cannot either see or hear or walk; nor did they repent of their murders or their sorceries or their immorality or their thefts.

A digression follows at Rev. 10:1, which introduces the angel who will offer John the little scroll, whose contents the audience learns in chapters 11–14. Elisabeth Schüssler Fiorenza compellingly shows that these later chapters form a cohesive unity within the Apocalypse.[37] Edith Humphrey builds on her arguments by showing how the cycle of visions in these chapters, especially those of the centrally located chapter 12 (the dramas of the woman clothed with the sun and the battle with the dragon), furnishes the key for interpreting the whole of the Apocalypse.[38] In this section John again depicts both idolaters and fornicators (Rev. 13:4, 14-15; 14:4, 9, 11). He offers a commentary in this "play within a play" on the wickedness of the unrepentant that Rev. 9:20-21 had described, together with a retrospective on events already portrayed and a foreshadowing of things to come. The contents of the little scroll communicated, the return to the action of Rev. 9:20-21 begins in Rev. 15:1, with the reference to the seven angels (thus echoing chapter 8). At 8:12 we had been promised three woes. Now the audience witnesses this third woe while the fate of those remaining unrepentant idolaters and fornicators of 9:20, who were commented on in the portraits of idolatry in chapter 13, unfolds.

These unrepentant characters make their final spectacular entry in chapters 17–18, which, like the seven messages, concern themselves with the fate of idolaters and the immoral. Those chapters are rightly interpreted as referring to the dangerous designs of the Roman Empire. But they also have an important literary function in developing the profile of idolaters and fornicators, who have appeared at significant points earlier in the narrative. Literarily, chapters 17–18 replicate the repetitive structure of the Apocalypse in which cycles of visions echo and build on one another as John reveals the contents of the scrolls. Social reference and repetition together prompt discovery: the (false) prophets of the seven messages are themselves imperial agents in saint's clothing; they represent the same danger, they deserve the same punishment. Consequently, chapter 17 recasts in the role of the harlot the rhetorically named Jezebel of Rev. 2:20, whose colorful Hebrew Bible career includes the charge of harlotry (2 Kings 9:22, 30). "Revamped" now in the garments of the "great harlot seated upon many waters" or of "those kings of the earth" who have slept with her (Rev. 17:1, 2), those staged earlier as sympathizers to Jezebel/Balaam/Nicolaitans now recognize themselves as accessories to the charges of fornication and idolatry that the author levels against these other figures (17:2, 4; 18:3, 9; 19:2). As John promised in Rev. 2:13, 22-23, they can now see the fate awaiting them as the judgment of the harlot and her royal paramours unfolds.

More dramatically, the true nature of their idolatry comes to light when John exposes the idolatry of the harlot as drinking the blood of the saints (Rev. 17:4, 5; 21:27—with the repeated use of *bdelygma* ["abomination"]). In this parodic, fantastic cast of characters, the alleged idolaters of Rev. 2:14-15, 20-22 thus unsuspectingly encounter themselves. It no doubt came as some surprise that those criticized in the seven letters shared the character of the one drunk on the blood of the Christian community's model citizens—the same community to whom John's enemies evidently appeal by their alleged false prophecy (2:20). It must also have been a shock that those sympathetic to "Jezebel's" teachings were thus excluded from the heavenly city of chapter 21. John, the master of surprise, offers in this tale of discovery and reversal world-shaking performances. His deft use of repetition unmasks an allegedly dangerous orientation to the Roman Empire, and by remasking opponents struggles to win resistance against his opponents. The charges of immorality and idolatry of chapter 2 thus signal to those who would otherwise be sympathetic to the teaching of the opponents a warning to regard the enemies of John as enemies of the churches. Indeed, their mythical titles already imply the danger that these enemies pose.

As John cycles to the climactic execution of the harlot of Babylon, the opponents he had introduced earlier in the seven messages, and then developed in chapters 9 and 13, now find themselves fully unveiled in this grotesque re-veiling. The lukewarm Laodiceans, moreover, who boast in their riches (Rev. 3:17), now see a vision of themselves in the dirges of the merchants of Babylon mourning the end of their profitable trade (18:11-24). The fate of the accused of the seven letters is sealed as John finally depicts the exclusion of idolaters and the immoral from the heavenly Jerusalem (21:8; 22:15). In such profiles, members of John's audience who would otherwise be sympathetic to messages that Balaam, the Nicolaitans, and Jezebel represent encounter themselves as objects of contempt.

Similarly, the ideal audience, whom chapters 2 and 3 exhort to endure (2:2, 3, 19; 3:10), to remain faithful (2:10), to conquer (2:7, 17, 26; 3:5, 12, 21), to repent of or resist fornication or idolatry (2:16, 22; 3:19), and to remain or become clothed in white garments (3:4, 18), also encounters itself in the apocalyptic narrative that commences in Rev. 4:1. John already foreshadows this ideal picture in Rev. 1:9, in his own self-portrait. "I John, your brother, who share with you in Jesus the tribulation and the kingdom and the patient endurance"—a depiction dissonant with the strong tones of censure that dominate the succeeding letters. But the rhetorically charged identity of the "authorial" John anticipates hoped-for future performances. As the Apocalypse unfolds, increasingly John is the one with whom the audience must identify in order to make sense of what is happening. Notwithstanding the contrary evidence of censure in the seven letters, John signals this call to identification with himself when he describes himself as "sharing" with his audience "the tribulation and the kingdom and the patient endurance." As he uses the first-person strategies outlined in the discussion of the previous chapter, the audience is lured into seeing things his way.

John casts his audience in roles he hopes they will perform, enticing them with scenes of reward or comfort. These characters, themselves (like their negative counterparts) caricatures for moral instruction, present in idealized settings of endurance and faithful witness the audience of Revelation to itself, offering visions designed to make listeners desirous of their better selves.

In contrast to the performances of idolatry and immorality offered by antagonists, John creates alternative identities as pure, white-robed witnesses who sing their way into the new heaven and earth (7:9-17; 14:1-5; 19:1-9), reign with Christ (20:4; 21:7), and enjoy the end of sorrow and suffering (21:4). The profile is the exact opposite of the lamenting, impure, idolatrous fornicators who suffer destruction with the Beast and his minions (18:9-24; 20:7-15; 21:8, 27; 22:11, 15). Those who encounter themselves in the choir hymning its victory over the destruction of fornicating, idolatrous enemies in Rev. 19:1-9 become John's guarantors that his call in Rev. 2:20, for resistance to false teaching, will not be in vain. Theirs will be the victory of the war that Rev. 2:16 promises and that Rev. 19:11-16 finally describes. John wants his audience to share with him enticing scenes of reward and comfort. To them, not to the minions of Babylon, belong streets of gold (20:15-21). Over that other city, praise instead of lament is heard (22:3). The Lord God, *dominus et Deus*, is not Domitian but the One who was, who is, and who is to come, and the Lamb upon the throne (21:22; 22:1, 3, 5, 6).[39] At the end, in jarring reversal, it is the slaves (*douloi*) of the Lamb (22:3), not the kings, merchants, and shippers of the earth, who inherit God's alternative empire.

Robert M. Royalty's brilliant study of wealth in the Apocalypse suggests that "opposition to the dominant culture in the Apocalypse is not an attempt to redeem that culture but rather an attempt to replace it with a Christianized version of the same thing."[40] Royalty astutely describes John's portrait of the fall of Babylon as a bricolage of Older Testament passages portending Yahweh's destruction of Jerusalem as well as pagan cities. But there is a significant omission. The prophetic pronouncements decrying injustices against the poor and disenfranchised, to accompany descriptions of love of money, are lacking. Thus, Royalty argues, John never questions economic injustice. In his vision of the heavenly Jerusalem or the apocalyptic Jesus, bedecked with jewels and gold and fine clothing (Rev. 1:13; 19:12; 21:17-21), John in effect changes the street signs and the names of the most-honored citizens, but replicates the basic economic structure of the Roman Empire.[41]

I am less convinced than Royalty that Apocalypse thus offers, as he goes on to conclude, "judgement with no justice."[42] We need to return to that claim in the final chapter when we attempt to tease out some social implications of John's death-defying reversal of fortune in the resurrected slain Lamb of God. For now it is enough to say that, at the end of the story, John points a way toward giving the followers of "Balaam" and "Jezebel" what they want (prestige, honor, status), but without the heavy price tag. The question John places before them is whether they will accept his terms. What is the Apocalypse if not an elaborate advertisement to make one envious of oneself as one could be and to inspire contempt for what one fears one is?[43] Such a discovery and reversal is a tour de force.

Remembering Apocalypse

*The whole life of those societies in which modern conditions of
production prevail presents itself as an immense accumulation
of spectacles. All that once was directly lived has become mere
representation.*

— Guy Debord, *The Society of the Spectacle*

Remembering Apocalypse on those breakfast mornings with my parents
made us feel part of a spectacle. From these conversations arose the profound sense of being visible. A panoptic sensibility arose out of the recollections of the voyeuristic Nazi state: my mother learning as a girl in
Poland to salute and say, "Heil Hitler!" instead of "Guten Tag"—the
visual token of the everywhere-surveilling state. It came with my father's
reminiscences of the whispered predictions of the loss of the war. I sat
wide-eyed as he recalled how you could be arrested for saying that the
war was lost, even as column upon column of German soldiers passed
through his German-Polish village in the disastrous and chaotic retreat
of January 1945. This was a world in which everything was seen, every
word heard.

But it was post-Apocalypse that magnified the power of observation
and focused it on the minutest particle of behavior: the fear of speaking
German in public in postwar Canada and of being publicly accused of
being a Nazi or beaten up. To be overheard speaking German was to be
told publicly to "speak English!" The broken and obviously German-
accented English located one instantly as foreign, suspicious, a monstrous other. The oddly fitting, awkward clothes marked one as refugee.

At the time my parents arrived in Canada, more than 80 percent of all
Canadians were of British, Irish, or French descent. Eastern European
displaced persons and refugees were thought to threaten that majority
and to counteract their flow into Canada, British immigration was
encouraged. "As many continentals and foreigners are now being permitted to enter Canada, we feel that it is essential that we maintain our
present percentage of British stock," claimed a Canadian agency in London in June 1947, in racist language reminiscent of the vanquished
enemy.[44] The threat of discovery took on mythic proportion even as the
truth of Nazi atrocity and German complicity came to be embedded in
popular culture.

As a young teen, living-room battles would ensue when I would watch my favorite TV show, *Hogan's Heroes*. In the hackneyed comedy series, clever American World War II prisoner of war Hogan and his fellow prisoners outsmart the half-witted concentration camp commander Colonel Klink and his overfed minion, Sergeant Schultz. The idiot Schultz, who every week would say under the interrogation of prisoner and commandant alike, "I know no-thing, No-Thing, NO-THING! I see noth-ing! I hear-r-r noth-ing! I say noth-ing! [canned laughter]." My parents would wince and tell me to turn the channel. "The Germans are always the stupid ones." I innocently defended it as "just a show." But was it German stupidity or denial that Hollywood was parodying? Coincidentally, Schultz's disingenuous claims to innocence mirrored the remonstrations of parent, relative, and German friend alike ("but we didn't know anything"; "they kept it all a secret"; "to stay alive you didn't ask questions") as this young German Canadian began to inquire about the horror of his cultural past.

Visibility threatens in the situation in which my parents found themselves. The task was to avoid discovery, by becoming invisible as quickly as possible and by performing the cultural script of the day. The path to invisibility, if paradoxical, was arduous but manageable. Heroic reversal of fortune through hard work is, after all, North America's favorite story line. To begin with, nonskilled Eastern European refugees and displaced persons were welcomed to Canada in order to fill the demand for unskilled workers created by a burgeoning resource-based economy.[45] This translated in turn into the extraordinary prosperity that would eventually characterize postwar expatriated Germans in Canada. In the western Canadian, German community in which I was raised, economic success mirrored back to the surrounding culture its own ideals. Becoming invisible meant simultaneously perfecting one's role in the show of postwar Canadian economic development. Paradoxically, becoming invisible gained one entry into a renewed form of visibility that characterizes the capitalism of a global economy—namely that of conspicuous consumption as the symbol of cultural belonging. We learned how to become in/conspicuous.

It was dress that marked our in/conspicuousness. We wore our difference and, through appearance, we paraded our economic transformation. The refugee culture of the post-Apocalypse German Canadian community in which I grew up pilloried the surrounding society for its

appearance. "Dirty Canadian," "cowboys," "typical sloppy Canadian"—
this was a way of marking difference and location, by dressing up non-
Germans in negative generalizations. By contrast we were tidy,
well-ordered, hard-working. Our yards with their manicured lawns and
gardens showed it; our spotless, firmly constructed, efficiently organized
homes showed it; the upright posture at table, on the street, in the car
showed it. We dressed for the part. To this day difference is marked by
contrasting the carefully ironed shirt of the German with that of the
frumpy "native." My school pictures, in which as a child I appear in
(apparently) imported German clothing and which even now are a
source of profound embarrassment, advertised an identity intended for
emulation. "Stop walking around looking like a Canadian," my mother
or father would say if my shirt was hanging out.

But was I not precisely that, a Canadian? How else should I look? For
us, I was to learn, the standards had to be higher. Since "we lost the war"
(again the positioning/dislocating first-person plural), it would be
harder for us. We were to become adept performers of the cultural script
outlined by the postwar economy, to be the obedient, reliable worker,
and so, inevitably, to prosper from the development of the postwar economy. Jerusalem the Golden beckoned with its promise of status and the
economic happy ending. This was a reversal of fortune, from refugee to
millionaire; Aristotle would have been satisfied with the plot. We aspired
to become the envy of others, through university education, business
ingenuity, and outstanding artisanship. We postapocalyptic characters
with our economic successes became advertisements for the surrounding culture's most cherished socioeconomic slogans concerning hard
work, industry, respect for law and order, decency, and cleanliness.

The French Marxist Guy Debord coined the phrase "the society of
the spectacle" to show how notions of the visible, of economic production, and of social alienation are interrelated. The "spectacle" is a "social
relationship between people that is mediated by images."[46] The spectacular is not a collection of images so much as a mode of producing ourselves by means of images. In this "social relationship," we agree to live
according to our representations to each other without stopping to ask
the socioeconomic function of our self-representations. Debord's analysis intends to explore the socioeconomic and finally alienating function
capitalism plays in rendering the world, especially oneself, visible. It thus
seeks, apocalypse-like, to expose "spectacular society" in order to return

readers to the real—the inevitable historical unfolding of late capitalism inching toward its demise.[47] More recently, Jean Baudrillard and David Harvey have further developed this critique. Baudrillard explores the terms *visual culture* and *ocularcentrism* to trace the ways contemporary global capitalism is centered in the production of signs, images, and sign-systems.[48] Harvey uses the word *simulacrum* to describe the rapid-fire replication of images and consumer identities as products for consumption.[49] Their impermanence obliterates any enduring notion of person, place, or location. "The good life" is the realization of economic success through the management of the spectacle.

In a world of rapidly changing representation, there are many paths into the panoptic sensibility of the spectacle. Recalling Apocalypse was my family's way. The memory of the ending of Eastern Europe's German community taught a new grammar of seeing the world, a (distorting) perspective that furnished sense with sensibility and proportion, the mirror by which to see the world and one's place in it. Memory created a form of theatricality. It shaped us to see ourselves performing a complex script, at once assimilating us into the Anglo-Saxon culture shaped by the Canadian establishment and marking us as different from it. Such a complicated script contributed to the transformation of Canadian society from the twin solitudes of British/Protestant and French/Catholic into a multicultural identity long before so-called English-speaking Canada was to adopt multiculturalism as the slogan of its national identity.[50] If it was not, exactly, God's eye that followed us, it was a nevertheless omniobservant gaze that demanded the faithful performance of economic prosperity. Under such a gaze we became a *pulchrum spectaculum*, a "fair spectacle" for the world to see.

But is not all this attention to the eye too one-sided? Was not the ancient world as interested in the ear as it was in the eye? To be sure, the Apocalypse lets you see things. It also makes you hear them—in hymn, lament, woe, and address. What sounds does the Apocalypse make? And how do its tones echo in post-Apocalypse? Let us continue our exploration of John's apocalyptic production, and listen more closely to the noises he makes.

4

Hearing Voices

For twenty-five centuries, Western knowledge has tried to look upon the world. It has failed to understand that the world is not for beholding. It is for hearing. It is not legible, but audible.

Our science has always desired to monitor, measure, abstract, and castrate meaning, forgetting that life is full of noise and that death alone is silent: work noise, noise of man, and noise of beast. Noise bought, sold, or prohibited. Nothing essential happens in the absence of noise.

—Jacques Attali, *Noise: The Political Economy of Music*

JOHN'S AUDITORIUM

The Apocalypse is the New Testament's noisiest book. Playing with the popular misnomer, we might rename it the Book of Reverberations. Its pages echo with the sounds of song and lament, cursing and praise, blasphemy and testimony, trumpet blasts and rolling thunder. Heaven, John tells us, is a place filled with uninterrupted song: "And the four living creatures . . . day and night they never cease to sing . . ." (Rev. 4:8). "I am John who heard and saw these things," says our hearer from Patmos, privileging the ear (22:8). Known in the tradition as a "seer," might he not more accurately have been named a "hearer," or better, picking up the metaphors of surveillance developed

91

in the last chapter, an "eavesdropper"? After all, what he sees are voices: "I heard behind me a loud voice like a trumpet. . . . I turned to see the voice that was speaking to me" (1:12). In fact, he hears voices even when there are no characters to speak: "From the throne issue flashes of lightning, and voices and peals of thunder . . ." (4:5; similarly, 8:5; 11:19; 16:18). The two faculties to which John returns throughout his Revelation are those associated with the auditory: ears (2:7, 17, 29; 3:6, 13, 22; 13:9) and mouth. "Blessed are those who hear" (1:3).

Blessed, too, are those who speak up. The Apocalypse's protagonists are always those who speak up against all odds, following the pattern of *the* Witness, Jesus (e.g., 1:2, 5), as in the case of the "two witnesses" of 11:3-13, whose prophetic speech does wonders (vv. 5-7). Or they are those whose testimony to Jesus we overhear in heavenly songs of praise and celebration (4:8, 10-11; 5:9-10, 11-14; 7:10-12; 11:15; 12:10-11; 14:2-5; 15:3-4; 19:1-8), what we may call a kind of ear and voice training for the down-to-earth testimony of John's listeners living below. The testimony given to and coming from Jesus (*martyria Iesou*, 1:2, 9; 12:17; 19:10—at once objective and subjective genitive) and prophecy are synonyms in the Book of Revelation. "The testimony of/to Jesus is the spirit of prophecy" (19:10). This is a startling equation that calls into question the popular view of John as a first-century futurologist, and takes the Apocalypse out of endtime visions and puts it back in the mouth. John the prophet from Patmos, as Hanna Roose brilliantly argues, does not see himself as one of a kind. Rather he typifies the voice of faithful oral witness to the costly testimony of Jesus Christ unto death, which John's listeners are to echo in their own testimony.[1]

Or, to repeat what I was arguing in the previous chapter, John embodies the ideal his listeners are to become. The listeners of the Apocalypse are to be like the two witnesses of Revelation 11, whose prophetic witness ends in death, resurrection, and the destruction of God's enemies. Like those two witnesses they are to bear costly testimony that conquers the dragon, the devil, Satan, and the later beasts of Revelation 12 and 13, "by the blood of the Lamb and by the word of their testimony, for they loved not their lives even unto death" (12:11). It is a testimony expressing the "true words" of John's Revelation (1:2; 19:9). The highest compliment John can pay the faithful is that they keep, that is, bear testimony to, "the word" (3:8, 10; 6:9; 20:4), again an identity our seer/hearer embodies (1:2, 9).

Hearing Voices   93

All this turns the Apocalypse into a particularly mouthy book. It is no accident that Revelation's Jesus slays his enemies with "the sword that issues from his mouth" (19:15, 21; see 1:16; 2:16). Nor is it a coincidence that the worst thing John can say about the Beast of Revelation 13 is that it possesses "a mouth uttering great and blasphemous words" (13:5, 6; 17:3), and that its followers "curse God" (16:9, 11, 21). One of its counterfeit signs is to make an image of itself speak (in John's parlance, false testimony), and so deceive unwitting pagans to worship it (13:15). When "the battle on the great day of God the Almighty" arrives, it is a showdown between Jesus, the "Word of God" (19:13), and the dragon, beast, and false prophet from whose mouths come "three false spirits like frogs, for they are demonic spirits, performing signs, who go abroad to the kings of the whole world, to assemble them for battle" (16:13-14).

These are not battles for the mealy-mouthed. The voices we hear coming either from heaven or its messengers are always loud, mighty, or great ones (1:10; 5:1, 11; 6:10; 7:2, 9-10; 8:13; 10:3; 11:12, 15; 12:10; 14:2, 6, 9, 15; 16:1, 17; 18:2; 19:1; 21:3). It is as though John would drown out his enemies with sound. He amplifies the voices he hears by likening them to rushing waters, thunder, roaring lions, harps, and blowing trumpets (1:11, 15; 4:1; 6:1; 10:3; 14:2; 19:6). He thereby expresses the prevailing religious sentiment of his Jewish and Hellenistic environment, that the sound of the divine is loud.[2] John's protagonists offer their listeners "sensurround" oral performances. The only time the Apocalypse's antagonists come close to matching the protagonists' volume is when they cry in terror while fleeing the advent of the wrathful Lamb (6:15), or lament the passing of Babylon (18:9-10, 11, 15, 18). In heaven, it seems, even silence is deafening (8:1); down below, in the ghost town of Babylon, silence symbolizes the impotence of the Beast's political order (18:22)—the opposite of heavenly Jerusalem's noisy wedding celebrations (21:2-3, 9).

Given all this sound, it is surprising that those quietly writing—contemporary exegetes of the Apocalypse—are so silent concerning all these noises. For example, the title of a representative study of the Apocalypse by Bruce Metzger, *Breaking the Code: Understanding the Book of Revelation,* speaks volumes.[3] It invites us to imagine the patient exegete silently laboring in a quiet study, working out the encrypted message and translating it into more readily understandable terms. The study remains uninterrupted by noise. As his book unfolds, it is the visionary and not the auditory that fixes Metzger's attention. The Apocalypse's visions "combine *cognitive insight* with emotional response. They invite the reader or listener to enter into the experience being recounted and to participate in it, triggering *mental images* of that which is described" (emphasis mine).[4] Notwithstanding the reference to listening, it is the eye that Metzger privileges. The eye serves the related faculty of intellectual understanding and the translation of weird symbolism into comprehensible ideas: "Some of the imagery in Revelation may seem unusual or even bizarre, but on further reflection, and with the use of disciplined imagination, the meaning will usually become clear. In any case, it is important to recognise that the descriptions are *descriptions of symbols, not of the reality conveyed by the symbols*" (Metzger's emphasis).[5] I do not wish to pick on Metzger's reading of the Apocalypse, only to cite it as a representative example of a long tradition that privileges the eye over the ear in studying Revelation.

Indeed, the eye has a winning pedigree. Treating the Apocalypse as a symbolic, theological, and/or lexical code to be broken and then translated into everyday parlance belongs to a time-honored tradition. Already in the third century, Dionysius the bishop of Alexandria (died 264 C.E.) confessed that the Apocalypse's code was too difficult for him to crack.

> I suppose that it is beyond my comprehension, and that there is a certain concealed and more wonderful meaning in every part. For if I do not understand I suspect that a deeper sense lies beneath the words. I do not measure and judge them by my own reason, but leaving the more to faith regard them as too high for me to grasp. And I do not reject what I cannot comprehend, but rather wonder because I do not understand it.
>
> (Eusebius, *Hist. eccl.* 7.25)

Later, the fourth-century Donatist Christian Tyconius (died ca. 400 C.E.) composed an exegetical handbook, *Liber regularum* (The book of rules), to help Christians interpret biblical symbolism and come to a correct understanding of the relation of the Older and Newer Testaments.[6] This work was to exercise a strong influence on Augustine of Hippo (354–430). Augustine's adaptation of Tyconius's rules is readily apparent in his theory of biblical interpretation outlined in his *De doctrina christiana*. More practically, Tyconius's rules provided Augustine with the ammunition for challenging the too-hasty identification by millenni-alist Christians of catastrophes in the latter days of the Roman Empire with those last days predicted in John's Revelation. In book 20 of Augustine's *City of God*, Tyconius's rules helped the bishop of Hippo to be a pastor to a jittery flock unsettled by the news of Rome's collapse and fearing that the incursion of barbarians into the empire signaled the onset of the Apocalypse's woes. In response, Augustine insisted that, though the Apocalypse was indeed describing a future time, it was not the time of his generation. For the present, however, Revelation offered important teaching concerning present-day spiritual realities, especially regarding the invisible warfare, waged since the days of Cain and Abel, of the city of God and of humankind. Tyconius's rules of exegesis furnished Augustine with the tools to crack the code of Revelation's encrypted spiritual teachings.

Augustine the *rhetor*, erstwhile writer of imperial speeches, was, of course, no silent reader. Nevertheless, the convert from Manichaeism via Platonism to Christianity remained a Platonizing reader. And the combination of Tyconian exegesis with a Platonizing Christian faith resulted in a treatment of the Apocalypse that has muzzled the Book of Revelation for two millennia and that has shifted attention away from ear and mouth toward sight, vision, understanding, and spiritual insight. It is on these latter faculties that the emphasis falls wherever Augustine outlines his theories of biblical interpretation.[7] Similarly, in the climactic twenty-second book of *The City of God*, in which Augustine describes the future bliss of the saints in the heavenly Jerusalem, it is the faculty of sight that dominates, not that of hearing or speech. "As far as the Lord deigns to help us see" (22.29), Augustine promises to describe what the saints in paradise will be doing with their resurrected bodies, though he has to admit that he has never actually seen these things, neither "with my physical sight" nor "with my mind." Nevertheless, it is eye and understanding that Augustine privileges. Thus, when Metzger struggles "to break the code" of the Book of Revelation, to use a disciplined imagination, and to excavate the theological, historical, or biblical terrain represented by apocalyptic symbolism, his exegesis is an eye-opener with a long tradition.

It is good for the eyes, but what about the ears? A few students of John's Revelation have allowed their silent readings to be interrupted by the Apocalypse's voices and noises.[8] These studies build on cross-cultural studies of oral cultures, as well as research into oral/aural aspects of the ancient world and biblical texts.[9] Orality, a relative late-comer to the field of biblical studies, seeks to understand the Bible in the context of a culture whose chief medium of communication is word of mouth. In the ancient cultures surrounding biblical writers, most were illiterate and the materials for writing and recording were clumsy and expensive. This resulted in an enduring focus on the oral aspects of communication, which did not shift until the invention of the printing press, revolutionizing the organization and self-understanding of Western society.[10] Walter J. Ong coins the phrases "oral sensorium," "visual sensorium," and "technological sensorium" to draw attention to the differing ways experience, knowledge, and cultural expectations are shaped and organized in cultures predominantly shaped by one or the other mode of communication.[11] In the "oral sensorium" of the Apocalypse, as in other oral cultures, sounded words are enchantingly power-ful, not so much because of what they mean after being translated into quotidian terms (or theological jargon), but because the very recitation of them has the power to conjure a blessing (1:3), or to bring a curse to anyone who takes away or adds to the words scripted for performance (22:18-19, privileging the ear). Is it any wonder that the power of the Apocalypse's Jesus as well as that of his followers is believed to reside in his/their mouth (1:16; 2:16; 19:15, 21; 12:11)?

Obviously, the Book of Revelation as written artifact is not purely oral. It represents a hybrid case in which the oral and the written overlap. The Apocalypse is at once *read* and *heard* ("Blessed is the one who *reads aloud* the words of the prophecy, and blessed are those who *hear. . .*" [Rev. 1:3]). It may be described oxymoronically as "oral literature," that is, like other rhetorical texts from Greco-Roman antiquity, it deploys writ-ing in the service of oral performance, and this with a view to persuade lis-teners.[12] In oral considerations of John's Apocalypse, attention shifts from *what* the text means, to *how* it means and persuades. Rather than viewing the text exclusively as a receptacle of meaning (a code to be cracked), such considerations treat it as a score for performance. Such exegesis pays as much attention to how listeners are affected in hearing an oral perform-ance and to the strategies for creating those experiences as to what listen-ers are meant to understand.

As an "oral score," Revelation gives attention to cues given the per-former (the reader, most probably in a public context of worship—1:3) of the text. Like other written documents of the period, John's Apocalypse was probably written on a scroll. Unlike modern writing, in which words are separated and punctuation marks off sentences and paragraphs from one another, first-century Greek documents were comprised of uninterrupted, unpunctuated streams of capital letters. The Apocalypse's reader, therefore, had to be fairly well acquainted with the work before s/he stood before listeners to perform it. S/he would also have committed to memory its structure in order to mark clearly for listeners the beginnings and endings of episodes, shifts in perspective, and the general unfolding of the apocalyptic plot. This must have resulted in much latitude on the part of the reader to interpret the text—hence the metaphor of text as score and reading as performance.

Nevertheless, through careful attention to structure, Revelation's author kept the performance within certain limits. In his groundbreaking essay on orality in the Apocalypse, David Barr explores the ways in which John structured his Apocalypse to help the reader and listeners keep their bearings during its recitation. John's visions are structured on recurring cycles of identically enumerated episodes (seven letters, seals, trumpets, bowls; three woes, portents, laments; two witnesses, beasts). The structure is made up of carefully marked transitions from earthly to heavenly perspectives (4:1; 11:1; 15:5; 21:1) and the opening of scrolls (5:1; 10:8). John keeps reader and hearer on track by associating places with images and actions, and by providing easily identifiable introductions and conclusions (2:1, 7; 2:8, 11; 2:12, 17; 7:1, 17; 9:20; 12:1, 17; 13:1, 11, 18; 17:1; 21:1; 22:8). Barr urges contemporary readers to give a listening ear to John's Apocalypse and to keep at bay some of the more natural assumptions of a visually oriented, print-based culture in interpreting a text.

Perhaps the most important implication of attention to orality in the Apocalypse is that one puts away timetables of the future, linear notions of time, analytical notions of conceptual consistency, strict succession of episodes and events, theological abstraction, and economy of expression. In other words, this means to be not so quick to "crack the code" of the Apocalypse, but to linger amid the weird and wonderful sounds of the text, and to pay attention to the experiences that they evoke. It means to ask of these sounds not so much, "What do they mean?" but, "What do they do?" To the analytical reader of a print-based culture, John's Revelation looks like what George Bernard Shaw described as "a curious record of the visions of a drug addict."[13] When assessed in terms of an oral culture, however, John's Apocalypse is at once less bizarre and more resistant to such an easy dismissal. Walter Ong furnishes a useful typology of the properties of orality that help build on Barr's initial treatment of Revelation as oral enactment.[14] Using Ong's typology I first seek to uncover the oral dimensions of a representative text and then to broaden the discussion toward treating the Apocalypse as a whole.

John's description of the 144,000 in Rev. 7:4-8 furnishes a good example for exploring the oral dimensions of the Apocalypse, as well as for a study of contrasts between readings formulated in the visual sensorium of the contemporary biblical exegete, and those echoing forth from an oral approach. In the hands of many interpreters, John's reference to the 144,000 becomes an occasion to crack a numerical code, an invitation prompted by John's own request for identification (7:13). Thus, Eugene Boring is surely correct when he writes,

> The church in this picture is not only big, it is complete. The number 144,000 is a complete, fulfilled number. (The 144 is obviously the multiple of 12 x 12, the twelve tribes of old Israel and the twelve apostles of the new Israel. . . . John declares that the eschatological hope for Israel is realised in the church.[15]

Nevertheless, something is lost in the translation. The Greek text piles twelve identical clauses on top of each other, thickening the description in an incantation-like recitation of numbers and names (*ek phylēs [Iouda/ Roubēn/Gad/etc.] dōdeka chiliades . . .*).

The Greek is musical. The repeated similar endings (homoioteleuta) of *phylēs* and *chiliades* offer a singsong assonance. Moreover, the repeated use of the perfect-passive participle *esphragismenoi* ("sealed") at the head of the list (v. 4b), then at the outset of the sequence (v. 5), and at its conclusion (v. 8c) offers both a neat demarcation of a narrative episode through chiasmus and is an instance of paronomasia, "the recurrence of the same word or word stem in close proximity."[16] All this represents an aesthetic experience resistant to the analytical abstraction of Boring's translation. These examples of wordplay (homoioteleuton, paronomasia) could be multiplied many times over. To them we could also add related examples of alliteration, homonym (parechesis), and onomatopoeia.[17] They indicate that while the translation of John's Revelation into more abstract theological categories is important, such translation plays a supporting role to the text's aurality/orality in drawing listeners into its world. One suspects that even if one did not know how to translate the words, the repetitious sounds would signal the importance of what was being communicated. Meaning here resides as much in the sound-event as in the theological notion it expresses.

The sonorous features of this vision introduce us to what Walter Ong calls the *redundant* or *copious* nature of orality.[18] We may contrast this with Boring's linear, analytical explanation of the text, centered in an economy of expression made possible by his being able to read and reread a text of the Apocalypse printed in a medium conducive to such analysis. The original listener had no recourse to such a tidy recorded explanation. In reading, one can linger and ponder. There is no stopping in listening, except when the reader pauses to take a breath. Words rush along. Thus in oral literature, time is made up through repetition and rehearsal of events and pictures. In the vision of the 144,000, John makes narrative time stop through sonorous repetition. This allows the listener time to grasp what the 144,000 might mean, not only analytically, but also experientially through being caught up in the reader's singsong recitation. A further example of the redundant and copious occurs in the continuation of the vision in verses 9-17. At verse 9, the vision shifts from the 144,000 of verses 3-8: "After this I looked, and behold, a great multitude which no one could number, from every nation, from all tribes and peoples and tongues. . . ." In a more linear, analytical reading, we might expect that this shift represents an identification of a second, perhaps larger, elect group, and that the narrative clock has moved on to see what John saw next. However, it is the nature of orality to rehearse the same idea in different words and from differing viewpoints, and to be more flexible with narrative time. This keeps the listeners' interest and draws them into an emotional experience of the vision.

Oral style, Ong notes, is *additive rather than subordinative.*[19] Oral performers win time through repetition, which they use to introduce new details. In 7:9-17, we are dealing with the same vision of verses 4-8, but from a different angle. The additive nature of the vision is again apparent through repetition. Three times we hear that the martyrs wear white robes (vv. 9d, 13c, 14e). The third time, John adds the significant epexegetical clause that "they have washed their robes and made them white in the blood of the Lamb." Without the earlier rehearsal, this notion so central to the Apocalypse as a whole would perhaps have been lost. Through repetition John endeavors to make the image and its explanation unforgettable. Making the vision further memorable is John's quoting of these characters in worship (v. 10), and his rehearsal at verses 11-12 of the elders and four living creatures of the throne room (chap. 4), as well (v. 12) as a virtually identical quotation of their song of praise (5:13).

A further example of the additive oral property of the Apocalypse appears in the seven-messages section (1:12—3:22). Heading the messages is a detailed description of "one like a son of man" (1:12-18) and the heavenly paraphernalia surrounding him (v. 20). This detailed imagery would be easily forgotten were it not for the fact that John rehearses each element by heading each of his seven messages with one or two of these descriptions. He thereby gives his listeners time to absorb the imagery and to become caught up in its mystery. As the letters unfold, the additive is again expressed, this time in the virtually identical structuring of the letters (greeting; "I know" section; blame/praise; admonition/exhortation; conclusion). The arrangement of these letters in an alternating pattern of blame and praise (see the discussion in chapter 1) helps make them more memorable. Again, John makes time for hearing. What might otherwise be an easily forgettable list of dos and don'ts becomes an experience of blame and praise. This realization carries with it an important implication for a historical understanding of the Apocalypse, namely, that one should not be too quick to take John at his word, that one or another church he describes typifies itself according to the properties or characters and teachings listed. It is as possible that John, the writer of a text for oral performance, links city churches and characteristics to achieve an additive oral strategy for outlining the behaviors and teachings to be embraced and avoided by his audience as a whole.

To illustrate another item in Ong's oral typology, *proximity to the human lifeworld*, we return to the concluding description of praise by the elect described in 7:15-17.[20] Again, a reader has time to stop and ponder an abstract concept and to think about his or her own experiences. Listeners have no such luxury. Oral literature therefore associates ideas with persons and experiences with which the listener can relate. The conclusion of the vision of the elect helps ground what might otherwise have become a heavenly vision, removed from earthly experiences. The descriptions are vivid, concrete, and rooted in human experience. "They shall hunger no more, neither thirst any more; the sun shall not strike them, nor any scorching heat" (v. 16). References to hunger, thirst, scorching heat and to shepherds, springs of water, and the wiping of tears keep the vision close to the human lifeworld of listeners and thus more memorable. The Apocalypse's theological categories are not analytical. As with texts and performances from other oral cultures, they seek to "conceptualize and verbalize all . . . knowledge with more or less close reference to the human lifeworld, assimilating the alien, objective world to the more immediate, familiar interaction of human beings."[21]

Keeping close to the lifeworld of listeners is closely related to two other dimensions of Ong's oral typology: the *empathetic and participatory*, and *the situational*.[22] If a picture paints a thousand words, getting into the skin of a character and feeling his or her emotions (*the empathetic*) helps make whatever lessons one draws from those experiences unforgettable.

Consider the cycle of laments of Babylon's allies (chap. 18). John invites us to experience their loss. Here the redundant and copious, as well as the additive, slow narrative time and give it over to exploring the loss of kings, merchants, and shippers. Three times John repeats the same lament (18:10, 16-17, 19), heightening the drama through onomatopoeia (*ouai, ouai;* "woe, woe") and assonant formulaic repetition (*ouai ouai, hē polis hē megalē, Babylōn hē polis hē ischyra;* "woe, woe, the great city, Babylon the mighty city"). The detailed listing of luxury goods that merchants traded with Babylon (vv. 11-13—75 words!) carry away listeners with the grief and size of the merchants' loss, an experience underscored by the extended use of repetition of words and phrases (homoioteleuta). The repetitive use of "and" (27 times) lengthens the text, making it weightier in its seemingly endless citation of luxury goods, as though it would overwhelm the listener through extravagant naming.

John has carefully prepared his listeners for this moment, first in 8:13, in which an angel utters *"ouai, ouai, ouai,"* pronouncing the three woes to come, and then in 11:14 through editorial aside. When the third woe comes, we experience a release of narrative tension. The third woe is not an abstract description of destruction, but a moment played out in high drama, in a way that invites our full participation. In the first place, John does not tell us, "And so Babylon was destroyed and that is the third woe," which would have been easily forgotten. The text does not "mean" but "does." His choice not to depict the actual destruction of

Babylon heightens the moment's pathos (foreshadowed in 17:15-18).

John rushes ahead to consider the setting after the destruction and takes his listeners for a walk amid the ruins in order to center on the emotional loss the ruins represent. If, as I have been arguing, the Apocalypse is a warning to Christian merchants to beware of getting too close to the economic benefits of the Roman Empire, then the experience conjured through these depictions of loss must have had an admonishing effect.

The situational aspect similarly keeps us located in the lifeworld of actors and their emotions. In Ong's typology, "situational" contrasts with "abstract" knowledge. That is, in oral cultures, concepts are not defined by their relation to other concepts, but by reference to lived situations. Conceptual abstraction gives way to living action, which serves to dramatize and thus to make enduring notions memorable.

Perhaps most notable is the Apocalypse's language of worship. Several studies have demonstrated the influence of Roman imperial-court ritual on John's depictions of heavenly worship in Revelation 4–5, as well as the use in those chapters of Roman language of imperial adoration to describe God and the Lamb.[23] I return to these aspects in more detail in the sixth chapter. It is enough to note that in what might otherwise be construed as highly abstract doxological, theological vocabulary, John always keeps his narrative relevant to the imperial situation. Practically, this has the effect of making John's Revelation one of the most political books of the New Testament, a property already noted a century ago by Friedrich Engels in his exposition of the Apocalypse.[24] That the doxological vocabulary John used to describe God was also the language of imperial politics keeps John's heavenly visions and worship of God down to earth. His language begins to open those churches in which his visions were heard as places of counterpolitics, in which the slain Lamb, not Caesar, is the one to whom imperial adoration is voiced.

We might say that John fights over who has the right to be called emperor—Caesar or, ironically, the one murdered by his henchmen, the Lamb. The most identifiable feature of the Apocalypse as oral literature is the way its plot and characters are *agonistically toned.*[25] What is to modern sensibilities an overly bloody story is par for the course in an oral culture, and belongs to a more general backdrop of struggle. "Many, if not all, oral or residually oral cultures strike literates as extraordinarily agonistic in their verbal performances and indeed in their lifestyle," writes Walter Ong.

Writing fosters abstractions that disengage knowledge from the arena where human beings struggle with one another. It separates the knower from the known. By keeping knowledge embedded in the human lifeworld, orality situates knowledge within a context of struggle.[26]

Here Ong has in mind the prevalence in oral literature of riddles, bragging, verbal challenges, and tongue-lashings in depicting human relationships. A little later Ong notes:

Not only in the use to which knowledge is put, but also in the celebration of physical behavior, oral cultures reveal themselves agonistically programmed. Enthusiastic description of physical violence often marks oral literature. . . . Portrayal of gross physical violence, central to much oral epic and other oral genres and residual through much early literacy, gradually wanes or becomes peripheral in later literary narrative.[27]

The explanation for this fact is found in the structure of orality itself: "When all verbal communication must be by direct word of mouth, involved in the give-and-take dynamics of sound, interpersonal relations are kept high—both attractions, and, even more, antagonisms."[28]

The Apocalypse is an agonistically intoned book both verbally and in terms of violent struggle. We repeatedly overhear protagonists and antagonists expressing extreme emotions of joy or grief, celebration or fear (1:17; 4:8-11; 5:4; 6:10, 16; 11:9-10, 13; 15:3-4; 18:10, 14-19; 19:1-8). Or we are promised that we will soon hear these things (1:7). John must tease explanations of his visions from his heavenly guide (Rev. 7:13-14; 17:6b-7). He is admonished for coming to wrong conclusions (19:10; 22:9). He sets numerical riddles for his listeners to solve (13:18; 17:9). His enemies or targets of admonition are often boastful (3:17; 13:4, 5-6; 18:6-7). Earthly characters demand explanations from God (6:9-11). Enemies curse God (16:9, 11, 21). God demands repentance (2:5, 16, 21; 3:3, 18). John is evidently in a battle with the prophet he agonistically labels "the woman Jezebel, who calls herself a prophetess" (2:20). This is the give and take of oral culture, a give and take that climaxes, of course, in the bloody battles of the Apocalypse, the chaos of destruction and death, and depictions of punishment.

I continue the exploration of the oral dimensions of the Apocalypse, now stepping several feet back from the work as a whole and making more general observations about its uses of metaphor and biblical citation. Here I am interested in the remaining three aspects of orality that Ong has identified—its *conservative* or *traditionalist,* its *homeostatic,* and its *aggregative* properties.[29] Ong's *conservative* or *traditionalist* dimension helps make sense of the fact that there is little in the Book of Revelation that is new, and to challenge some prevalent modern academic methods of reading the Apocalypse.

As has been amply documented in numerous studies, most of the Apocalypse's imagery has numerous parallels in other literature. Indeed, one of the more challenging tasks facing any exegete of the Apocalypse is the identification of the innumerable parallels, sometimes as imagery, sometimes as direct quotations, of Older Testament and Second Temple Jewish texts. Reading some of the detailed modern exegesis of the Apocalypse, however, in which close comparisons are made between minute portions from earlier Jewish texts and the Apocalypse, gives an impression of John as a bookish intellectual. When such similarities are discovered in literate cultures they are presumed to be examples of citation or a form of literary dependence.

It is obvious that John quotes, and sometimes very carefully. But in oral cultures, including the hybrid oral-literary culture of Greco-Roman antiquity, what is too quickly assessed in a print-dominated culture as simple literary dependence has a deeper social explanation and cultural meaning. In oral cultures, older stories are repeated and remembered, rather than written down and recorded. In literary cultures originality is often expressed through intellectual experimentation with recorded knowledge. But in oral cultures, written knowledge is more difficult to come by and, as in the Greco-Roman environment of the Apocalypse, often unwieldy and resistant to the quick cross-referencing and allusion typical of print cultures.

Originality in oral situations is more like composing variations on a theme than striking out with bold new melodies. Commenting on the conservative nature of originality in oral cultures, Ong writes:

> Narrative originality lodges not in making up new stories but in managing a particular interaction with this audience at this time—at every telling the story has to be introduced uniquely into

a unique situation, for in oral cultures an audience must be brought to respond, often vigorously. But narrators also introduce new elements into old stories. . . . In oral traditions, there will be as many minor variants of a myth as there are repetitions of it, and the number of repetitions can be increased indefinitely. Praise poems of chiefs invite entrepreneurship, as the old formulas and themes have to be made to interact with new and often complicated political situations. But the formulas and themes are reshuffled rather than supplanted with new materials.[30]

Again, John's Apocalypse expresses a hybrid literate orality. The recycling of older materials and the reshuffling of inherited traditions is obvious even on the most superficial reading of Revelation. John's descriptions of the "one like a son of man" in Rev. 1:12-15 rehearses images prevalent in Older Testament and early Jewish texts, as does his vision of the heavenly throne room (chap. 4).[31] In particular, Ezekiel's throne-room vision (chaps. 40–47) furnishes John with many of the details of his own temple visions as well as those of the heavenly Jerusalem of Rev. 21:1—22:5. John's treatment of the fall of Babylon is a reworking, among other Older Testament texts, of the oracles against Babylon and Tyre found in Jeremiah 50–51 and Ezekiel 27–28, respectively. The representation of plagues in Revelation 16 is patterned after those in the account of the exodus from Egypt. The apocalyptic section of the Book of Daniel (chaps. 7–12) furnishes John with beasts and hybrid monsters (for example, Daniel 7; cf. Revelation 13; 17:9-12), a book of life, last judgment, and resurrection (Dan. 7:9-14; 12:1-4; cf. Rev. 20:11-15).

John reworks such texts and images not in a way that suggests slavish quotation of individual passages, but a redeployment of inherited metaphors—what Ong describes in the quotation above as making older formulas and themes interact with new situations. John's Apocalypse expresses and thereby conserves an inherited tradition.

Revelation thereby tends toward *homeostasis*—Ong's term for that feature of oral culture that preserves the memorable and forgets the rest. This is the social dimension of John's citations of older traditions that contemporary scholarly attention to John's literary dependence on earlier texts passes over. John evidently had at his disposal a large but nevertheless circumscribed stock of metaphors and literary tropes with which to communicate his Apocalypse.

In its visions, the Apocalypse rehearses the grand narratives of the Older Testament (creation, exodus, exile, restoration, day of wrath, holy war). These provide the framework for John's more precise quotations of biblical texts and his allusions to inherited metaphors. In Rev. 8:6-12, there is a "de-creation" as the order of Gen. 1:1-25 is reversed. John describes the destruction first of one-third of all plants, then of sea creatures, followed by destruction of one-third of the moon, sun, and stars. He represents his faithful listeners as the children of Israel liberated from slavery and singing the song of Moses (15:3), or as people called forth from exile in Babylon (18:4-8). The warrior on the white horse riding forth to punish his enemies and to destroy idolaters (Rev. 19:11-16) echoes the traditions recorded in Joshua and Judges associated with the military victories over the idolatrous inhabitants of Canaan. The image also recalls the terror of Older Testament representations of the Lord's day of wrath (Zeph. 1:14-16; Jer. 30:7; Joel 1:15; 2:1-2, 11, 31; Mal. 4:5; see Rev. 1:7). Further, by depicting opponents as Older Testament antagonists (Balaam, Jezebel—Rev. 2:14, 20), John keeps his story close to the legendary narrative templates hallowed by memory. Such homeostasis tends further toward the conservatism valued in oral cultures. By invoking well-known legends, John's stories preserve traditional modes of understanding and interpretation of human behaviors and experiences and encourage listeners to understand the world in terms of older patterns. Clearly he wants his audience to hear him as representing the voice of a time-honored sacred past, and his opponents as innovators representing inferior characters.

Finally, as an example of orality, John's language is *aggregative rather than analytic*. The aggregative describes the pleonastic aspect of orality. This occurs first through the drawing out of nouns by placing them in identical or similar adjectival/participial phrases, or through the association of nouns and verbs with a discrete set of adjectives and adverbs. Or, second, aggregation occurs by placing clauses parallel to one another, or antithetically.

As the Apocalypse unfolds, one notices that John draws out particular nouns in similar ways. Almost without exception, when John hears a heavenly voice, it is loud. When he speaks of the Lamb it is usually as "slain" (5:6, 9, 12; 13:8). The heavenly throne belongs to God ("the one seated on the throne"), and from chapter 5 onward also to the Lamb (3:21; 4:2, 10; 5:7, 13; 6:16; 7:9, 10, 15, 17; 12:5; 19:4; 20:11; 21:5; 22:1, 3).

God is the "one who is and who was and who is to come" (1:8; 4:8;
11:17), "the Alpha and the Omega," "the first and the last" (1:8; 21:6; 22:13;
1:17). The Beast, in memorable contrast, "was, and is not, and . . . is to go
to perdition" (17:8, 11). Usually when heaven is invoked, the four living
creatures and/or the twenty-four elders are nearby (4:4, 10; 5:5, 6, 8, 11, 14;
7:11; 11:16; 14:3; 19:4). Witness or testimony in the Apocalypse is faithful
(1:5; 3:14); one either gives it to Jesus, or receives it from him (twice with
the verb *echein;* 1:2, 9; 12:17; 19:10). On account of witness the faithful are
slain (6:9; 11:7). By means of it they conquer the Beast (12:11). Elsewhere
the Apocalypse employs more extensive formulas, especially in describing worship (for example, 4:4, 6-8, 10; 5:6, 9-10, 12, 13; 7:12), or when representing the universal creation, or humankind (5:13; 6:15; 7:9; 10:11;
13:7-8, 16; 15:4; 16:14; 17:2, 8, 15; 18:9, 11, 17; 19:18; 21:24).

John often employs parallelism of various kinds: direct (the idea of a
first line repeated in a second), staircase (one clause building on another),
and antithetical (the second line contrasting with the first). This is especially true when he recounts expressions of worship, or admonishes (for
example, 3:17; 7:15-17; 15:3). Repeating phrases or echoing/contrasting
phrases in quick succession has an important function in solidifying what
is heard in a listener's mind, as well as helping to promote a more vivid listening experience. Functionally, repeated phrases help to make what is
heard memorable. It is easy to forget that Jesus is a faithful witness; it is
more difficult to wrest from one's mind the image of a figure with a two-
edged sword coming from his mouth. Semantically, such phrases train the
listener to keep the many characters of the Apocalypse straight and to
identify more easily what makes them blameworthy or laudable.

Ong's typology helps to identify the oral features of the Book of Revelation, to resist an overly quick translation of its imagery into theological meanings, and to recognize how it might have functioned to persuade
hearers to understand and pursue its ideals. The typology moves us
toward a general appreciation of the oral qualities of John's Revelation.
Naming, however, is only a first step in understanding. The next task is
to investigate more closely what might be described as the heavily
accented tonalities of John's orality. Phrases like "the oral literature of
Greco-Roman antiquity" conceal as much as they reveal, for the state-
ment covers oral performers as diverse as Cicero and the hearer of Patmos. We need to listen more closely.

MAKING NOISES

Moreover, it can also be shown that the diction of the Gospel and Epistle differs from that of the Apocalypse. For they were written not only without error as regards the Greek language, but also with elegance in their expression, in their reasonings, and in their entire structure. They are far indeed from betraying any barbarism or solecism, or any vulgarism whatever. For the writer had, as it seems, both the requisites of discourse, that is, the gift of knowledge and the gift of expression, — as the Lord had bestowed them both upon him. I do not deny that the other writer saw a revelation and received knowledge and prophecy. I perceive, however, that his dialect and language are not accurate Greek, but that he uses barbarous idioms, and, in some places, solecisms. It is unnecessary to point these out here, for I would not have any one think that I have said these things in a spirit of ridicule, for I have said what I have only with the purpose of showing clearly the difference between the writings.

—Dionysius of Alexandria, Eusebius *Hist. eccl.* 7.25

Dionysius, the third-century bishop of Alexandria, is right. John's Greek is peculiar. It differs from that of the Fourth Gospel and the Johannine Epistles. In fact, it differs from anything else one finds in the Newer Testament. In terms of "barbarism or solecism, or any vulgarism," perhaps only the Gospel of Mark comes close. No other Newer Testament text has as many textual variants as the Book of Revelation. The critical apparatus for the Apocalypse contained in the Nestle-Aland Greek New Testament apparatus, growing more complex with each new edition (now the twenty-seventh), reveals generations of scribes trying to save the Apocalypse from the glaring grammatical errors and infelicities of style to which Dionysius alludes in his panning of Revelation.

A reading of contemporary translations of the Apocalypse, however, would not reveal this complexity. The Book of Revelation translated in modern English Bibles reflects a cleaned-up Greek text and, especially when it comes to translation of verb tenses, a far more orderly account of the things John heard and saw than the original suggests.[32] John's part-

ner in grammatical crimes, the gospeler Mark, has been similarly rehabilitated. Are we not dealing here with the politics of biblical translation?
Maybe. Were all the glory of the Apocalypse's grammatical inconsistencies and "barbarism" to be captured in a modern translation, would this
not open the book of the Bible most known to audiences outside the
Christian church to that "spirit of ridicule" Dionysius of Alexandria
wanted to avoid?

It is understandable, therefore, that scholars should try their hand at
bringing some order to Revelation's grammatical mayhem. Early in the
twentieth century, R. H. Charles included in a preface to his commentary
on Revelation "A Short Grammar of the Apocalypse," until then, and
perhaps since, the boldest attempt to identify some system in John's
"not accurate Greek."[33] Charles gathers all the grammatical peculiarities,
errors, and inconsistencies of the Apocalypse's Greek, organizes them
according to type, and then seeks to account for them either by reference
to the author's idiosyncrasies of style, grammatical slips, or by primitive
scribal corruptions. His remains the most accessible listing of grammatical peculiarities to date. "It would seem," observed Charles, "that the
author of the Apocalypse deliberately set at defiance the grammarian and
ordinary rules of syntax. But such a description would do him the gross-
est injustice." No, he argues, John "has no thought of consistently breaking any rules of syntax. How then are we to explain the unbridled license
of his Greek constructions? The reason clearly is that, *while he writes in
Greek, he thinks in Hebrew*, and the thought has naturally affected the
vehicle of his expression."[34]

In the years since Charles's commentary there have been many would-
be champions concerning the Apocalypse's grammatical style, but few
victors.[35] There is a wide spectrum of views to account for the peculiarities of the Book of Revelation's Greek. The more robust thesis is that
Revelation is a Greek translation of a Hebrew or Aramaic original.[36] Less
ambitious is the argument that it reflects the philological know-how of a
Hebrew or Aramaic native speaker whose second language was Greek
(Charles's Hebrew thinker).[37] Others have argued that John's is "Jewish
Greek." That is, it reflects a Hellenistic Greek syntactically related
to Hebrew and spoken by Hellenistic Jews.[38] Another group argues
that John deliberately "modelled his grammar on the pattern of the classical Hebrew of the Old Testament."[39] Still others insist that John knew

Greek well, but that he deliberately broke its grammatical rules, and grammatical transgressions can largely be explained by dependence on the Septuagint.[40]

It lies beyond the philological competence of the present author to offer arguments that add to or detract from any of these views. Instead, my interest is in the sounds of the text. Whichever account is correct, all would agree that the Apocalypse *sounded* strange to Greek ears, hence Dionysius of Alexandria's reference to it as containing barbarisms, solecisms, and vulgarisms. That middle space between speaker and audience tells volumes. It moves us once again away from static explanation, in this case of a philological kind, toward the unfolding event of orality. The interest is not, Why did John write such strange Greek? It is rather, How might strange-sounding Greek have affected listeners?

In groundbreaking studies, first John E. Hurtgen and more recently Allen Dwight Callahan have endeavored to stay within the sounds of John's Apocalypse to consider the social function the idiosyncrasies of the Apocalypse's grammar might have had for an audience. Hurtgen uses the phrase "anti-language" (coined by Michael A. K. Halliday) to describe Revelation's syntax as "a language displaying all kinds of verbal play that a group employs to register its opposition to a dominant group in the culture."[41] To borrow a phrase from Wittgenstein, apocalyptic anti-language in the Book of Revelation takes its listeners on an apocalyptic holiday into social dissent. Word/sound plays of the types outlined above (similar endings, inversions of words, etc.) invite listeners into a strangely sounded world that gives voice to countercultural resistance.

Hurtgen further notes instances of "relexicalization" and "overlexicalization," terms borrowed from Halliday.[42] Relexicalization describes the ways in which the Apocalypse overturns conventional descriptions of the world by renaming it in surprising ways. Overlexicalization occurs when a single aspect of experience or culture is given focus through lengthy description, or through the piling on of synonyms and metaphor to describe the same phenomenon. The Apocalypse's slain Lamb is a good example of relexicalization. John renames his social world by ascribing to the Lamb language of imperial might and prestige usually reserved in court ritual for the Roman emperor (in chapter 6 I discuss this political usage of doxology in more detail). Overlexicalization occurs when John names the dragon of Revelation 12 variously as "the great red dragon" (vv. 3, 4, 7, 9, 13, 16, 17), "ancient serpent" (v. 9), "the Devil and

Satan" (v. 9), and later links it with the two beasts (13:1, 11) and the whore of Babylon (17:3). By means of re- and overlexicalization, John linguistically constructs a dissenting countersociety to imperial authority, centered in the worship of the slain Lamb.

Hurtgen does not consider the oddly textured grammar of John's Apocalypse. This is what Callahan offers in a study that, while not citing Hurtgen's earlier arguments, comes to similar conclusions. According to Callahan, the grammatical peculiarities of the Apocalypse reflect John's use of "the language of the Septuagint to weave a biblical texture for his text."[43] John consciously deploys this language to develop a counterdiscourse to Roman power. "The language of the seer is a subaltern language, the language of one who is disenfranchised from mainstream discourse, but must appropriate its articulations simply to be understood." A little later he continues that John, "with strategy and premeditation, transgressed grammatical norms as an exercise of his own discursive power."[44] The grammatical difficulties of John's Greek reflect neither an improperly learned Greek nor a Jewish Greek idiolect.

The medium is the message: John's grammar is difficult because *John* wants to be difficult. "The language of the text—its discourse, the word of God—*is* the struggle. The terrain of contestation is the discourse itself."[45] What R. H. Charles names "solecisms," derived from "slips of our author which a subsequent revision would have removed, if the opportunity for such a revision had offered itself," are, according to Callahan, neither slips nor evidence of lack of proofreading.[46] John's grammatical howlers are intentionally designed to alert listeners that, upon entering the realm of apocalyptic language, they are in a place that contests accepted ways of naming and organizing the world. We may add that they also express the agonistically toned property of orality.

Most famous, and conspicuous because it appears at the outset of the Apocalypse (1:4), is John's misuse of the preposition *apo* with the nominative prepositional phrase *ho ōn kai ho ēn kai ho erchomenos*, instead of the grammatically correct genitive. Close on its heels (v. 5) comes another error, again with the preposition *apo*, this time complementing the preposition correctly with a genitive appositive (*apo Iēsou Christou*), but then continuing incorrectly with an appositive in the accusative *ho martys, ho pistos, ho prōtotokos*. Since in other uses of *apo* in verses 4-5 John correctly links preposition and case, it is most probable that the error is intentional. Notably, these errors occur in formulaic phrases charged with significance. "By leaving the words of each of these phrases in the nominative case," Callahan concludes,

> he [John] showed that they are not be understood as individual lexica, but as inseparable parts of an indeclinable whole. He has privileged the integrity of these epithets over the dictates of Greek grammar: they are not declined, but bent down to the rule of standard language. He has dropped the syntax "in an effort to effect and affect."[47]

John's difficulties of grammar communicate a "decolonising discourse."[48] He is in this regard not unlike a Rastafarian who has learned English metaphors, phrases, and grammatical structures from English colonialism, but who redeploys them to subvert the imperial discourse that mediated those linguistic features in the first place. Here is Hurtgen's "anti-language" in grammatical dress.

In other words, John's Apocalypse makes noises that resist translation into either abstract theological conceptions or correct English. Oddly compounded chains of description (Hurtgen) as well as odd grammar (Callahan) result in a text whose meaning lies in its surplus. Both scholars urge us to linger amid the Apocalypse's sounds instead of beating a hasty retreat to the commentaries when met with weird symbolism and mystifying grammatical constructions. In these readings, Revelation does not mean—it does. As orality, it does so through an application of noise, designed to call into question the very system of meaning and signification the traditional commentary represents.

"Noise is violence: it disturbs," notes Jacques Attali, brilliantly analyzing what he calls the political economies in the history of Western music. "To make noise is to interrupt a transmission, to disconnect, to kill."[49] Music, and, by logical extension, language, is organized noise—noise brought to heel through organization. Music and language remain vulnerable to disruption by their very source. "A network can be destroyed by noises that attack and transform it, if the codes in place are unable to normalize and repress them."[50] On the other hand, nothing happens without noise. Systems normalize and repress noise—turn what would otherwise be interruptions into new tonalities and expressions of speech. But in this very act noise modulates and shifts preexisting systems.

Describing the social orchestration of noise in the eighteenth and nineteenth centuries in representational systems of harmony, Attali outlines the relation between music and noise and the way the latter is naturalized by the former.

> Harmony is . . . the operator of a compromise between natural forms of noise, of the emergence of a conflictual order, of a code that gives meaning to noise, of a field in the imaginary and of a limit on violence. Harmony theorizes its usage . . . by affirming that it has a pacifying effect. . . . Harmony is in a way the representation of an absolute relation between well-being and order in nature. In China as in Greece, harmony implies a system of measurement, in other words, a system for the scientific, quantified representation of nature. The scale is the incarnation of the harmony between heaven and earth, the isomorphism of all representations: the bridge between the order of the Gods (ritual) and earthly order (the simulacrum).

"This explains," Attali concludes later, "the fundamental political importance of music as demonstration that an ideal order, the true image offered by elemental religion, is possible."[51]

Attali's observations alert us to the social role of John's noisiness, that is, to those extra sounds silenced by commentary and explanation. Noise does not mean, it disrupts—that is, until it is accounted for as a further instance of meaning, until it is coded and then cracked. John's "subaltern grammar" is a noisy breakout from a Roman prison of imperial signification. If such noise is resolved in the loud testimony of heavenly characters to the slain Lamb, the resulting harmonics modulate an inherited imperial order to a different key and express a logic that calls the order's conventional modes of signification into question. To this idea I return in the final chapter. The relexicalized Roman emperor, the slain Lamb, is the object of sung praise, voiced in a broken grammar that finally *talks* imperial might and domination off its throne.

Appreciating the way John's grammatical noisiness disrupts conventional rules of Greek syntax, Callahan urges that one read the Apocalypse "with a poetic sensibility."[52] The invocation of poetry in a discussion concerning broken grammar is especially apt, and dovetails nicely with Attali's exposition of the relation of noise to music/syntax and their development.

Nora Chadwick in an anthropological study of the social function of poets in oral societies describes shamans as mantic poets mediating, through poetically intoned speech, listeners' access to the divine.[53] Contained and orchestrated through ritual, the inspired speech of shamans consolidates the social organization in which such speech occurs. In a related study treating the social context of oral poetry, Ruth Finnegan pays close attention to the careful restrictions societies place on performances of oral poetry, whether in shamanic ritual, or among members of industrialized society gathered to sing protest songs.[54]

In the preliterate societies Chadwick investigates, oral poetry mediates the divine. There is also evidence of this in the first-century courtly culture of the early Roman Empire. Horace and Virgil, poets active in the late Republic and early Augustan age, believed their role was not only to celebrate, but also to mediate the eschatological political realities they believed that Octavian heralded in his ending of civil war and creation of a subsequent political order. Horace's *Carmen saeculare* and Virgil's *Eclogues* (especially *Ecl.* 1, 5, 6, and 9), as well as the eighth book of his *Aeneid*, offer revelatory celebrations of a divinely established political peace. Dieter Georgi in a sociohistorical study of Horace's *Carmen saeculare* (a panegyric to the political order established by Augustus) identifies Horace socially as a medium who delivers through his poetic speech a divinely revealed political eschatology celebrating Augustan rule. Horace saw himself, however, as more than a mere court poet. In his Augustus Epistle (*Ep.* 2.1.134–37), he celebrates his divinely inspired poetry as mediating power both in the divine and human spheres. Not only does his poetry celebrate the principate as established by the gods. It in fact helps to place the principate firmly among the gods.

Such speech could, however, be put to other uses. Georgi goes on to treat the Apocalypse as political mantic speech analogous to contemporary political poetry. But in John's case, divinely mediated visions do not cement the imperial order into place among the gods. His visions contest that position. Georgi assesses John's unique grammar as belonging to this challenge to imperial power. By placing John alongside Horace and Virgil in this way, Georgi recovers the political dimensions of John's orality, and insightfully places him in a social context of competing oralities believed to mediate and solidify divine realities.

John is conscious of the creative dimension of language and literary composition. The peculiar Greek style of the book is not an expression of linguistic incompetence or barbarism but proves to be an original creation of the singular language with its own rather consistent grammar, syntax, and vocabulary. John uses this language not, as Apocalypticism does, in order to create another supernatural reality but in order to get hold of historical reality with the help of prophetic magic.[55]

The Apocalypse is counterpolitical poetics. It upsets the earthly political order through the charged speech of divine revelation.

A revolution delivered by poetry? According to contemporary Freudian/ Marxist theorist Julia Kristeva, poetry is the seedbed of revolution. In its challenging of grammar and semantics, poetry expresses a poet's breaking free of the symbolic, that is, the conventional socioeconomic signification of culture. For Kristeva, poetry promises a liberation from a Freudian/Lacanian psycho-sexual "fall" into language as compensation for frustrated desire. Infant sounds (the semiotic) in time become words (the symbolic), which carry with them the medium of their speaker's self-alienation. Between these stages, occupying a kind of threshold between sound and meaning, is the "thetic," "that crucial place on the basis of which the human being constitutes himself as signifying and/or social." Poetry offers a reversal of the symbolic, carrying the poet/audience back not to the pre-linguistic semiotic, but to that productive liminal space of the thetic, after sounds and before words, when intoned desires are co-opted by signifying systems.

The Freudianism here is elaborate, but in an intriguing way celebrates the surplus noise of signification, which results in the revolutions of society Attali chronicles in his political exposé of music. One need not adopt Kristeva's account of the transformation of infant noises into words to agree that the

> textual experience [of the thetic, i.e., poetic] represents one of the most daring explorations the subject can allow himself, one that delves into his constitutive process. But at the same time and as a result, textual experience reaches the very foundation of the social—that which is exploited by sociality but which elaborates and can go beyond it, either destroying or transforming it.[56]

It was surely the destroying "textual experience" that Plato had in mind when he exiled poets from his ideal city-state. It is no accident then that John of Patmos should be all but exiled from the church and handed over to the experts, talked about behind closed doors, explained, and interpreted. Poets (and apocalyptic eavesdroppers) have the power to destabilize the most idealized of political and religious fantasies, through their peculiar grammars and metaphorical constructions.

But it is not only Plato who fares ill on this account. So do those decoders who want to discover a poetic text's hidden meaning, as do the commentators who would domesticate noisy texts by excavating their symbolic meaning. To hear the Apocalypse with a "poetic sensibility" is to resist the temptation to write grammars to make John write more perfect Greek, and to overcome grammatical dissatisfaction with its text. A poetic sensibility lets the errors howl amid apocalyptic intonations. It hears in them a challenge to the imperial order surrounding John's listeners and the possibility of a new heaven and a new earth.

Let every word howl.

REMEMBERING APOCALYPSE

With Freud . . . foreignness, an uncanny one, creeps into the tranquillity of reason itself, and, without being restricted to madness, beauty, or faith anymore than to ethnicity or race, irrigates our very speaking-being, estranged by other logics, including the heterogeneity of biology. . . . Henceforth, we know that we are foreigners to ourselves, and it is with the help of that sole support that we can attempt to live with others.

—Julia Kristeva, *Strangers to Ourselves*

Nothing important happened in my family in the absence of grammatical noise. Worlds were overturned and created in the adventurous grammar of our oral culture of remembered apocalypse. Memory now reconstructs in perfect English the stories told around the family table about that traumatic winter of 1945, of flight and rapine, escape and murder, immigration and adaptation. This is a trick of the brain, or perhaps it is the product of the self-reflective commentary of a second-generation child who has a home and who has learned to crack the assimilating culture's code. The stories were not told thus. In setting forth to tell stories, our immigrant family wandered across languages as though, having fled once as refugees, grammatically they would never set down roots again. The stories would inevitably begin in German, migrate to English punctuated by German words, or contrariwise. As recitations unfolded, tellers braided language, coining nonsense words—English embedded in German sentences, jammed into a foreign language by the hasty addition of German suffixes and prefixes. Word order strayed. Invented nouns and verbs skirted both languages. And every now and then, usually in mockery, a stray Polish word. Here was syntax in free fall; words in no dictionary, grammar without rhyme or reason.

In the mouths of these immigrants familiar topics of conversations, descriptions of the most routine aspects and objects of everyday life, became uncanny—as though *Heimatlosigkeit* ("statelessness") gave expression to itself in the *unheimlich* ("uncanny strangeness") grammar of a two-forked tongue. Listening in as a child, it was the sound of this immigrant grammar that mesmerized, carrying teller and listeners beyond the believable, to the limit of the imagination.

Some were better tellers than others. My maternal grandmother was the best. She was a linguistic *bricoleur.* Although barely literate, by the time I was born she had learned enough English and forgotten enough German to speak in a tongue of her own making—Oma's *Wanderungs-grammatik,* the perfect tool for wringing out the last drop of emotion from the recalled tales of Apocalypse 1945, recited like a litany of deprivation and loss. In December 1945, following a daring escape from a Soviet-military work camp, she shepherded elderly parents, and three children, one of them a toddler whom she carried much of the way on her back, hundreds of kilometers overland out of Poland to Germany. My earliest memories are of weekends, Christmases, and holidays spent overhearing her aggregative recitation of an epic journey. To sit at her kitchen table and hear her recite was to be an apocalyptic eavesdropper on testimony to the loss of heaven and earth, by someone who lived to tell the story.

The grammar endures. However much the world now orders nouns, verbs, adjectives, and adverbs, there remains a background noisiness that refuses to be drowned out by the order of things. It is the noisiness of the kitchen table—crosstalk that speaks a language countering the glowing progress reports of a post-industrialized society. But we should not kid ourselves. There is little room for crosstalk in the increasingly rationalized society of global economic production. We may illustrate this by reference to Jürgen Habermas's description of modernity's "incomplete project"—the creation of a domination-free society of communicative action.[57] In this idea, a society would grow ever more rational through its citizens' continued commitment to conversing with one another concerning warrants for actions, values, and structures of belief, especially when they find themselves in fundamental disagreement. Habermas hopes for a society of growing consensus and allegiance to a liberating categorical imperative of rational discussion.

Habermas's *Theory of Communicative Action* models such a conversation: theoretical exposition punctuated by careful discussion of the views of sociological, philosophical, and political conversation partners.[58] It is intriguing, therefore, that the one philosophical tradition Habermas does not engage in his theory of communicative action is aesthetics. This is because, according to Habermas, aesthetics plays only a supporting role to reason. Art serves reason by commending its version of truth to its audience's senses and making it thereby persuasive.[59] Poetry and metaphor have no intrinsic meaning in themselves—they are a means to a more rational sensibility. If there is a way to exile the poets from the ideal state without physically removing them, this is surely it—to treat art as an epiphenomenon of reason. The *unheimlich* in this account is "merely rhetorical," an aesthetic to make the rational more compelling.

One fears, then, that on the way toward consensus, there is little room for poor grammar. Would not a goal of Habermas's ever more rational consensus be to filter out crosstalk? Would this not be the domination of the domination-free society? Modernity's "project," as Charles Taylor, a critic of Habermas, notes, hides its accent—that is, its value-laden mooring in a particular cultural tradition, the European Christian culture of Immanuel Kant.[60] Intriguingly, the Canadian philosopher Taylor, having an Anglophone father and a French Canadian mother, grew up in a bilingual household. "Another language is also another way to conceive the world."[61] In this view, the noisiness of a strange tongue is not something to fit into an overarching rational grammar. Like poetry that means what it says rather than signifying some deeper, hidden truth, the unruly grammar of an immigrant tongue inhabiting several languages at once would be a reminder of the foreignness without which there is never reason, and, therefore, the particularity of truth.

On this view, the good society does not always aim toward rational convergence. In fact, it gets nervous when too many people believe in the same slogans. (It is not so long ago that the citizens of Habermas's Frankfurt were burning books in the name of reason.) Good societies let people make noise, speak in strange tongues, and insist upon difference. The good citizens of such good societies nurture social gatherings in which talking funny takes place. Inhabiting several languages at once, speaking in strange tongues: could this be a way for the sidelined churches of once-powerful Christendom to re-vision their self-understanding and come to play an enlivening role in post-Christian secular society? What if a Christian contribution to an ever more rationalized postindustrial society were to sound voices of unreason, in testimony to the foolishness of God's wisdom in the cruciform Jesus Christ, Revelation's slain Lamb? Here I only raise the question and reserve fuller discussion for my final chapter. What if Christianity were to recover a strange grammar of confession with which to urge citizens to be kinder, less cruel, more life-preserving people?

Another account of social conversation preserves the accents. For Julia Kristeva, Habermas's communicative action would not lead toward rational consensus so much as to a recovery of the foreignness lurking in the most familiar aspects of oneself and one's neighbors, a strangeness the rational hides and overcomes. Kristeva, too, insists on conversation, but on a special form of conversation, namely psychoanalysis, leading not to convergence but difference. In her punchy section of *New Maladies of the Soul*, "In a Time Like This, Who Needs Psychoanalysis?" she champions psychoanalytical conversation as liberating praxis.

> The psychic realm may be the place where somatic symptoms and delirious fantasies can be worked through and thus eliminated; as long as we avoid becoming trapped inside it, the psychic realm protects us. Yet we must transform it through *linguistic activity* into a form of sublimation or into an intellectual, interpretative, or transformational activity. At the same time, we must conceive of the "psychic realm" as a *speech act*, that is, neither an acting-out nor a psychological rumination within an imaginary crypt, but the link between this inevitable and necessary rumination and its potential for verbal expression.[62]

On this account the rhetorical is not an epiphenomenon of reason, but takes us to the foundations of the rational and the madness that lurks therein. "Revitalizing grammar and rhetoric, and enriching the style of those who wish to speak with us because they can no longer remain silent and brushed aside: do such projects not mirror the new life and new psyche that psychoanalysis wishes to unearth?"[63] Indeed, such a revitalized grammar and rhetoric focuses not on conversation as a means toward generalized consensus, but asks how individuals make their souls: "We must ask how a soul is made. What kinds of representations and which logical varieties constitute the soul?"[64] Like Habermas, Kristeva writes that linguistic activity is utopian, but centered in individual difference: "In a roundabout manner, the psychoanalyst is . . . asked to restore psychic life and to enable the speaking entity to live life to its fullest."[65]

Kristeva's championing of psychoanalysis in these quotations teeters on the edge of an individualism ill-equipped for meeting the challenges of societal exchange. But it is finally a societally embedded "revitalized grammar and rhetoric" that is for her the goal of psychoanalytic conversation. Kristeva herself is a Bulgarian immigrant to France. In her *Strangers to Ourselves* she offers a meditation on the experience of foreignness by redeploying Freud's notion of the *unheimlich* as "strangely uncanny."[66] In Freud's fully developed psychoanalytic treatment, the *unheimlich* expresses anxiety associated with daily recurring objects that possess a strange ability to unsettle us. Upon closer investigation the strangely uncanny reveals repression by the unconscious of a fear or anxiety now projected and externalized onto a familiar object through which the repressed fear returns to haunt us. Kristeva reworks this notion, noting that, among the many definitions Freud lists on his way toward an accurate definition of the *unheimlich,* is the Greek notion of *xenos* ("stranger"). On Kristeva's account, Freud, the theoretician of uncanny strangeness, is himself, as Jew wandering from Galicia to Vienna and, later, as émigré to London, the stranger.

What is in Freud's account an exploration of the unconscious becomes in Kristeva's treatment a discussion of xenophobia. The strangeness of foreigners—which greets me daily in the color of their skin, their odd clothing, the way they talk, how their houses smell—is the visible token of my own strangeness to myself and the invitation (at least ideally) to explore my own foreignness. More usually such strangeness is so unsettling that we would rather drive it away through expulsion or exclusion. In Canada, for example, we set stringent immigrant rules. In the United States, foreigners are given green cards imprinted with numeric codes that gather and organize strangeness as a means to police and render it predictable. Canadian and American governments are today envisioning an impregnable defensive perimeter to surround the continent. What is this if not a fear of uncanny strangeness? Is it not an impotent attempt to exorcise the irreducible strangeness that we all carry within us, to project outside our borders that which ceaselessly seeks to infiltrate our well-devised schemes, and, more hauntingly still, that which greets us when we are forced to live alongside the strangely other? To let foreigners in—would this not bring us face to face with ourselves? There are many ways civilized governments exile the poet, who might otherwise bring a revolution, and render our anxieties manageable, even reasonable: by appealing to fears of terrorism, unemployment, poor economic growth, the national debt, overcrowded schools, and so on.

> The ethics of psychoanalysis implies a politics; it would involve a cosmopolitanism of a new sort that, cutting across governments, economies, and markets, might work for a mankind whose solidarity is founded on the consciousness of the unconscious—desiring, destructive, fearful, empty, impossible. . . . On the basis of an erotic, death-bearing unconscious, the uncanny strangeness . . . which adumbrates the work of the "second" Freud, the one of *Beyond the Pleasure Principle*, sets the difference within us in its most bewildering shape and presents it as the ultimate condition of our being *with* others.[67]

"The foreigner is within me, hence we are all foreigners," writes Kristeva earlier. "If I am foreigner, there are no foreigners."

This final paradox returns us to the kitchen table and its peculiarly intoned speech. It insists upon noise at the table of "communicative action," and wins a place that Habermas too often reserves for "experts." Certainly, anxiety propelled those part-German, part-English conversations overheard as a child: anxieties not only concerning the dominant culture from whose fragments of grammar a private family language was built, but anxiety concerning our own selves. "People, when they are starving and afraid, are animals," was the refrain to these tales of horror.

The animal we carry around within ourselves, I was told, was barely tamed by civilization. What I *heard* was that it also was barely contained by grammar. Still, we were animals *talking* to each other and, in the uncanny intonations of grammar, anxiety was given a voice.

Reflecting years later, I cannot say that these conversations opened us to a way of "being *with* others." At worst the grammar shut others out (in any case one had to have the rudiments of German to understand what was being talked about). At best it helped the family be *alongside* others. Nevertheless, the ungrammatical orality of the foreign/not foreign tongue provided a means for expressing an identity at once fully immersed in Canadian life and the Anglophone culture that surrounded us, and one step removed from it, addressing it in the most jarring syntax. The syntax turned inward kept immigrant troubles at bay. But what if it had been turned outward?

I return in due course to the theological power of an address that confounds grammar, taking cues from both John of Patmos and the recollections of post–World War II apocalypse. In chapter 6, I again listen in on the political "crosstalk" of the Apocalypse to its Roman Empire, and the poetic revolution implied in testimony to the slain Lamb, the crucified Jesus Christ. For now, however, let us linger amid the memories. Long overdue, let us take a journey through apocalyptic time, keeping our eyes and, yes, our ears open along the way.

5

Games with Time

Both read the Bible day and night,
But thou read'st black where I read white

—William Blake, "The Everlasting Gospel"

POST-APOCALYPSE

The Book of Revelation is a post-Apocalypse. Framed by an epistolary opening and closing (Rev. 1:4-5; 22:8-21), John stuffs his Apocalypse in an envelope and sends it from Patmos hoping, as we saw in chapter 3, to make listeners envious of the sights and sounds recorded from his exotic trip through the end of the world.[1] Revelation requests that John's audience indeed share with him "in Jesus the tribulation and the kingdom and the patient endurance" in the same way that Paul urged his listeners to be "in Christ," and thus share in Jesus' suffering and resurrection. It is a "wishing-you-were-here" letter addressed to a Christian audience that, John insists, has sidled up too closely to Roman imperial culture and the desire for its economic benefits.

But, once sent, not all letters arrive, and the ones that do are not always on time, or even intact. From the island of Patmos to the seven churches of Asia Minor is a relatively short distance, but our letter has taken a rather longer route.

> There is no destination, my sweet destiny
> you understand,
> within every sign already, every mark or every trait, there is dis-
> tancing, the post, what there has to be so that it is legible for
> another, another than you or me, and everything is messed up
> in advance, cards on the table. The condition for it to arrive is
> that it ends up and even that it begins by not arriving. This is
> how it is to be read, and written, the *carte* of the adestination.[2]

When will the post-Apocalypse arrive? John's answer: sometime soon! The Apocalypse is a letter that notoriously defers the arrival of its contents: "The revelation of Jesus Christ, which God gave him to show to his servants what must *soon* take place . . ." (1:1); "He who testifies to these things says, 'Surely I am coming *soon*.' Amen. Come Lord Jesus!" (22:20). When the subaltern saints of Rev. 6:10-11, "slain for the word of God," ask how much longer it will be before their blood will be avenged, each receives a white robe and the instruction "to rest a little longer."[3] Jesus, like Godot, is just around a corner that is never turned. In the meantime . . . there is the meantime left to wonder what content the letter will bring when it finally does arrive, and to make up time in the wake of its absence.

"We notice," comments Northrop Frye, "that while the Book of Revelation seems to be emphatically the end of the Bible, it is a remarkably open end." Frye goes on to argue that the "panoramic apocalypse" at the Bible's end "gives way . . . to a second apocalypse that, ideally, begins in the reader's mind as soon as he has finished reading, a vision that passes through the legalized vision of ordeals and trials and judgments and comes out into a second life."[4] Indeed, the Apocalypse is known in popular culture as *the* biblical book dominated by the future tense. Pop culture's Book of Revelation does not end with the epistolary retrospective of John concerning the visions he communicates but with the vision of the descended heavenly Jerusalem of 20:1—22:5. Notably, Frye in the above quotation is commenting on the Apocalypse minus the letter ending. For it is that Apocalypse which has influenced the shape of English literature. As for the conclusion, perhaps it was lost in the mail, or the letter carrier decided to deliver only the contents and to throw the envelope away. Endings, however, are important, for they help us make sense of middles and beginnings, and to John's sense of an ending we will return.[5] But not before we linger a little longer at the postbox to look more closely at the form of Revelation that the Western tradition delivers.

Revelation, I suggested in the opening chapter, is the apocalyptic troublemaker. That version of the Apocalypse, expressly futurist in orientation, is notorious for the speculation concerning when and how the world is to end and for the church's resulting nervousness over including it in the biblical canon. It is tucked in at the end of The Book because it is about The End. Could its canonical location also reflect mainstream anxieties concerning its potential for misuse and even abuse? It is a text *in extremis,* the book at the edge for an edgier audience. Traditionally it has been those at the margins who have most enthusiastically welcomed the Apocalypse.[6] Those inhabiting the comforts of the center have been less welcoming. In many parts of the Christian East, Revelation's canonical authority remains disputed. In the West, its inclusion in the Bible, if late, was due in part to its acceptance among early Latin Christian authorities (especially Tertullian and Jerome). The most notable of its Latin champions was Augustine of Hippo, whose interpretation of the Apocalypse "won the West" and came to exert a profound influence on its culture. Augustine's *City of God,* written from 413–425 C.E., was the crowning achievement of his literary career and became a Western classic. Its influence on the Christian West can hardly be overestimated. More than any other work of Christian antiquity, it assured a place for the Book of Revelation in the Bible and in the subsequent mainstream Western Christian tradition.[7]

Augustine did so by blunting the Apocalypse's political edginess and saving its trouble for a latter day. The final four books of Augustine's *City of God,* arguably a loose, running commentary on world history guided by Revelation's final four chapters, proceed by insisting on Revelation's use of the future tense and on its deferrals of an ending.[8] Addressing end-time speculation, among other matters, the *City of God* is a long apology, or interpretation, of Jesus' saying that "of that day or that hour no one knows, not even the angels of heaven, nor the Son, but only the Father" (Mark 13:32).[9] The Gothic sack of Rome by Alaric in 410 had given incentive to Christian apocalyptic expectation that these were the last days before the second coming, and to pagan criticism that the pagan deities were punishing the Roman Empire for embracing Christianity. Augustine countered both notions by challenging the prevailing assumption shared by Christian and pagan alike that the rise and fall of political powers and their societies were to be explained by reference to divine favor and punishment. Instead he insisted on an opaque history in which the providential arrangement of historical events, though affirmed as an article of faith, remains inscrutable.

Robert Markus describes this notion of the opaque as Augustine's "secular" understanding of history. For Augustine, secular history is that record of time belonging to the present, between the ending of the Book of Acts and the descriptions of the last days, in which sacred scripture is silent concerning God's orchestration of history.[10] Augustine insists that the Bible outlines in chronological detail an inevitable ending to human history. He formulates a kind of "harmony of the end," a chronological ordering of endtime events gathered from the Apocalypse and other apocalyptic Older and Newer Testament texts (for example, *City of God* 2.20.30). His harmony in hand, he concludes that the sack of Rome cannot be the harbinger of the second coming, because it fails to coincide with the course of future events he gleans from the Bible. A consequence of this argument is to turn Revelation into a text that speaks of an inevitable future but that remains silent concerning the ambiguities of the present. Revelation is a text for a rainier day.

So it was that Augustine tamed the apocalyptic troublemaker and thereby assured a means of keeping the Book of Revelation in the canon. In insisting on the future tenses of the Book of Revelation, Augustine removes it from the present. Augustine's Revelation does not end in the present in which John is writing, that is, with the epistolary closing of Rev. 22:8-21, but in the vision of the descended heavenly Jerusalem and in the creation of a new heaven and earth of 20:1—22:5. Guided at least in part by Revelation's vision of Jerusalem bliss (Rev. 22:1-5), Augustine concludes the *City of God*, referring to the "eighth and eternal day, consecrated by the resurrection of Christ." "There we shall rest and see, see and love, love and praise, this is what shall be in the end without end. For what other end do we propose to ourselves than to attain to the kingdom of which there is no end?" (22.30).[11] The *City of God* ends not on Patmos, but in Augustine's imagined, unending eighth day of creation, a day whose time is firmly in the future.

Thus Augustine took one of the Bible's most politically oriented texts, with its potential for supporting utopian aspirations, toward greater justice *within* history, and, according to Robert Markus, "pushed such fundamental commitments as a man's religious beliefs and the values he lives by outside the field of political discourse."[12] What remains at

the conclusion of the *City of God* (book 22), in which Augustine medi-
tates on the heavenly Jerusalem of Rev. 21:1—22:5, is not the hope for a
more just political order in the wake of Rome's collapse but the paradoxical attempt to imagine the unimaginable, "the end without end" of a
purely timeless heavenly Jerusalem. Augustine effectively takes Revelation out of the realm of this-worldly flesh and blood, and delivers it to an
immaterial imagination. Frye's invocation of the "second apocalypse"
that "ideally forms in the reader's mind once he has finished reading the
Apocalypse" is thus a thoroughly Augustinian sentiment.

Such a docetically oriented reading strategy, however, comes with a
price. Catherine Keller, building on Robert Markus's assessment, argues
that the *City of God*'s rejection of this-worldly millennialism lands its
author in a dangerous paradox. "It is not apocalypse per se which has
been undermined by the Augustinian triumph, but rather the apocalypse
of collective, utopian aspirations for greater justice in history. The anti-
apocalyptic impulse produces an anti-apocalyptic impulse *precisely as a
form of apocalypse*."[13] The Augustinian relegation of justice and the city
of God to a remote and *imaginary* endtime fails to address the human
need for a life *before* death as much as after it. Further, Keller argues,
those who remain ignorant of apocalypse are doomed to repeat it. The
Augustinian ending of history, in which the total war of the dueling cities
finally occurs, closes off future possibility by a predetermined end. It
leads to what Keller names "the apocalypse habit," that scripting of the
self and culture in view of an inevitably destructive ending.

Frye's "second apocalypse that, ideally, begins to form in the reader's
imagination" thus seems a less-than-ideal reading. Keller's argument
prompts me to remember that the majority of citizens of the most milita-
rized society in human history, the United States, believe that the world
will end in cataclysm.[14] Michael Ortiz Hill finds apocalyptic expectation
in American culture so high that he is able to write a kind of Jungian
vademecum for interpreting recurring nightmares of the end shared
nightly by the rank and file of American citizens, including, astonishingly, children. Hill offers his guide to help apocalyptic sleepers make
sense of their dreams of unmitigated horror, and to urge them to face
their nightmares as symptomatic of civil helplessness in the shadow of
the bomb and as an invitation to resist the Manichaean dualism that the
violence expresses. Apocalyptic dreaming, as his subtitle indicates, can
serve, more positively, to invite the responsible to a "rite of passage" in

which they face nuclear-age terrors and begin to unlock the tight grip of military domination on the collective imagination.[15]

Hill's study supports Keller's contention that we are addicted to the apocalypse habit. For that reason, Keller criticizes as naive those who plead, especially in more liberal Christian circles, to "just say no" to the Apocalypse and to stop reading it. She also critiques those who reinscribe apocalyptic gestures in their call to bring apocalyptic ways of thinking to an end. The Apocalypse is too much with us for such simple solutions, and too dangerous to begin flirting with endist scenarios, however kinder and gentler they may at first appear. Instead, Keller insists on a sustained counterapocalypse as a strategy to pry open the end of history and to imagine a more material end without end, a planet freed from endist scenarios and returned to open-ended possibility.[16]

Have we been preprogrammed by our culture to produce the imaginary "end without end" of a nuclear nightmare? Catherine Keller traces the origin of the apocalypse habit to John of Patmos. In Revelation is the foreclosed sense of an ending that she finds most dangerous. Augustine helped in securing for Revelation a canonical place in Western culture, but "the security of a single history numbered from The Beginning to The End is an effect of the text of Revelation. . . ."

> Yet already in John's hands a relentless temporal oneness penetrates its confusing multiplicity of images: the Alpha which is one with the Omega, one global history directed by one God, culminating in one final judgment issuing in one redemption— for those "at one" with its End. While the narrative structure of Apocalypse does still express, like a basso continuo, the rhythmic Hebrew sense of time—neither line nor circle, but "purely and simply a rhythmic alternation"—its cadences propel it frantically forward, toward its unnerving *ultimo*.[17]

John tells the Apocalypse "as the story of his already *past* revelation. The tense is that of the future-past. . . . The point is that this particular inscription of the future as though it has already transpired, this strange privilege of The End, has framed the Western Story. It at once wedges open and slams shut that future."[18] The ending of John's letter thus makes its appearance once again, but now with a vengeance. It is John's "post–" that Keller finds most unnerving. Tucked in at the epistolary closing, it reminds one that what one has read is after all a *recollection* of the end, the future-past. The Apocalypse brings its audience, in the very act of listening, not to predictive anticipations of the future but to the future *through the remembrance of things past*. There is, then, in this reading, a predetermined future orchestrated by John's vision of the future, sealed shut by his rehearsal of it as time already concluded.

Still, I find myself lingering after John's ending. My love of receiving mail keeps me returning to the post. Reading and re-reading Keller's argument I find her most convincing when she addresses the effects of the Apocalypse in Western culture. Yet when she writes that the Apocalypse's "cadences propel it frantically forward" I think that the rhythms of her prose have begun to carry her away. To be sure, this is the version of the Apocalypse that has been passed down to us. Indeed, Keller's sense of the frantically forward-propelled Apocalypse is itself an intriguingly Augustinian reading of the Book of Revelation. How often Augustine complains in reciting his epic tale of two cities that it is taking him too long to get to the unimaginable bliss of its ending (e.g., *City of God* 16.37; 17.11); for Augustine, life is, like time, a headlong race toward death and the end (13.10, 14–24). Is it not an *Augustinian* apocalyptic habit that Keller is trying to break?

I wonder how completely we remain captives of an Augustinian vision of history when I read James Berger's study of how North American culture is framed by a struggle between competing utopian or dystopic imaginings of life after Apocalypse. Such a vision is apparent in Western governments celebrating the inevitable victory of capitalist democracy over communism. One can discern it again in the jingoist rhetoric of "the first war of the twenty-first century," against terrorism, or discover it in the dystopic anguish of apocalypse-inspired entertainment. Linda Hamilton, protagonist of *Terminator II: Judgment Day*, sees the future and pronounces: "You're dead, don't you understand that? You're already dead." For Berger, the Book of Revelation *is* a post-apocalyptic discourse: "A post-apocalyptic representation is a paradoxical, oxymoronic discourse that measures the incommensurable and speaks the unspeakable; a discourse that impossibly straddles the boundary between before and after some event that has obliterated what went before yet defines what will come after."[19] "In nearly every apocalyptic presentation," Berger writes earlier, "something remains *after the end*. In the New Testament Revelation, the new heaven and earth and New Jerusalem descend."[20]

Maybe a way of overcoming the apocalypse habit is to remember our love of getting mail. A careful exegesis notices that utopia and dystopia, imagined or realized, are not the Apocalypse's final word. The Book of Revelation stubbornly does *not* end in an imagined vision of heaven coming down to a new earth, but it happens in John's here and now, in a letter ending in the present. Whatever its cultural effects, the text itself resists any easy futurist or postfuturist appropriation.

Looking more closely at the verb tenses of the Apocalypse, one discovers a multivalent sense of time. John's opening verses describe what follows as a revelation of what "must soon take place" (1:1). But what he offers is a tensely narrated story (or better, series of stories). Reading the succeeding chapters, what strikes me are the delays and how relentlessly that promised "soon" is eroded in the story's telling. Is Revelation not a rather *long* telling of an ending? It takes up fully twenty-five pages of the Nestle-Aland's twenty-seventh edition of the Greek New Testament, and weighs in as the fourth-largest of its twenty-seven books. And for a text that is supposed to fall over itself to get to its ending, it takes an overly circuitous route, with its repetitious piles of sevens and confusing interludes, fast-frame forwards and retrospectives. Its cocktail mix of future, present, and past tenses leaves exegetes stumbling as they struggle to work out the timeline inscribed by John's narration.

The confusing mix of tenses brings time out of joint, intoxicating readers and listeners so that they no longer quite know where (or when!) they are, other than in the middle of things.[21] Narrated time continues and a remainder follows, giving the false impression of a linear story line. What in fact happens, though, is that John leads his audience in circles: "The parallelism of the three seven-fold visions has always attracted attention.... The arrangement of the actual apocalyptic section (Rev. 4:1 to 22:6) is ... governed by the fact that the same eschatological period is predicted three times" (i.e., on this reading, 6:1—8:1; 8:2-14:20; 15:1—22:5).[22]

Narrative time in the Apocalypse is vertiginous time: the deft master of achronicities makes one sick with envy for what one is not, and sick unto death for what one is. It is as though, tucked between the lines of the impatient call for the Lord to come soon, is the wry acknowledgment that the end will not in fact come too quickly; a "soon but not yet" eschatology. Could it be that the Apocalypse, like advertising with its urgent

appeal to buy "while quantities last," uses the threat of an imminent end
to break open an urgent reconfiguration of the present, that it creates a
sense of the present carved out of an imminence made more urgent
through delay? "'O sovereign Lord, holy and true, how long before thou
wilt judge and avenge our blood on those who dwell upon the earth?'
Then they were each given a white robe and told *to rest a little longer* . . . "
(Rev. 6:11). What if the letter, with its promised coming, is unremittingly
delayed in the mail? Is it possible to write a letter that defers its own
arrival? a letter that arrives by not arriving? It would not be the first time
a letter was delayed by the mail. Apocalypse postponed?[23] This "not yet"
opens up time in a way that Keller does not explore. It is a "not yet" unlike
Augustine's, which delays the coming of the Lord and the promises of
justice and equity so that one is left wondering, given the ambiguity of the
saeculum, whether it will ever come at all. Would it be better, given the
seemingly insuperable problems facing our planet, to give up on politics
and to tend one's own garden by working on the inner life?—recom-
mended in that secular version of Augustine's apocalyptic imagination,
known as the "self-help book."

Revelation is rather a "not yet" that insists on present action. Its *basso
continuo* is not "a rhythmic alteration," which effectively reduces John's
playfulness with narrated time to an aesthetic dimension that serves the
relentless move toward an ending. Its counterpoint is formed by the
repeated calls to repent, and by the recollection of that other apocalyptic
moment when the sun was darkened, the earth shook, and the dead rose
from their tombs, namely the crucifixion of Jesus of Nazareth (Matt.
27:45-53; cf. Mark 15:33-38; Luke 23:44-45). In Revelation, the historical
death of Jesus is theologically transposed with the metonym "the Lamb,"
even the "Lamb slain since the foundation of time," and linked with costly
testimony.[24] In tales of successful and failed repentance, as well as in the
witness of/to Jesus unto death, time finds its rhythm and unveiling. The
Apocalypse makes time for repentance and testimony. "What must soon
take place" is after all not only the end, it is also repentance, as five of the
seven letters to the seven churches indicate (2:5, 16, 21; 3:1, 19). What do
John's numerous recitations of heavenly hymns (4:8, 10-11; 5:9-14; 7:9-12;
11:15-18; 12:10-12; 15:3-4; 16:5-7; 19:1-4, 5, 6-8; cf. 14:3, 7; 22:3) provide if
not a kind of voice training for faithful witness?[25]

Could this not yet be a site for counterapocalypse? Perhaps. I return
to that possibility in my final chapter. For now it is enough to anticipate

some of the ironies inherent in a reading more faithful to the complexity of tenses in the Apocalypse by posing questions.

What if the Apocalypse were invoked against those who cite it reverently for its fatalistic timetables of the end, as a call to return to this-worldly time and the mess of politics? Could its urgent appeal to costly testimony in our first-world situation be a demand to stop waiting for the end, and instead to start living another ending to insatiable first-world desires for more material wealth? Could the alternative be found in justice-making, creation-loving, penitent, worshipful hopefulness? Can we imagine a time-sensitive reading of the Apocalypse that urges us to nurture allegiances among peoples and movements that protest greed, which makes the majority of created beings, humans and other forms of life, slaves to economic growth?

In what follows I want to return to the mailbox, to fetch the letter and read it again—this time not for what it portends, but for how it delays. In doing so I hope to open a space for being fully present in time, for living in the middle of things made possible by the *delayed* conclusion. The Apocalypse, after all, not only contains past and future tenses. It is full of present tenses as well. The Apocalypse's epistolary closing drives us back into the present. The happy ending of the Apocalypse, with its vision of the New Jerusalem and renewed creation, is only penultimate. At the end, it is what you are doing in the meantime that counts.

MAKING TIME

For such a timely text it is surprising that so little exegetical attention has been given to time in John's Apocalypse. That territory seems to have been relinquished to those inclined to read the Apocalypse as though it contained the headlines of tomorrow's news.[27] Perhaps as a corrective to that reading strategy, or maybe embarrassed by it, mainstream scholarly treatments of the Apocalypse of the past three decades have been more preoccupied with form and structure than time and narrative in the Apocalypse. The prophecy "that there should be time no longer" (Rev. 10:6—KJV) seems to have been fulfilled by more form-critical and structuralist readings of the Apocalypse. Time, where it is considered, has been assessed in terms of its function in mediating formal apocalyptic structures.

This is certainly the case in reigning scholarly morphologies that treat ancient apocalypses as sharing the characteristics of a common literary genre. J. J. Collins's now definitive outline of features shared by the apocalypse genre formulates differing categories to describe the overarching temporal purviews of ancient apocalypses (protology; history; eschatological crisis; etc.) and then assigns the dozen or so apocalypses loosely contemporary with Revelation accordingly. But applied to a text as temporally varied as Revelation, this effectively levels narrative diversity in favor of a formal coherence. Collins's morphology generalizes the complexly textured timescapes of the Apocalypse as instances of "cosmic and/or political eschatology," thereby passing over the complex narrative games with time that John's apocalyptic visions play.[28]

David Hellholm's return to Collins's typology aims at a more precise definition through a more systematic analysis of Revelation.[29] Initially the promise of systematic attention to such temporal connectors as adverbs promises an analysis of time more sophisticated than Collins's paradigmatic model. But once again formal features take over, evidenced in particular by Hellholm's near-mathematical breakdown of Revelation according to structural categories of communication, and his treatment of the text in terms of overarching events.[30]

In recent, more narrative-sensitive studies of the Apocalypse, Elisabeth Schüssler Fiorenza and Adela Yarbro Collins promise, at first glance, a more precise excavation of the Apocalypse's narrative timescapes, but end similarly in subordinating time to morphological considerations, this time considerations of structure. Concerning time and the Apocalypse, Schüssler Fiorenza observes:

> The author of Revelation is, indeed, aware of time, but he knows only a "short time" before the eschaton. The eschatology of Revelation is, therefore, not dependent on or legitimated by a certain course of historical events. Rather time and history have significance only insofar as they constitute the "little while" before the end.[31]

Penning those words in the mid-1980s, during the heyday of the Christian right's influence on American politics and its apocalyptic dispensationalist reading of secular history, Schüssler Fiorenza reveals her commitment to a biblical exegesis fully conscious of its political effects.

Still, this quotation is notable in the way it treats "time and history" synonymously. To say that, in the Apocalypse, time is short or that history only has a little while before the end ignores Revelation's varied temporalities and their rhetorical importance. Schüssler Fiorenza's interest is in a more structurally oriented reading of the Apocalypse. She focuses on its architectural composition, generalizing Revelation's individual characters into structuralist abstractions or spheres of action, to help identify the coded structural arrangements determining the Apocalypse's movement.

Her study indicates how strained linear notions of plot and narrative become when applied to the Apocalypse. Schüssler Fiorenza rightly insists that Revelation does not proceed linearly but in a concentric spiral, picking up elements represented in earlier portions of the text, rehearsing them, and then developing or slightly inflecting them. The Apocalypse does not hasten to an ending, but folds in on a middle (10:1—15:4), and the chapters around it radiate outward like so many circles from an epicenter. The epistolary ending (22:8-21) corresponds to its opening (1:1-8); the punishment and vindication of the saints of 19:11—22:7 rehearse the threats and promises of the seven letters of 1:9—3:22; the bowls of destruction poured out from the opened heaven of 15:1, 5—19:10 echo the cycles of destruction radiating from the heavenly throne room of 4:1—9:21; 11:15-19. Schüssler Fiorenza names these the "the architectonic designs controlling the arrangement of the materials and the organisation of the whole book."[32]

Adela Yarbro Collins also argues for a non-linear structuring of the Apocalypse—a recurring narrative pattern of increasing opposition, igniting in battle, and resolved in victory, adumbrated through repetition from chapters 4–11, fully unveiled at the text's center in chapter 12 (the dragon's persecution of the woman) and hastening in subsequent chapters to a final recapitulation and resolution of the primordial conflict of chapters 13–19.[33] These observations help her to explore the impact of such a recurring narrative structure on a listening audience, especially in generating and naming negative emotions toward Rome.[34] If there is attention to time in all these studies, it is to the ticking clock advancing the structures of the Apocalypse's spirals. Time exists to make structure possible.

Still, do not characters inhabit these morphologies of genre; do they not live amid the Apocalypse's architecture? And as soon as one speaks of character, must one not begin again to speak of time? John, after all, finds himself in the Spirit "on the Lord's day" (1:10), thus, at the Apocalypse's outset, insisting that one pay attention to time. There is not here the impasse of an either/or. The organizing principles of Revelation can continue to walk to their own beat, but on the level of the characters who live inside the text, time can seem quite different. In fact, Schüssler Fiorenza's sense of the architectonic and Yarbro Collins's tracing of a literary spiral are indispensable to a fuller appreciation of the fictive structure of time in the Apocalypse. Literature, unlike everyday language, is extraordinarily resourceful for the way it creates time by its wedding of narrative structure to temporal content. This is because the worlds that fictive texts generate are created by the interplay between their characters, who experience and express time in various ways, and the ways that the structural and temporal arrangements of a narrative modulate those expressions. Nevertheless, a fuller appreciation of the Apocalypse's temporal richness requires a certain resistance to "reducing," as Schüssler Fiorenza describes her structuralist project, "an infinite set of variables (the various personages and actions of the narrative) to a limited number of structural elements (actantial roles or spheres of action)."[35] Truth, the saying goes, lies in the details; and in the Apocalypse it is in the temporal details that literary metaphor finds its power to rule, both as it discloses and gives rise to a world in which to live.[36] It is the confluence of time *in* narrative and the structural arrangements of the time *of* narrative that *together* make the Apocalypse rich.

Schüssler Fiorenza's and Yarbro Collins's studies walk us to the doorstep of the classic literary distinction between narrated time (the time that fictive characters inhabit) and the time of narration (the time it takes to tell their stories). To cross the threshold into the fascinating world established by the combination of narrated time and the time of narration, it is necessary first to explore the world(s) of time that the Apocalypse's characters inhabit. The discussion will shift to an analysis of Revelation's variations in attention span as it narrates the life and times of its characters. I do not intend the following to be a complete description, which, were it possible, would require undertaking a full-scale study, but to explore by way of representative excavation the varied terrain of time and narrative in the Apocalypse.[37]

A Special Kind of Middle

Clov: *The ending is terrific.*
Hamm: *I prefer the middle.*

—Samuel Beckett, *Endgame*

"*Tick* is a humble genesis, *tock* is a feeble apocalypse; and *tick-tock* is in any case not much of a plot," comments Frank Kermode on the role of time in works of fiction. "We say they differ. What enables them to be different is a special kind of middle." This middle he calls *kairos*, the intervals fictions open between beginnings and endings and the times through which characters move. Fictions arrange time, moving their characters from *kairos* to *kairos*, or enveloping them in *kairoi* in the course of reading.[38] The Apocalypse, too, moves from *kairos* to *kairos*.

Not all its *kairoi*, however, are created equal. The *kairos* of the Laodiceans invited to repent and answer the door (3:20) differs from that of the Smyrnaeans, with enemies who are about to throw some of them into prison (2:10). The *kairos* of the praising hosts of heaven who punctuate the Apocalypse differs from the *kairos* of the lamenting merchants of Revelation 18. Nor are all *kairoi* of the same interval. Arguably, for example, the question of the subaltern saints of 6:10 ("O Sovereign Lord, holy and true, how long before thou wilt judge and avenge our blood on those who dwell upon the earth?"), a mere nineteen words in the Greek text, sets off an enduring moment of *kairos* "ticking" as long as the apocalyptic narrative unfolds, and thus exerts a kind of gravitational pull on the Apocalypse far in excess of its mass. It exerts a pull greater even than that of the weightier chapter 18, with its serial laments and dirges. It is possible to read the entire Apocalypse, including the letter ending, as a response to this age-old question. Admonishing, praising, lamenting, suffering, fleeing, hoping, and comforting: this list names only a few inflections of *kairos* in the Apocalypse and indicates how characters in the same Apocalypse inhabit differing frames of time. John constructs out of the "and" of "I am the Alpha and the Omega, the first and the last, the beginning and the end" (22:13) an astonishingly variegated kind of middle.

John's post-Apocalypse treats us to playful games with time.[39] John presents us with an Apocalypse that is a first-person retrospective telling of what is and will be. A. A. Mendilow, commenting on the use of first-person narration in novels, observes that, contrary to what one might expect, such narration does not create a sense of immediacy, but rather "tends to appear remote in time."

> The essence of such a novel is that it is retrospective, and that there is an avowed temporal distance between the fictional time—that of the events as they happened—and the narrator's actual time—his time of recording those events. There is a vital difference between writing a story forward from the past, as in the third-person novel, and writing one backward from the present, as in the first-person novel. Though both are equally written in the past, in the former the illusion is created that the action is taking place; in the latter, the action is felt as having taken place.[40]

This observation helps us recognize an important characteristic of the Apocalypse. Surprisingly, John's is a first-person narration that does *not* seem temporally remote. At first glance it fulfills Mendilow's prediction. First-person past-tense recitation marks distance: "I *was* in the Spirit on the Lord's Day. . . . I heard behind me a loud voice. . . . Then I turned to see the voice that was speaking to me . . ." (1:10, 12); "I John am he who *heard* and *saw* these things" (22:8). Yet events seem to unfold either in the present tense or communicate imminence. John may tell us where he *was* when he recorded what he saw, but he is commanded to write what he *sees* (*blepeis*—present indicative), suggesting contemporary duration (1:11).[41]

Indeed, were it not for the epistolary frame locating the visions as belonging to an apocalypse recalled, one might wonder with Käte Hamburger and Harald Weinrich whether, as in other fiction narrated in the past tense, the past tense in the Apocalypse had lost its ability to designate the past, and instead referred to a kind of zero degree, or canvas background, of narration in relation to which events revolve around central characters.[42] Yet as Gérard Genette observes, Hamburger's (and, by implication, Weinrich's) observations concerning the illusionary past of past-tense discourse is valid to the degree that stories are pure fictions. Since no narrative, however fanciful, can ever be *pure* fiction, the past of narrative retrospection makes its return in the act of mimesis, or imita-

tion of the world of lived time (the actions of characters, their motivations, their response to the succession of events, and so on).[43] Otherwise
we would have no way to gain entrance into the force field of fictional
time that stories erect around themselves. John's epistolary frame takes
the Apocalypse out of the realm of pure fiction and gives his fantastic stories a lever to affect the lived world of the audience. He offers a
mythopoeic conception of lived time into which he invites his audience
to make actors of themselves, or to discover what kind of roles they have
been performing.

The temporal modalities of a narrative present rendered past through
retrospection, and an active sense of the present through stenographic
"freeze-framing," create extraordinarily rich earth for John's tales. From
it he harvests a vivid sense of the imminent and nurses an ever ripening
immanence of the lived present, with its call to live decisively amid the
world's ambiguities and to make (or oppose—Rev. 3:16!) the gamble that
life is found in being cruciform. John, "the rounding wizard of times
gone by," does not seek to overcome the paradox Mendilow describes,
but to exploit it.[44] He can thus enjoy what August Wilhelm Schlegel
described as "the composed sobriety of the narrator" of epic story,
standing at some distance after the narrated events, interjecting editorial
commentary (14:12) or explanations (12:9; 13:18; 19:10), anticipating endings (9:12), assured of the story's outcome (3:12; chaps. 21–22), and
arranging events accordingly.[45] Or he can get caught up in the story,
obliterating narrative distance through direct quotation in the present
tense (e.g., chap. 18).[46] In various ways John both overcomes and insists
on the temporal gap between his actual time of recalled narration and the
fictional time of the events as they happened. In doing so he wrests from
what was (the heard and seen of 22:8) an abiding sense of imminence
("what must soon take place"—1:1), and even immanence ("what is"—
1:19). The traversal of this interval opens the present to new possibility.

How, then, does John overcome the space created by writing "backward from the present"? Chief among the strategies for transforming
Apocalypse recalled into an immanent account is John's use of editorial
interjection (e.g., Rev. 9:11, 12, 19; 11:4; 13:18; 14:4, 11, 12; 15:1; 16:14; 17:9-
11; 19:10d, 11; 20:5b-6) along with editorial comments embedded in his
descriptions of visions (e.g., 5:6; 8:2; 13:6; 19:8; 21:22). These allow him
to remind his audience that what he once saw and what they now hear is
about the present.

Further, John bridges the temporal distance by a narrative mixing of tenses. For example, the battle sequence of 19:11-21 (see table 1 below), introduced in the past tense (v. 11a), moves quickly into a present-tense description of the warrior on the white horse (vv. 11c-13, 15, 16), a description interrupted first by the past (v. 14) and then the future tense (v. 15b). The episode ends (vv. 17, 19, 20-21) in the past tense, but John fills the temporal space, again, by the present-tense quotation of a command (vv. 17c-18). Such remarkable temporal variations, repeated regularly throughout the Apocalypse, bring vividness and a sense of the audience's participation to what would otherwise be a more epic-style recitation in the past tense, tending toward inertia. The interjection of a command in the present tense ("Come, gather for the great supper of God, to eat the flesh of kings . . ."—v. 17) reinforces this lively sense. We quickly forget that this is to be a future event (v. 15b), and even when John rehearses the event in the past tense, as something that has already happened (v. 20, 21), the more vivid narration remains.

Quotation is perhaps John's favorite means of closing temporal distance. Again, chapter 18, with its sequence of quoted laments, makes us hear what John heard and so brings a recalled transcription of what will be into the present. We experience the loss of these characters in our present. These two examples could be multiplied many times over, but they will suffice to show how John overcomes past-tense inertia and propels his narratives back into the present.[47]

The past tense of recollection, then, is an obstacle John overcomes in order to close the gap separating the narrative time of his apocalyptic narratives from the time John shares with his audience. Traversing time in the ways just identified creates an abiding sense of the imminent—the "soon" of John's "soon but not yet" eschatology. John's apocalyptic stories do not, however, obliterate the "not yet"; they insist on it. The distance from the narrated events, created because the implied author is situated temporally after the cycle of visions, allows him to shift and arrange the details of the narratives, to reorder their sequence and thus to arrange powerful juxtapositions.

John stitches time in sometimes predictable and sometimes surprising patterns. Routinely, the Apocalypse offers *tick-tock* kinds of stories, or a predictable arrangement of narrative time. This we saw in chapter 3 above, for example, in which I traced the careers of enviable and detestable characters presented by John in partial fulfillment of the

Table 1. Revelation 19:11-21

Past*	Present	Future
[11]Then I saw heaven opened,		
	and behold, a white horse! The one sitting on it is called Faithful and True, and in righteousness he judges and makes war. [12]His eyes are like a flame of fire, and on his head are many diadems; and he has a name inscribed which no one knows but himself. [13]He is clad in a robe dipped in blood, and the name by which he is called is The Word of God.	
[14]And the armies of heaven, arrayed in fine linen, white and pure, followed him on white horses.		
	[15]From his mouth issues a sharp sword with which to smite the nations,	
		and he will rule them with a rod of iron;
	he treads the wine press of the fury of the wrath	

(continued on next page)

* For sake of economy, "past" here and in table 2 refers to varieties of the Greek past tense: aorist (a single event in the past whose duration and effect are past); perfect (a past event whose effects endure); and imperfect (an event continuing to unfold in the past).

	of God the Almighty. [16]On his robe and on his thigh he has a name inscribed, King of kings and Lord of lords.	
[17]Then I saw an angel standing in the sun, and with a loud voice he called to all the birds that fly in mid-heaven,		
	"Come,** gather for the great supper of God, [18]to eat the flesh of kings, the flesh of captains, the flesh of mighty men, the flesh of horses and their riders, and the flesh of all men, both free and slave, both small and great."	
[19]And I saw the beast and the kings of the earth with their armies gathered to make war against him		
	who sits upon the horse and against his army.	
[20]And the beast was captured, and with it the false prophet who in its presence worked the signs by which he deceived *(column continues on next page)*		

(continued on next page)

**A punctilinear aorist imperative denoting a command of limited duration.

those who had received the mark of the beast and those who worshiped its image. These two were thrown into the lake of fire		
	that burns with brimstone.	
[21]And the rest were slain by the sword issuing from his mouth. And all the birds were gorged with their flesh.		

promises and threats associated with the messages to the seven churches of 1:4—3:22. And we walk the same temporal path in the warning that those who add to or subtract from the Apocalypse can expect punishment (22:18-19), or in the appeal to Jesus to come quickly (22:20). Such statements make time in a way with which we are generally accustomed: threat giving way to punishment, promise to fulfillment.

But the narrative distance of Apocalypse recalled also creates room for the more playful possibility of *tock-tick*, or the rearrangement of narrative time in unexpected permutations. This makes time in quite another way. At chapter 18 we hear laments over fallen Babylon, and, in 19:1-11, celebration. This is already anticipated at 14:8-11 and 16:17-21 and, as others have observed, such a narrative achronicity is an instance of foreshadowing, or even the creation of suspense relieved by the later account.[48] Yet if we read these passages not for the expectations they raise to be fulfilled later, but for their own inscription of narrative time, we discover marked differences between them and observe them carrying out different functions in the overall apocalyptic narrative. The passages anticipate coming destruction, but they inhabit very different kinds of time.

One (16:1-21) is a story of the *tick-tock* variety: seven angels roughly repeat the plagues of Egypt of Exodus 7–14, the last of which, as in the Exodus account, the most decisive one, anticipates the destruction of Babylon. Placed here, 16:1-21 seems to function as a narrative transition to chapter 17 and to prepare the way for the full description of Babylon's destruction that will follow. Time flows from one episode into another. The other story (14:6-11), however, is jarringly *tock-tick;* the events do not follow such a tidy sequence. The visions of anticipated destruction (14:8, 9-11) are not the culmination of a cycle of seven, but are spliced halfway between the proclamation of a gospel of repentance to be proclaimed to the nations (14:6-7) and a call for endurance (v. 12). Here, time does not flow. It lurches. Through these verses it shifts abruptly from one temporality to another, and, in so doing, it allows John to inflect time dramatically and to make it serve a far more productive end than a simple foreshadowing of what will occur from 17:1—22:5.

John's playfulness with time in 14:1-13 (table 2 below) deserves closer analysis for, as we will see below, it reveals a theologically charged treatment of time arising out of the distance of the implied author from his narrative. *Tock-tick*, we may say, asks us to reappraise how we estimate *tick-tock*, even in its most routine forms. In what follows I look more closely at 14:1-13 and then present how its achronicities point to a more neglected feature of the Apocalypse's chronological orderings.

Revelation 14:1-13 comprises a tidy *inclusio* interjected between the account of the beast of the land (13:1-18) and a vision of "one like a son of man" with a sickle ready to bring judgment to the beast's followers (14:14-20; cf. 15:1-4). It begins with a narrative transition at 14:1 ("Then I looked, and lo, on Mount Zion stood the Lamb . . ."). Temporally what follows in 14:1-5 is a kind of still-life portrait of praise of the 144,000 who are described in the past tense as the redeemed of the world and undefiled, and in the present tense as chaste, obedient (vv. 4b, 5), and spotless (v. 5) followers of the Lamb. At 14:6 a second episode follows, with an introduction narrated in the past tense of an angelic vision, giving way (v. 7) to aorist imperatives to fear and worship God. Here the past tense communicates an imminent present: the aorist Greek imperatives denote commands of limited duration to alter behavior in advance of the judgment that is first announced (v. 7c) and that then arrives in verse 8.[49] The next episode ("Another angel, a second") depicts Babylon's fall, again first in the past tense (v. 8) and then in a third angel's quotation mixing present (vv. 9, 11) and future (v. 10) tenses. There follows (v. 12) an editorial admonition in the present tense. Finally, verse 13 returns us to the vision of the 144,000 in the form of quotation in the present tense, blessing those who die in the Lord. Now, however, the quotation offers a more dynamic orientation, by bringing the past of verses 4-5 and future into dramatic relationship: "Blessed are the dead who die in the Lord *henceforth*."

Table 2. Revelation 14:1-13

Past*	Present	Future
¹Then I looked, and lo, on Mount Zion stood the Lamb, and with him a 144,000 who had his name and his Father's name written on their foreheads. ²And I heard a voice from heaven like the sound of loud thunder; the voice I heard was like the sound of harpers playing on their harps		
	³and they sing a new song before the throne and before the four living creatures and before the elders.	
No one could learn that song except the 144,000 who had been redeemed from the earth. ⁴It is these who have not defiled themselves with women,		

(continued on next page)

* For various forms and meanings of the Greek past tense, see the note attached to table 1 above.

	for they are chaste; it is these who follow the Lamb wherever he goes;	
these have been redeemed from humankind as first fruits for God and the Lamb, ⁵and in their mouth no lie was found,		
	for they are spotless.	
⁶Then I saw another angel flying in mid-heaven, with an eternal gospel to proclaim to those who dwell on earth, to every nation and tribe and tongue and people; ⁷and he said with a loud voice,		
	"Fear** God and give him glory,	
for the hour of his judgment has come		
	and worship him	
who made heaven and earth, the sea and the fountains of water." ⁸Another angel, a second, followed, saying, "Fallen, fallen is Babylon the Great, she who made all nations drink the wine of her impure passion." ⁹And another angel, a third, followed, saying with a loud voice,		

(continued on next page)

**The imperative verbs in verses 7 and in 13b are in the aorist tense and denote a command of limited duration (hence, a punctiliar aorist). An appropriate English translation of verse 7 would be, "Fear God, right now and give him glory, right now . . . and worship him, right now. . . ."

(continued from previous page)

	"If anyone worships the beast and its image, and receives a mark on his forehead or on his hand,	
		¹⁰he also shall drink the wine of God's wrath, poured unmixed into the cup of his anger, and he shall be tormented with fire and brimstone, in the presence of the holy angels and in the presence of the Lamb.
	¹¹And the smoke of their torment goes up for ever and ever; and they have no rest, day or night, these worshipers of the beast and its image, and whoever receives the mark of its name." ¹²Here is a call for the endurance of the saints, those who keep the commandments of God and the faith of Jesus.	
¹³And I heard a voice from heaven saying,		
	"Write this: Blessed are the dead	
		who die in the Lord henceforth."
	"Blessed indeed," says the Spirit, "that they may rest from their labors, for their deeds follow them."	

In this example, the episodic juxtapositions and their respective temporalities do more than foreshadow. They open, even demand, a time for repentance, endurance, and costly testimony. Stasis contrasts with movement in the arrangement of these passages. The 144,000 are at a still point ("in their mouth no lie was found, for they are spotless"—v. 5) and so they spend their time learning (indicative present tense—designating continuous action) the song before the throne of the four living creatures and the elders. It is an enduring narrative moment, for we have learned earlier that this is a song the four living creatures sing day and night without ceasing (4:8-11).

By comparison, those "who dwell on earth, ... every nation, tribe and tongue and people" (v. 6) face the moment of decision and possible transformation from idolatry toward repentance (v. 7). A stasis is represented at verse 11 ("And the smoke of their torment goes up for ever and ever and they have no rest, day or night, these worshipers of the beast and its image"), but this is clearly a description of the future (v. 10), and so is in the service of a dynamic forward orientation. A future-oriented stasis appears again at verse 13, but now clearly in contrast to the stasis of verse 11. The interjection of verse 8 ("Fallen, fallen is Babylon the great. . . .) in the aorist form, thus expressing the city's fate as something past, sharply limits the length of time for repentance, already delimited by the use of the aorist in verse 7.

So imminent is the time for repentance that the punctiliar point shrinks. The possibility for such a temporal opening is indicated in fact by the shift from the first angel (v. 6) with its gospel to that of the second and third angels of verses 8 and 9, announcing punishment. Nevertheless, John inserts a temporal space, however limited, between verses 7 and 8 that has now become alive with possibilities, alternatives that verses 1-5 and 9-11 explore and contrast.

This example shows how productive John's distance from the events being recounted can be. He organizes past, present, and future to draw his audience into an abiding sense of the imminent—here a moment filled either with a call to repentance (v. 7) or to endurance (v. 12).

Additionally, Rev. 14:1-13 shows how John can exploit narrative distance by lingering closer or farther away from various characters and events. The characters of verses 6-7 and 12-13 are presumably equidistant from the events of verse 8; for both there is a marked sense of imminence. The punctiliar aorist imperative of verse 7 defines the endurance of verse 12; the latter will need to endure for as long as the angel's command can be obeyed. But John is closer to the characters of verse 12 than to the characters of verse 6 (hence, 1:9), and, of course, farthest away from the tormented of verses 10-11 (see 19:20-21).

Revelation 14:1-13 shows John nurturing an asymmetrical narrative distance from the protagonists and antagonists of his apocalyptic narrative, an asymmetry that functions rhetorically to convince his listeners to adopt his point of view. In this example, Apocalypse recalled makes time by combining achronicity with varied narrative distances. John thereby opens a "special kind of middle" and fills it with hopeful possibility—for repentance, endurance, and testimony.

PLACING TIME

Before returning to considerations of how John organizes his apocalyptic visions, I want to linger a little longer amid the achronicities of John's narratives. But now, instead of excavating one or two sites, I want to survey the lay of the apocalyptic narrative landscape and account for the various modes of time associated with Revelation's various topographics. Again, I am interested in the special kind of middle that John opens and the way retrospective Apocalypse makes that kind of middle possible. I have room here only for marking some of the boundaries. But once surveyed we will be ready to return to a consideration of how John tells time, that is, the time his Apocalypse takes to tell its revelation.

Like other contemporary apocalypses, the Book of Revelation entails a journey from the earthly to the heavenly domain. More atypically, the Apocalypse crosses the space between heaven and earth repeatedly. Such traversals result in highly charged narrative achronicities. Generally, the Apocalypse's narratives revolve around a consistent spatial opposition between heaven and earth and the characters who inhabit them. There are, first, to borrow a phrase from Thomas Mann's *Magic Mountain*, "the Flat Landers": the earthbound nations, or their pagan representatives, tangled up in idolatry and the forward thrust of visionary cycles. Contrasting these are John's heavenly or heaven-blessed characters, the worshipers of God, who break into and disrupt the narrative sequences with varying apocalyptic prospects, at once slowing earthbound clocks and making them beat ever faster.

This is most clear in chapters 12–14, the accounts of the casting out of the dragon from heaven, the two beasts, and the account of the praise of the 144,000. These chapters, significantly located at the center of the Apocalypse, have been repeatedly noted for the way they offer an interpretive key to the Book of Revelation as a whole. It is not surprising, then, that the spatial topography should here be most explicit—a kind of legend for John's apocalyptic map.

At 12:9, following a war in heaven, the dragon (later serpent, devil, Satan) is cast down to the earth. Heaven and its inhabitants now rejoice (v. 12), but the earth is warned: "Woe to you, O earth and sea, for the devil has come down to you in great wrath, because he knows that his time is short!" At verse 13 the dragon, now on earth, pursues the woman of verse 2 and pours "water like a river out of his mouth . . . to sweep her away with the flood" (v. 15). The dualism of heaven–earth/sea is disrupted slightly at verse 16, in which the earth comes to the help of the woman, but the association of the dragon with the earth and sea of verse 12 now continues in the narratives of the two beasts of the land and sea in 13:1-10 and 11-18, respectively, and with those who "dwell on the earth" (13:14; cf. v. 12) who worship or obey them. Here the Apocalypse defines what has been implicit, at least topographically, all along and what in the following chapters will become increasingly explicit. In chapter 13 the earth is named five times, and is implied in a sixth reference (v. 16): at verse 3, "the whole earth" follows the beast; it has authority "over every tribe and people and tongue and nation" (v. 7); those who "dwell on earth" worship it (v. 8; also vv. 12, 14). From chapter 6, John has consistently named the earth as the site of opposition to God and the place where God's punishment falls (6:10; 8:13; 11:10; cf. 1:5; 6:15). Following chapter 13 this continues, but now with increasing intensity until the final showdown at 19:17-21, where we see the beast and its followers destroyed.[50] Further, given the power of the dragon over the sea as well, it is no accident that the laments of chapter 18 over Babylon's fall include those of seafaring merchants (18:17).

John punctuates these earthly scenes with heavenly ones. Spatially, heaven is, of course, above the earth (4:1). From chapter 4 onward, John's protagonists either inhabit or are more or less directly associated with heaven and from thence punishments fall (chap. 6ff.). Some of the earth's inhabitants, however, have a more elevated status. Thus, in 14:1-5 we meet the Lamb and 144,000 "on Mount Zion." The latter are, significantly,

the "redeemed from the earth" (*apo tēs gēs*), and are possibly the same
as those named in 13:6 as "those who dwell in heaven." Their spatial
elevation already indicates their removal from the earth; their behavior
expresses it. They are chaste (i.e., not fornicators, the Apocalypse's
favored designation for the idolatrous—2:14, 20; 17:1, 2; 18:3; 19:2; 21:8;
22:15) and "follow the Lamb wherever he goes" (14:4). Further, they truly
worship God whose throne room, significantly, is in heaven (4:2-5)—in
contrast to those who worship the earth- and sea-dwelling beasts (13:4, 8,
12-14; 14:9; 16:2; 19:20; cf. 20:4; 21:8). Again, the two witnesses of 11:4-13,
upon their resurrection, are assumed into heaven (v. 12), from whence, if
we may assume they are Moses and Elijah, they originated (the former in
popular tradition did not die but was assumed into heaven [Jos. *Ant.*
4.326], as was Elijah [2 Kings 2:11]). Finally, John himself "in the Spirit on
the Lord's day" (1:10) anticipates his removal from the earth at 4:1, and the
address to "the angel" of each of the seven churches, together with references to their lampstands (2:1, 5, 8, 12, 18; 3:1, 7, 14; cf. 4:5), represents an
identity associated with heaven. But if these heroes and churches have
their heads in the clouds, their feet are nevertheless firmly planted on the
earth, and they must always be alerted to its gravitational pull. Hence the
warnings against idolatry in the seven messages (2:4, 14-16, 20-23; 3:2-3,
15-18). Even "spirited" John slips too easily into near-idolatry (19:10;
22:8-9) and reveals the origins of his species, however much it has evolved
toward a prophetic consciousness.

The middle region, named *mesouranema* ("midheaven"), forms a
kind of sacred "no-fly zone" that the beast nevertheless transgresses by
counterfeit performances of God (13:13), but over which God retains
control (8:13; 14:6; 19:17).

We thus have a consistent topographical contrast that John main-
tains until he envisions the creation of a new heaven and earth (21:1),
when Jerusalem comes "down out of heaven from God" (v. 2). Significantly, John, marking an end to the earlier conflict between heaven and
earth/sea, now comments: "and the first earth had passed away, and the
sea was no more" (21:1b-c). Furthermore, this new topography seems at
least in part to have ended the earlier enmity between the flat-landers
and heaven/mountain dwellers. Now we see the kings of the earth, who
had earlier been duped by the beast and the whore of Babylon, bearing
"their glory into it [Jerusalem]," whose gates remain forever open
(21:24-26; see, however, v. 27). In fact, the Apocalypse now states that

the New Jerusalem's tree of life possesses "leaves . . . for the healing of nations" (22:2).

John surprises us. Did we not just hear in 19:18-21 that the nations who conspired against God were slaughtered in their war with the mounted warrior and that their carcasses were fed to the birds? True, a "twist-ending" was already anticipated at 11:15, in which a heavenly voice proclaimed, "The kingdom of the world has become the kingdom of our Lord and of his Christ, and he shall reign for ever and ever." Still, in the vision of the descended heavenly Jerusalem, the careful topographical lines John has been drawing seem smudged. Indeed, verse 21:27 seems to presume the continued existence of "Flat Landers," and this is confirmed by 22:15. The apparent refusal of at least some to repent and their seemingly miraculous ability to avoid extermination has given rise to a lively exegetical debate over whether John envisions a universal salvation of the nations, or whether his soteriological scheme indicates a more sectarian interest.[51]

It is not my goal here to resolve the Apocalypse's conflicting soteriological hopes, but only to signal the ambiguity and how temporally productive the ambiguity becomes at Revelation's conclusion. We are led by John to expect a final resolution with the epistolary closing, a return from narration of what will be to John's present. At first this expectation is satisfied in the transitional 22:8 ("I John am he who heard and saw these things . . ."). That verse returns us to the time of 1:9, and to the firm ground of Patmos. But John lurches us back into the vision of the heavenly Jerusalem at 22:14-15, where we learn that the idolaters of the preceding visions remain outside its open gates. Narrative present and future thus collide; the former envelops the latter. John is no longer speaking of what will be. In a way the narrative does not resolve, he now tells us that he has been writing about "what is" (1:19).

This is startling. "Dogs, and sorcerers and fornicators and murderers and idolaters, and everyone who loves and practices falsehood," are outside the gates of the heavenly Jerusalem, a territory that is supposed to have been cleansed of their presence at 20:15. John's post refuses to deliver an ending. It erases it and instead insists that its listeners make a choice. Will one enter Jerusalem's gates along with the repentant nations or stay outside the gates? As for the gates, they will not close. Only the members of the Apocalypse's audience can bring the story to a conclusion, a conclusion brought not by a kind of *deus ex machina* or fanciful escape into a beatific future, but by the decision either to choose a life of costly testimony or to refuse it. In the Apocalypse the present moment is made heavy with the weight of decision.

Of course, John believes there is only one choice, and to make it as easy as possible he sketches the Apocalypse's actors with dramatic poses in their respective topographies and moving in characteristic ways through time. The temporality of the inhabitants of the earth is, to borrow a phrase that seems particularly apt, that of "one damn thing after another."[52] These characters are swept away by time. They occupy sequences, most usually of sevens, and thus find themselves assigned to a temporality whose conclusion is divinely worked out from the start. They are there at the conclusion of the sixth seal (6:12-17), at the climax of a series of disasters, hiding in fear from the wrath of the Lamb and shaken by the cycle of preceding calamities (6:1-7). In the seventh seal (8:1) they find themselves again, this time in the midst of the fifth and then the sixth trumpets, first tortured by locusts (9:1-6), then killed by the cavalry of the four angels of the Euphrates River (9:13-15).

The survivors of this sequence (9:20-21) live on to succumb to further series of woes from chapter 16 onward. At 16:1-21, a series of calamities reminiscent of the plagues of Egypt befalls them as seven angels pour out "the seven bowls of the wrath of God" (16:1). The invocation of the legendary Egyptian plagues, together with sharp staccato performances of each of seven bowls, makes the Apocalypse rush feverishly forward toward a foregone conclusion. It even stumbles ahead of itself when, at verse 16, with the reference to the gathering of the final battle of Armageddon, John anticipates the final showdown of the last battle of 19:17-21. By this point, these characters are little more than caricatures of obdurate wickedness—cartoonlike victims of heavenly assaults. John furnishes the idolatrous earth dwellers with a form of serialized narrative time broken by brief staccato performances of resistance to God and resulting punishment. Fragmenting time in such narrative sequences persuasively enacts the promise to the dragon/devil/Satan, cast out from heaven to the earth, "that his time is short" (12:12). Brief self-enclosed episodes help us to experience time as though it were short of breath and to catch us up in its urgency.

If time rushes ahead of itself in the earthly domain, in the heavenly domain, it slows down, even stops. When we learn, for example, of the four living creatures of 4:8 that "day and night they never cease to sing, 'Holy, holy, holy, is the Lord God Almighty, who was and is and is to come,'" and that "whenever the living creatures give glory" the twenty-four elders similarly hymn their praise (vv. 9-11), the narrative clock has given up time. This is not a staccato moment never to be repeated, but a time without end, a *ritardando* that makes time linger. Here, somewhat unnecessarily, John directly names the unending interval, already implied by the use of the present tense. Later, John hears more music (5:9-10, 12, 13), and once again the present tense slows narrative time and successfully draws it out so that its echo can be heard reverberating through the labyrinthine passages that follow. It is therefore all the more notable when John interrupts the mad rush to an ever more violent ending with heavenly scenes. Strictly speaking, of course, these too belong to the unfolding of an apocalyptic sequence.

Others have commented on these hymns as the means by which John offers a narrative commentary on the events "down below," keeping track of what has been happening and what is yet to occur, or that they serve a narrative function in creating suspenseful anticipation, later relieved in fulfillment.[53] Such interpretations, however, seem too linear. True, when we hear at the conclusion of 11:1-13 (the two-witnesses episode) a hymn of praise by our twenty-four elders that "the kingdom of the world has become the kingdom of our Lord and of his Christ, and he shall reign for ever and ever" (v. 15), and their subsequent celebration of the victory of God (vv. 17-18), there is both commentary and foreshadowing. But more importantly there is a temporal apposition between the tightly scripted narrative sequence of "one thing after another" of verses 4-13 and 19 and the description of praise—a lengthening of storied time. The apposition is itself productive of meaning. Such an achronicity produces an eddy of narrative time as a more routine recitation of events is disrupted, gathered, and made to whirl around its temporal obstructions: alternative moments of *kairos* appear face to face, the one staring the other down. Mimetically this enacts the text's claim that if the text is a linear recitation of things to come, it is also a revelation of *what is* (1:19).

The interjection of hymns now celebrating what is going to come later opens the present moment in a startlingly fresh way. They help give sense to the wager that hangs over the Apocalypse as a whole, that Revelation is an unveiling not only of one who is going to come, but who is, in fact, in the very present moment of Revelation's reception and recitation, *coming* (1:4, "Grace and peace from him who was, who is and who is coming [*ho erchomenos*, a present participle]).

Revelation 11:15 is a shorter example of narrative apposition.[54] At chapter 7 we find a much longer one. Again, John splices a rapid-fire recitation of the seals with a vision that slows narrative time to a crawl. The vision of the 144,000 is a "back to the future" story that catapults the listening audience ahead of the cycles of destruction unfolded in its neighboring chapters. When John asks who the white-robed characters are, he learns, in jarring achronicity, "These are they who have come out of the great tribulation; they have washed their robes and made them white in the blood of the Lamb" (7:14). The great tribulation is of course what we have been hearing about through chapter 6 and to which we will return in chapter 8. Further, the martyrs' hymn at verse 10 as well as the responses of the elders and four living creatures at verse 12, with the paean to the Lamb as Savior (*sōtēria*), implies events already completed, namely the destruction of Babylon (19:1-10). If the title of Savior is intended in its military sense, it further implies the victory of the white rider in the battle of 19:11-21. And armies' description that they are before God's throne, bear God's seal on their foreheads, no longer hunger and thirst, and that the Lamb guides them to living water (7:4, 15-17) expresses the ending of 21:4 and 22:1-5. Narrative time leapfrogs.

In verses 4-8 time is given up altogether. The listing of the twelve tribes offers a narrative *sostenuto*. John puts a spell on and halts story time through an incantation-like naming and identical numbering of each tribe. Twelve times we hear *ek phylēs . . . dōdeka chiliades esphragismenoi* ("from the tribe of . . . twelve thousand"). Coming as it does at the center of the narrative description of these members (vv. 1-4, 13-17), and including (with vv. 9-11) roughly the same number of words as either wing of commentary, the episode thus tends to fold in upon itself. John enchants narrative time with heavenly arithmetic drawn from Hebrew Bible legend of the twelve tribes of Israel and so makes time give up its count.

In this episode, achronicity combined with the heaviness of repetition makes time, if it moves at all, lumber—in marked contrast to the charge of calamities that sprint in the episodes of seals and trumpets that race around it. There is perhaps no more startling a contrast of narrative time in the Newer Testament.

Finally, there is the lengthening of narrative time in contrasting laments and dirges of the kings, merchants, and seafarers of chapter 18 and the victory songs of chapter 19. If, until now, earthly time has been speeding along through its route of seals, trumpets, and bowls, now, coming to its end, it slows down and invites listeners/readers to enter into the disappointment of Babylon's judgment and collapse. John lingers in its details. The listing of the luxury goods the merchants can no longer trade (18:11-13) occupies more than sixty-five words of the Greek text. The length of its recitation is only increased by the application of the repetitive "and" as well as the sustained use of homoioteleuton (identical endings of words). The threefold onomatopoeic lament *ouai, ouai* at verses 10, 16, and 19 also lengthens the section. Similarly, the heading of each series of lament with reference to "the great city" (*hē polis hē megalē*), or, in verse 10, the longer *hē polis hē megalē, Babylōn hē polis hē ischyra*, with their assonances, and the formulaic conclusions of each lament ("In one hour has thy judgement come / all this wealth has been laid waste / she has been laid waste"—vv. 10, 17, 19), thickens what has been until now a more recitative unfolding of disasters on the earthly stage into aria-like performances of grief. Throughout this sequence, repetition of words and phrases, grammatical structures, sustained use of parallelism, and formulaic expression serve to gather and slow narrative time, even to monumentalize it. Direct quotation together with these grammatical elements draws us into and makes us experience firsthand the disappointment of those who have learned too late that their lives are a shipwreck of misbegotten fortune.[55]

The shift in tone at 19:1 ("Hallelujah! Salvation and glory and power belong to our God") could not be more dramatic. From the extreme low of earthly tragedy to the extreme high of heavenly joy, the Apocalypse dipsy-doodles along a roller-coaster course of emotion. Again, John deploys all the elements deployed in chapter 18 to make the emotions as vivid as possible and to retard narrative time: repetition, repetitive use of "and," and words with identical endings (vv. 1, 3, 4, 6); concordances of grammatical structure (vv. 2, 6, 7) and formulaic language (vv. 4, 5, 8) drawn from tradition. Nor is it an accident that the threefold *allēlouia* of verses 1, 3, and 6 mimes, if not mocks, the refrain of *ouai* of 18:10, 15, and 19, in a brilliant deployment of assonance designed to bring opposing "still-lives" of despair and of joy into sharpest relief.

Placed side by side as they are, two monumental moments of *kairos* unfold before and face their audience and ask it which life it will live, and to whose sounds of testimony John's listeners will join their voices in chorus. The contrast between temporalities could not be more dramatic or sharp. Flat-landers and heaven dwellers face off in these chapters, each inhabiting their respective time. In one place we hear wedding music (19:7, 9); in the other that of a funeral—two senses of an ending. For as long as the moment lasts, John awaits a decision.

TAKING TIME

We are now ready to face the "rhythmic alternation," to borrow an apt phrase from Catherine Keller, of the Apocalypse's structural organization. My intent is not to outline yet another structure of the Apocalypse (there are as many of those as there are readers of Revelation), but to remark on what the majority of reconstructions in one way or another observe, namely, the way the Apocalypse moves along in blocks. And, more important, I intend to register how Revelation's narrative movements beguile time by stealing it away through omission or increasing it through detailed attention. Whether those movements form a spiral, as I myself think, following Schüssler Fiorenza, or a more linear plot of suspenseful foreshadowing and relaxation in fulfillment of expectation, will not, I think, affect the following discussion. The point is rather to indicate how the time of narrative, or of telling, joins with the narrative time that characters inhabit, to observe that confluence of times, and to remark upon the world that arises before the text as its result.

We owe a tremendous debt to the patient attention of Günther Müller and Eberhard Lämmert and their remarks concerning the way fictions organize time and make or lose time in their telling, and to Erich Auerbach, whose work, if preceding the later more scientific approaches, anticipates their insights.[56] These studies ask us to pay careful attention to the time within narrative (what happens when), as well as how long it takes to tell the episodes that make up fictional texts. For these writers what is at stake is no less than an awareness of how the consciousness of time makes possible a particularly human appropriation of the world. For, if other natural phenomena unfold according to a predetermined blueprint more or less unconscious to itself, humankind distinguishes itself by its awareness of this unfolding. Authors of fiction celebrate this consciousness in their ordering of the events and actions of their characters and their furnishing of events with an infinite array of temporalities. In fiction, time moves backward and forward, now hastening ahead of itself, now returning to a point before itself, now stopping altogether at any moment of past, present, or future.

In reading, however, the clock, like life, beats unrelentingly forward in step with the heavens and their time-marking revolutions. But when narrative time and the time of narration meet, the one transforms the other and so gives rise to creative human responses to "natural time," which is not pure fantasy, still less the stark empirical realism of the biological clock, but an enriching of time set in motion by their mutual acquaintance. The confluence of story and storied time signifies an important means by which we fashion ourselves into thoughtful human beings.

It is now time to apply these insights to the experience of reading the Apocalypse. Thus far we have been treating John's expressions of narrative time—the ways he accelerates or slows down, jumps forward or backward, or freezes storied time in the telling of his visions. Along the way we have stopped to notice the time of John's narration—the time it takes him to tell his Apocalypse. He lavishes time on hymns of praise and the lives of their performers; he speeds through the succinct moments of disaster unfolding in serialized time. He makes story time thicken through repetition.

How much time does John take to tell the Apocalypse? One requires roughly a half-hour to read the Apocalypse silently to oneself, one and a half hours if read aloud. In this half-hour to ninety minutes, however, one leaps across weeks, months, years, even millennia and arrives at the end to a time which, in the absence of nighttime (22:5), can no longer sustain any resemblance to natural time. Heavenly bodies may mark the 1,260 days of Rev. 11:3 and 12:6, or the forty-two months of 11:2, and the thousand years of 20:2, 7, but these numbers do not measure solar/lunar time. They mark theological time, as the halved seven (three and a half years) these numbers represent indicates.

The Apocalypse suspends the time that readers and listeners inhabit. But such suspension paradoxically depends on the unremarkable beating of the everyday clock in order to attain this end. Quotidian time conspires with the words, phrases, and sentences of the Apocalypse to make up the episodes that in turn restitch time into a theologically charged pattern. As one may expect, the author gives over more time to telling what is most remarkable: the throne-room vision (chaps. 4–5); the account of the 144,000 (chap. 7); the judgment of "the great harlot" of Babylon (chap. 17) and the subsequent laments of chapter 18; the creation of a new heaven and earth and the descent of the heavenly Jerusalem (21:1—22:5), to name only a few instances. John gives these narrative sections the most careful detail, suffusing them with symbolism that gives them a weightiness consistent with their mass. Or he repeats a narrative sequence with different words, adding new details in each repetition (12:1-6, 7-12, 13-17; 13:1-10, 11-18) and so lengthens the time of reading/listening. Or, again, in the contents of the "little scroll," he inserts a large narrative block into an unfolding sequence (10:1—14:20). Lengthening the time of narration in this way disrupts the progression of narrative time by delaying the sequence of events that would otherwise hasten to their conclusion.

More detailed descriptions, then, are one way the Apocalypse inscribes a sense of "a little longer" duration before "what must soon take place" arrives (1:1; 6:11). Further, John lengthens the Apocalypse by compounding time—namely, adding unanticipated episodes where we would otherwise expect a conclusion.[57] We are prepared for a swift conclusion to the Apocalypse by chapters 6–8. Here in quick succession John treats us to the breaking of six of the seven seals introduced in 5:1. The time of narration is lengthened at chapter 7, between the sixth and seventh seal, giving a heightened sense of drama to the opening of the seventh seal at 8:1. However, even as the seventh seal gives way to some fourteen more chapters of apocalyptic visions, it is not clear where or even whether the contents of the seventh seal end. Indeed, the introduction of yet another scroll at 10:1-11, together with a return to heaven (10:1; 11:1, 19), seems to rewind the narrative clock and to mark the beginning of still more Apocalypse. By the third time we return to open heaven at 15:5, we have learned to suspect the promise that the seven angels with the seven plagues John sees "are the last, for with them the wrath of God is ended."

The suspicion is not unwarranted. For although the plagues unfold rapidly and we are even told climactically that, with the seventh and final plague, "It is done!" (16:17), the narrative clock keeps stubbornly ticking. John draws Babylon's ending out with a lengthy description of the whore's transgressions and coming fate (chap. 17), the rehearsal of laments (chap. 18), and then the threefold shout of victory (19:1-8). Yet not even this will bring the Apocalypse to a close. And John now gives up counting his angels (for perhaps by this time even he has lost track of them) as his heavenly characters mark dramatic transitions (19:9, 17;

20:1; 21:9). There follows yet another "war to end all wars" (19:11-21), and then another (20:7-15). Finally, we meet this sense of a delayed ending in the epistolary closing and its exhortations to the evildoer and righteous alike to continue their behaviors (22:11). In fact, the letters, conclusion brings us back to the beginning of the Apocalypse, where the time of narrative began, and thus returns us by post to the present.

This is the fictional present inscribed by the author's description of himself on Patmos (22:8; 1:9). It is the present his work has been anticipating all along—the yawning present of a world his work has opened before itself and into which his audience has stepped in their listening to his visions and exhortations. It is a present that no longer remains what it was. Narrative time and the time of narration have conspired to invest the world of his listeners and readers with an urgent demand. John returns his audience, not to where it was before it began its apocalyptic journey, but to the present moment of the seven letters, which places before them the decisions it must make (1:4-5; 22:21). It is a time soon but not yet. John borrows from the time marked by the rising and the setting of the sun to conjure "eternity in an hour."[58] It is a moment rich with possibility: John requests the favor of a reply to his call to costly testimony to the crucified Jesus Christ.

Remembering Apocalypse

There are moments that hang over a life, that give it form and substance, to which one returns again and again to make sense of things—moments that for decades radiate out from themselves, shape the present, and sketch the future's horizon. Perhaps the moment is an unrequited love, a courageous decision, or an instant when all was lost or found. Upon their passing, seasons no longer turn as they once did; the sun loses its capacity to measure time; they make time gain weight and draw the routine passing of hours, days, weeks, and years into their orbit. We humans—are we not whirling eddies of time?

On Sundays my father made time for me by recalling such a moment. He liked especially to take time to describe his father. In spring 1944 a German military courier delivered by hand the news that my grandfather, Emil Maier, had been reported missing in action on the eastern front during the siege of Ternopol in present-day Ukraine. Few exact details were known, only that he had disappeared sometime after the beginning of the spring Soviet offensive against the southern flank of the German army on March 4, 1944. Vigorous attempts to break out the army encircled near Ternopol had succeeded, but only at an incalculable cost in human life. Soldiers literally starving and freezing to death fought for their lives to retreat toward the northwest to join the main army.[59]

My grandfather's body was never recovered, leaving open the possibility for decades to come that perhaps he had been deported to a Soviet labor camp and was still alive. I now look for his face in pictures of German soldiers marched through the streets of Moscow a month later, or in photos of prisoners of war in gulags. Perhaps one of those nameless ones was my grandfather's friend? Maybe, when I look closely into the eyes of those who line the photos, those thousands of anonymous eyes, I am, without knowing it, looking into the eyes of one who witnessed the panic and fury of that spring.[60] Here is the living trace of Apocalypse. My father was fifteen years old. He remembers the weather that day, the slow approach of the courier to his farm, the chores that were interrupted by the news. As a child I fantasized what it would be like if my grandfather suddenly returned; I imagined my father's joy at seeing him again, the tears that would be shed, the stories told. I dreamed of the questions that I would ask him. The passing of time and the tragedy of his disappearance had made him larger than life, and telling had smoothed the more troublesome edges away. Through my father's testimony he became the idealized grandfather of a young boy's imagination: kind, gentle, good-humored, playful, generous, wise.

Or, in any case, the yawning gap of his absence in my own father's life had transformed him into the ideal father he never had. Even his death was a heroic ideal. *Das Heldenlied von Tarnopol* [The Hero's Song of Ternopol] was how my father heard the siege described in which he died, a phrase coined by the divisions that broke free and survived. *Heldenlieder* belong to the epic recitation of the German legendary past—to the stories of Sigfried, Tristan, and Parzival. *Heldenlieder* are what medieval poets gathered to perform in the court of that icon of German national identity—the Wartburg Castle—the nineteenth-century representations of which decorate its walls to express a burgeoning imperial identity, immortalized by no less a "court musician" than Richard Wagner. *Das Heldenlied von Tarnopol* represents the Nazi propaganda of the era—the attempt to redeem through legend the senseless slaughter of people, the result of egomaniacal decision making. The "heroes" of Ternopol were in fact ciphers in one of the greatest military reversals of recorded history, as Soviet forces drove back a German army that only three years before, on a front that stretched from the Black Sea to the Baltic, had advanced forward to the very gates of Moscow, only to be stopped in its tracks by the worst winter in a generation. *Das Helden-lied von Tarnopol* mystifies the tragic reality of terrified men fighting to save their skins. It is an unlikely term to describe the wagers of modern war. My grandfather the epic courtly hero? Was he not in fact a farmer scratching out a relatively poor existence and drafted into an impossible war that brought his life to an untimely end?

These two senses of an ending were furnished years later by competing versions of apocalyptic history; now the beginning outline of a renewed present offering a choice.

For most of my life all we had were the stories. Pictures, family mementos, all other means of recollection were swept away in the chaos of the "ethnic cleansing" of Germans from Eastern Europe, begun in the winter of 1945. Then, suddenly, there was a letter with a picture saved by a relative. In fact, it was the last picture taken of the family before they were separated by war. At last there was a face, a body, and the image of a person on which to pin the loving testimony—an instant of light captured in the camera's container and inscribed on paper; a freeze-framed split-second, forever rescued from the scrambled time of Apocalypse recalled. So it is that a moment past can throw open the future, and swell the present.

It is a remarkable picture. Not only is my grandfather in it, but the whole family—my grandmother, father, aunt and uncle, and great-grandmother—appears in front of the house in which they lived shortly after being resettled from eastern to western Poland. They had ended up there as a result of the German-Russian Ribbentrop-Molotov nonaggression pact of 1939, in which Poland was divided between the two powers, Slavic peoples were repatriated east to the Russian occupation zone, and ethnic Germans (*Volksdeutsche*) were resettled west. In the picture my grandfather and grandmother sit beside each other in the foreground; behind them are the three children with their grandmother. A closer look shows more: my grandmother visibly pregnant with my youngest uncle conceived just before my grandfather left for war, her arms crossed as though in benediction over her lap. My grandfather and my uncle are in suit jackets hastily donned for the photographic occasion. Clearly, both have just been at work on the farm—my grandfather is not wearing a shirt under his Sunday jacket and vest. My grandfather's hands are dirty from the day's work. The jackets fit clumsily, not tailored for the brawny physique of these farmers.[61] My great-grandmother stands behind her son with her hand on his shoulder; behind him, moving left, is my uncle, himself about to be drafted into the army. Next stands my aunt, behind her mother, and finally at the left end, again behind his mother, my father, age ten—the only surviving picture of him from Europe. The midday sun casts shadows on their faces.

There is more. My father—the ten-year-old—is dressed in a Hitler Youth uniform. The camera now refocuses, and captured light opens into story. The pregnant mother, the land-tilling father with his devoted mother behind him, the eldest son behind his father, the daughter and younger son behind their mother, the picture outside the family home on the farm—the picture tells a disturbing story etched out of an instant of captured sunlight, and opens a distressing invitation. No, we are not in the realm of the *Heldenlied*. Still, the photo makes from an innocent captured second of sunlight a monument of time.

Without much exaggeration, one could say that a more ideal German family photo could not have been taken in the spring of 1940. For it was a goal of the Nazi state to reverse the urbanizing trends of the Industrial Revolution and their attending social problems by returning Germans to the land, the mythic symbol of national identity. There hearty, decent, clean-living agriculturists were to grow their own food, to flourish in tight family units and, of course, to produce children for glorious military campaigns and the spreading of German culture. This picture contains all these elements. It portrays the farmers who were, in the National Socialist imagination, the outposts of the realized millennium of Rev. 20:2, the Thousand-Year Reich cultivated from land sown with German blood.[62] The photograph gathers apocalypse, freezes it, and invites its viewer into a world shaped if not assaulted by the reigning ideology of its day.

When my father told the story of his father's sudden death it was as if two times opened before us—one symbolized in the abundance of the Sunday breakfast feast, the other carved in ruin and loss and the betrayal of a generation. The times were double-sided. There arose in the same telling gratitude for the present and the hopes that sprang to life before it, and the heaviness of loss. There was praise and lament: two times no longer marked by the course of the sun and the moon, but brought to life by the time and place of storytelling. From the apposition of these times, questions began to address me as an inheritor of Apocalypse. What form will a life take in response to such a history? What demand does the luxury of recalling Apocalypse make? The very notion of Apocalypse recalled expresses first-world privilege. Much of the two-thirds world is so busy *living* Apocalypse, it has no time to remember it.

The questions shape the present. If the Apocalypse calls for costly testimony, is this the kind it demands—obedience to power and its ideologies, and the fashioning of oneself into the epic hero or heroine? Do we dare to return to the Apocalypse to find voices to respond to these questions when, so often in Western history, the Book of Revelation has produced testimonies that have ended in bloodied lament over the disappointment of utopian dreams? Can we accept their invitation? We have been speaking of "costly testimony," and it is now time to calculate its expense and to ask ourselves if we can afford it.

Let us begin by seeking an alternative legend to make sense of our brief span of months and years. No longer will Apocalypse recalled guide our way. Now we come face to face with its wager and the gamble that can cost a life.

6

The Praise of Folly

*Come, now that I have "put on the lion's skin," I shall show this
also, that the happiness of Christians, which they pursue with so
much travail, is nothing else but a kind of madness and folly.*

—Erasmus, *The Praise of Folly*

Making Fun

Can it be that biblical scholars have taken all the fun out of the
Book of Revelation? To stroll once again through my opening
chapter's gallery of conflicting judgments concerning the Apocalypse is to be met with seriousness at every turn. What person, having
come face to face with the Apocalypse in all its goriness, does not want to
edit Revelation's visions? John of Patmos, remarked Elizabeth Cady
Stanton more than a century ago, was "evidently the victim of a terrible
and extravagant imagination and of visions which make the blood cur-
dle."[1] Because of its misogyny and violence, she later remarked, taking
her chances with John's parting warning (22:18-19), that Revelation
numbers among those biblical texts "that should no longer be read in
our churches."[2]

Who, indeed, does not pale at Revelation's two-hundred-mile-long
river of human blood, as high as a horse's bridle, pouring out from the
winepress of God's wrath (Rev. 14:20)? Whose stomach does not turn at

that vision of birds gorged on the flesh of the dead (19:17-18)? Who can warm to the damned thrown into lakes of burning fire (19:20; 20:14-15)? Who can idly stand by while the whore of Babylon is first raped and then cannibalized by erstwhile paramours (17:16)? What ecologically responsible person does not feel uneasy about the Apocalypse's easy disposal of thirds of land, sea, and sky creatures (8:7-12) as its visions rush toward a new heaven and earth (21:1)?

If Revelation's contents are not enough to make one sympathetic to the censorship of an Elizabeth Cady Stanton, surely its results are. Who does not cover their eyes in horror upon witnessing this text's history in culture? To convert the Apocalypse's violent imagery, through the application of utopian constants, into social equations is to shudder at the resulting violence. Who can estimate the apocalyptic sum of all those gulags and concentration camps designed to usher in a Revelation-inspired millennium? What scale can weigh the mass of human suffering brought about by competing religious and secular incarnations of Apocalypse? Who, having faced squarely the dangers of simplistic dualisms, does not swallow hard when confronted by the Apocalypse's stereotypical oppositions of gender, of whores and brides, fornicators and virgins, beasts and angels, victors and vanquished? Which person who hopes for a humane and tolerant social pluralism does not bristle at the Apocalypse's uncompromising versions of salvation and eternal damnation, of insiders and outsiders, purity and corruption?

Surely it is a matter of ethical responsibility that those who try to understand the Book of Revelation bring with them a profound earnestness in their exegesis and interpretation. There is little room for kidding around when so many unhappy things happen on the way to the Apocalypse's happy ending. "Its existence and its place in the canon," remarks Jack T. Sanders, "are, in the fullest sense of the word, evil."[3] No wonder biblical exegetes are so somber around the Book of Revelation.

To be earnest, however, some have detected in Revelation a play of mistaken identity. And a few have even had a hard time stifling a smile amid all the carnage. To be sure, the Apocalypse serves up some of the bloodiest violence in the Bible. But it garnishes it here and there with a sprinkling of fun. *Parody* is the term exegetes have fastened upon to describe the Apocalypse's more ironic moments. In a definitive study, David Aune traces the influence of Roman imperial-court ceremonial on John's visions of God's throne room (Revelation 4–5). He concludes that our seer's vision of heavenly liturgies "bears such a striking resemblance to the ceremonial of the imperial court and cult that the latter [imperial liturgy] can only be a parody of the former [right Christian worship]."[4] Elsewhere Aune argues that the seven messages to the seven churches imitate the structure of imperial decrees, in which case the imperial publishing of edicts might also be interpreted as a parodic arrogation of divine authority.[5]

Sophie Laws extends Aune's discovery of parody in Revelation's throne room to include John's representations of the beasts of Revelation 13 and their claims. She argues that the vision of the beast which "seemed to have a mortal wound, but its mortal wound was healed" (13:3) parodies that of the Lamb, which stood "as though it had been slain" (e.g., 5:6). The return of the eighth king, once fallen and returned now as beast (17:9-11), parodies the return of the crucified Jesus (1:7), "the living one" who "died and behold I am alive for evermore" (1:18). Other examples she cites include: God "is . . . and was and . . . is coming" (1:8), the beast "was and is not . . . and it goes to perdition" (17:8, 11); God's servants are sealed on their foreheads with the name of the Lamb and his Father (14:1), the beast's allies bear his mark (13:16); throughout the Apocalypse protagonists worship the Lamb with God, the beast with the dragon demands worship (13:4). From such contrasts Laws concludes that the Apocalypse's antagonists represent "a parody theme" with "variations" of Revelation's leading character, the slain Lamb.[6] M. Eugene Boring, in a more recent commentary, follows Laws's lead, arguing that John intended the dragon, the beast, and the false prophet (named together at 16:13) as an "evil trinity" which parodies God, the creator; Christ/the Lamb; and the Spirit—the source of true prophecy.[7]

The term *parody* in these studies describes the masquerade of an emperor and his minions wanting to play God. The Apocalypse's parody capitalizes on mistaken identities. For John, power and might do not belong to the Roman Empire and its henchmen, but to God and the Lamb. God/the Lamb, not the emperor, is the one who goes forth to conquer the nations (19:11-16). John makes fun by representing the emperor and his supporters as dissembling fakes.

Such fun, however, comes at a price. If Aune, Laws, and Boring discover John cracking a smile, others return it with a scowl. "Why is violence condoned when it is in scripture and when God is the actor?"[8] asks Tina Pippin, cross-examining John of Patmos. The Apocalypse's

"Achilles' heel," observes Elisabeth Schüssler Fiorenza, is "its envisioning of God and Christ in analogy to the Oriental Great King and the Roman Emperor." This "calls for theological evaluation" because it risks inscribing in heaven oppressive "kyriarchal relations of domination," thereby making them sacrosanct.[9]

The purpose of the Apocalypse, argues Robert M. Royalty, is not, contrary to Adela Yarbro Collins, to help otherwise decent Christians living in a sometimes hostile Roman Empire deal with their negative feelings toward their government that, left untreated, could have dangerous consequences. No, John does not want his audience to get mad; he wants it to get even. The heavenly Jerusalem, not Rome, will be the capital city of their empire; wealth will flow to God and his slaves, not to the pagan emperor and his allies; the Lamb, not Caesar, will be emperor.[10]

Stephen Moore adopts an arch, if not satirical, tone in his own exposé of the Apocalypse's moral vision. Moore builds on numismatic studies showing Revelation's depictions of the Lamb, together with the symbols of rule and honor ascribed to him, modeled after representations drawn from first-century imperial iconography. Noting further the many parallels between honorific titles ascribed to the Roman emperor and those given to the God/Lamb of the Apocalypse, Moore argues that the Lamb of the Apocalypse is a larger-than-life apotheosized ruler dressed up in emperor's clothing. Together with the one seated on the throne, God/Jesus flexes his manly muscle and kicks sand in the face of that wimp beast of Rev. 13:1 who stands on the seashore.[11]

For these interpreters, the Apocalypse is no laughing matter. Its treatment of imperial power and imagery as a parodic representation of *true* divine power replaces one tyrant with another without addressing the ethics of domination and bloodlust. Friedrich Nietzsche described the Book of Revelation as "the most rabid outburst of vindictiveness in all recorded history."[12]

To apply the term *parody* to John's Revelation is to trouble the waters of Apocalypse scholarship. Aune, Laws, and Boring deploy the word *parody* loosely as a synonym for *counterfeit*. In doing so they introduce, if inadvertently, the closely associated notion of irony. Now, to speak of parody and irony in the Apocalypse is to open a Pandora's box. We may question, for example, the direction of the parody in the Apocalypse. Is it the empire that parodies God's dominion, or the other way around? Do God and the Lamb dressed up in emperor's clothing parody the empire and its institutions of domination? Sophie Laws briefly contemplates a reverse flow of parody when she employs the term *counter-parody* to describe the ceremonial imperial court language in Revelation 4:

> As with his development of the images of the adversaries, so John's presentation of heavenly worship has a strongly polemical edge, and here its impact comes through counter-parody: as the beast falsely claimed the status and character of the Lamb, so now the Lamb truly claims and gives content to the beast's own forms of worship.[13]

Yet when one admits the term *counter-parody* into the conversation, it is no longer clear what precisely the phrase "the Lamb truly claims and gives content to the beast's own forms of worship" means. Where does the "counter" in "counter-parody" end? Where does John stop joking around and get serious? What is to keep us from reading the entire Apocalypse as a sustained parody? These are foolish questions, were it not for the way Revelation sets up from its very outset the profoundest of reversals of fortune, reversals we have explored in previous chapters.

What if even John's happy ending of golden Jerusalem bliss were given some reversal? An exegetical folly? Perhaps, but then again, as we saw in the previous chapter, even here in that most purified vision of Jerusalem, destabilizing impurities lurk. All those once hostile kings and nations whom we thought were slain, deceived by Satan, or cast into the lake of burning fire (Rev. 19:17-21; 20:7-10, 15) now appear suddenly on the scene again. No longer enemies, they are worshipers, bearing their honor and glory into the city (21:24, 26).

What if we read this ending as a final, grand reversal, a self-parodying of the apocalypse-style dualism for which, according to contemporary formulators of the genre, ancient apocalypses are so famous? Notwithstanding the confident scholarly identifications of formal literary properties of ancient "apocalypses" and the straightforward taxonomies in which the Revelation of John is supposed to find its place, this mess of parody begins to alert us to some destabilizing possibilities. In fact, the term *parody* nowhere appears in the now-classic taxonomies of ancient apocalypse. With good reason: parody opens a can of worms that the ready-to-hand generic descriptions of the biblical academy concerning apocalypses, apocalyptic eschatology, and apocalypticism are ill-equipped to handle.

This is only the beginning of our exegetical troubles. Once parody is allowed to stick its nose into the tent of apocalypse scholarship, the rest of the beast is not far behind. For parody is but the poor cousin of its wealthy relation, irony. Even if one feels confident about making a truce with parody in Revelation, irony keeps skirmishing along agreed-upon borders, contesting allegiances and breaking the firmest exegetical treaties.

Consider, for example, our hero, John of Patmos, the one my prior discussion has marked as the ideal with whom the audience is to identify (Rev. 1:9) in order to come to a solid understanding of the work. There he is, our prophet John sharing his prophecy at the start of his Apocalypse letter (1:3), confidently numbered among the prophets at its close (22:9), pillorying Jezebel and Balaam for false prophecy (2:20, 14), gloating over the warm ending of the beast's "false prophet" (20:10). See him railing against the false worship of the beast (13:15).

Nothing prepares us for our hero's liturgical blunder: his falling down to worship the angel who delivers his prophecy—not once (19:10), but twice (22:9), and this at the end of his visions, at a point when he should surely have known better. "Worship God!" the angel commands John, now suddenly pitting ideal reader against implied author in the latter's fall from grace. Irony, quipped Friedrich Schlegel, is "transzendentale Buffonerie."[14] Our erstwhile "transcendental" prophet John is now suddenly playing the buffoon. John leaves us high and dry and wondering what's up.

A condition of irony is that the *eiron* or ironist enjoys a detachment from his/her ironized subject so as to explore its incongruities. This the Apocalypse certainly offers. Following John to heaven we enjoy with him the *eiron*'s distance from everyday society, placed in the position to observe the incongruities in which the ironist revels. His apocalyptic tales give us the elevated God's eye perspective explored in an earlier chapter. Disentangled from the daily round we look down upon the *alazon*'s or hubrist's (i.e., Rome's) arrogance. From our lofty position we enjoy the exposure of incongruity, especially the impotence of brute imperial power and the wholly misguided claims of the ruler and his minions to enjoy honor, worship, as well as the arrogance arising from their prosperity.

John assures us of the Apocalypse's conclusion from the start (1:7), an ending which the majority of the characters populating his visions remain woefully unaware, putting us in the know and so again privileging us with a posture that results in the exposure of ironical incongruity. Ironies unfold as trumpets blow and bowls fall and thirds of creation are wiped out, but pagans hostile to God remain obdurate in their wickedness, clinging, laughably, to soon-to-be-demolished idols (e.g., 9:20-21).

Enjoying the full awareness of what they fail to see, we look down and smile at the arrogant blindness of their enduring wickedness. Perhaps we even grin with bemused incredulity. Thus we might remain smug in our heaven, smiling that all is so unwell in the world below, were it not for John's sudden plummet into this mess of idolatry. For now, at the Apocalypse's end, alone on high, we are less certain of ourselves, not wholly immune from our own laughter. If such a prophet like John can be shot with his own gun, what of us lesser mortals?

Parody and irony, then, introduce instability not only to the Apocalypse's literary world, but also to confident exegetical conclusions regarding its meaning. One must exercise some caution in coming to overly stable conclusions when met with a text in which parody can point equally to the beast *or* the Lamb. We should wonder what is going on when a narrator, having spent the better part of his tale convincing us of his trustworthiness, pulls the carpet out from under himself and assaults himself with the censure launched against his enemies.

Before we decide to laugh along with Sophie Laws at the parodies of the Apocalypse, or to cry over them with Tina Pippin and Stephen Moore, we need to take a longer look at irony, and to explore how irony relates to parody. This will help us register some of the more memorable parodic and ironic moments of John's Revelation and their implications here, in the contemporary world, at memory's end. There follows first an exploration of definitions, an exegesis of the Apocalypse's deployment of parody and irony, and finally the possible consequences for existence of such a destabilizing narrative. Never far in the background, of course, lurks an autobiographical folly.

IRONY'S STAGE

Let us consider some definitions of irony and from there move into the Apocalypse and a consideration of a series of ironical moments that unfold into larger parodies. The *Oxford English Dictionary* offers two definitions relevant to our study. Irony is, first, "a figure of speech in which the intended meaning is the opposite of that expressed by the words used." Second, it is "a condition of affairs or events of a character opposite to what was, or might naturally be, expected; a contradictory outcome of events as if in mockery of the promise and fitness of things." These are definitions drawn from modern usage, but they may be traced to ancient sources. The first definition, the saying of one thing while meaning another, was already offered in the fourth century rhetorical handbook composed by Anaximenes, and later found its way into the Roman rhetorical manuals of Cicero and Quintillian.[15] The more formal linguistic definition (irony as antiphrasis), however, quickly broadened to express the second usage. For example, included among Theophrastus's (fourth century B.C.E.) handbook of civic characters is *eirōneia* (the Dissembler), a social type who intentionally appears to be something s/he is not."[16] Aristotle pairs *eirōneia* (by which he means "self-deprecation") with its opposite intemperance, *alazoneia* ("boastfulness"), both of which, left untrained by virtue, occur naturally.[17] More positively, dissembling as a strategy for unmasking ignorance and discovering truth appears in Plato's appreciation of Socrates as the prototypical *eirōn*.[18] In these examples, irony as "a condition of affairs or events . . . opposite to what was, or might naturally be, expected" takes us beyond a strictly linguistic definition to a social one.

D. C. Muecke in a now classic study of irony calls the first definition cited above "verbal irony." The second form, extending the definition beyond figures of speech to the drama of life, he names situational.[19] Something like Muecke's twofold classification is found in ancient treatments. Quintillian distinguishes between a mere ironical phrase or gesture and the sustained rhetorical deployment of incongruity.[20] Situational irony describes Odysseus's undercover homecoming and Oedipus's blindness. It also describes the Older Testament stories of fleeing Hebrew slaves occasioning the destruction of Pharaoh's army, and the description of pagan Cyrus as the Lord's "anointed one" (*meshiach*) and "shepherd" to restore the remnant Israel (Isa. 44:28; 45:1). Finally, situational irony plays a leading role in the Gospel stagings of Jesus' mock coronation (Mark 15:17-20; John 19:1-3, 17-22)—most sophisticatedly in John the Evangelist's reversed roles of the fully-in-control condemned "criminal" Jesus against the "innocent" imperial/cosmic stooge, Pontius Pilate (John 18:28—19:16).

Close attention to the situational ironies in the Apocalypse attunes us to hitherto unrecognized possibilities of verbal ironies, and leads us finally to a reappraisal of Revelation's uses of parody. Incongruities abound in John's Apocalypse, but nowhere more so than in John's address to the seven churches and his descriptions of the ecclesial realities that follow. These frame the whole of the Book of Revelation in a situational irony, inviting its listeners to consider a series of contradictory outcomes "as if," following the definition cited above, "in mockery of the promise and fitness of things." Indeed, so numerous are the contradictory outcomes in the Book of Revelation that we finally must doubt our senses and give ourselves over to the resignification of the world I explored in chapter 2.

This is an unrecognized aspect of what has rightly been named the "hermeneutical function" of the opening message section.[21] John hardly prepares us for the incongruities that follow the opening address to the inhabitants of the seven churches, referring to them as God's "slaves" (*douloi*—1:1), who together make up "a kingdom, priests to [Jesus'] God and Father" (v. 6), and who share with him "in the tribulation and the kingdom and the patient endurance." Our expectations of further panegyric are disappointed by the mixed bag of censure and praise that follows. We soon discover that many of those censured have no idea of their deathly, impoverished condition. Some of them are even confident that they are in the bloom of life and health. In disappointing expectations in this way, John begins to till the rich metaphorical soil of his Apocalypse with irony.

The incongruities become, as we discovered in the first chapter's discussion of the "architecture" of the letters, increasingly pronounced. The Ephesians "cannot bear evil people but have tested those who call themselves apostles but are not, and found them to be false." Nevertheless, "you have abandoned the love you had at first" (2:2-4). The church at Sardis has "the name of being alive." Nevertheless, "you are dead" (3:1).

John may be training us not to trust our senses, but nothing prepares us for the full-scale polemical application of irony in the message to the Laodiceans. Here John goes beyond an exposé of a true reality masked by appearances; he rails at the massive incongruity of a community that celebrates, "I am rich, I have prospered, and I need nothing," but is in fact "wretched, pitiable, poor, blind, and naked" (3:17). This prepares us for later exposing of God's boastful enemies who entrust themselves to their prosperity, revealing themselves as fornicating idolaters. The implied author's voice, thrown here into the mouth of the revelatory Jesus, creates the ironist's stance of observation from a distance, and the detachment necessary to mock the apparent fitness of things as presently constituted.

Further, John's representation of his opponents first as Balaam (2:14) and then as Jezebel (2:20) charges his polemic with what Linda Hutcheon in her study of irony names "assailing irony," that is, an irony that offers a satirical corrective function through sharply subversive critique.[22] To charge a prophet as false is one thing; it is another to dress her up in the clothing of one of the Bible's most booed antiheroes. "Jezebel" here is the picture that speaks a thousand words, "the one who calls herself a prophetess and is teaching and beguiling my servants to practice immorality and to eat food sacrificed to idols" (v. 20). The apparent fitness of things could not be more mocked, their present constitution rendered scarcely more questionable.

On the other hand, not all is bad in the seven churches, even if John has a funny idea of what "doing well" means. Irony abounds in letters of praise. "I know your tribulation and poverty," says "the first and the last, who died and came to life," "but you are rich" (2:9). Likewise, the Philadelphian church, which has "but little power," is nonetheless promised that the day is coming when those who say they are Jews and (ironically) are not will "bow down before your feet, and learn that I have loved you." This is more than reversal of fortune. When read together with the other examples just cited, it contributes to a construction of reality that is counterintuitive and that, again, explores a condition not normally expected, and that prepares us for that "contradictory outcome of events as if in mockery of the promise and fitness of things." These praiseworthy churches express the larger theological ironies developed in the Apocalypse's opening three chapters.

The ironical incongruities of the character and experiences of the seven churches center for John in a cosmic theological irony. He inscribes this theological irony from the outset, though only in outline, through the use of christological sketches. Creedal familiarity with the notion of the second coming has perhaps made us immune to the deeply ironical assertion that "all tribes of the earth will wail" upon the appearance of the Palestinian nobody, the crucified one (1:7), or that such a political loser should be "the ruler of kings on earth" (1:5).

Less familiar, and more readily available to us as ironical, are the titles that open the various decrees (indeed, calling them decrees is already to give irony admission to the Apocalypse's show). Contradictory outcomes abound in Revelation's titling of Jesus as the one "who died and came to life" (2:8), as the "pierced" one (1:7) luxuriously robed (1:13), with a two-edged sword (2:12), "eyes like a flame of fire" (2:18), "the beginning God's creation" (3:14). These ascriptions, like the letters they head, mock whatever notions of expected outcomes our work-a-day world brings with it. They set the stage for the play of irony that follows.

Revelation's opening three chapters, then, function as a kind of primer in John's uses of irony. Upon entering the throne-room visions of chapters 4 and 5, the training moves to a more advanced level. As in the seven "decrees," the unfolding sequence of visionary events fails to prepare us for the incongruities erupting in this episode. The vision is one of an imperial court: repetitive acclamations shouted by subjects and court attendants to the emperor, torches of fire, bowls of incense, dignitaries surrounding the throne, the luxuries of dress and architecture, *proskynēsis* or ritualized obeisance to the divine ruler, the opening of a scroll to read a decree (4:3-11; 5:8-14). All this belongs to the drama and ritual of the Roman court—from the acclamations of might and power ascribed to God, down to the Jovian-sounding reference to lightning and thunder issuing from God's throne (4:5).[23] In the latter case, emperors from Julius Caesar onward wrapped themselves in Jupiter's clothing to reinforce the claims of their dynasty to divine sonship and inevitable apotheosis.[24] Having witnessed with John all the splendor of the heavenly emperor, we readily sympathize that none can be found worthy to break the seven seals of the heavenly imperial decree and to read it (5:1-4).

John scarcely prepares us for the incongruity that follows. At verse 5 one of the elders comforts John with the promise that "the lion of the tribe of Judah the root of David, has conquered so that he can open the scroll and its seven seals." The promise builds first on messianic promises of the Older Testament and Second Temple Judaism of a coming David-like figure. It also continues to develop the Roman political ideology of apotheosis, whereby divinization of a deceased emperor was accorded by senatorial decision based on a ruler's merit.[25] In fact, the adjectives of adulation that follow in 5:12-13, echoing those used to praise "the Lord God Almighty"—(4:9-11) while also drawing on Older and extratestamental adjectives associated with God—parallel favorite terms of praise reserved for emperors, notoriously that self-apotheosized "Lord and God" Domitian.[26]

What follows, however, is sharply disjunctive. John sees the "Lamb [*to arnion*—the diminutive form of *arēn*], standing, as though it had been slain, with seven horns and with seven eyes." This vision of the Lamb, standing in profound tension with the immediately preceding image of the conquering "lion of the tribe of Judah," marks an outcome that contradicts, if not mocks, all the high-sounding court language that precedes it. As if parodying the ideology upon which it draws, this Lamb now receives imperial shouts of acclamation and *proskynēsis* by imperial-looking attendants (5:11-14).

The move from lion to Lamb has been too disjunctive for some exegetes, so they have found in the reference to the seven horns of verse 6 evidence that the innocent "lambkins" is a messianic killer. Hence a chorus of commentators discovers in the horned Lamb echoes of an allegedly widespread conquering ram/messiah tradition in (apocalyptic) Judaism.[27] There is, indeed, in early Judaism evidence of lambs becoming rams (thus, *1 Enoch* 89:42-48 [Saul and David]; 90:9-10 [the Maccabees]), as there is an iconographic tradition in the ancient Near East of the ram/goat as a symbol of divine leadership.[28] The author of *1 Enoch* adopts the Older Testament metaphor of Israel as God's flock (e.g., Isa. 40:11; Jer. 23:2-4; Ezek. 34:2-16), and uses the ram metaphor to signal divine appointment of leadership.[29] But this is not an analogue to the Apocalypse's usage.

The notion of a messianic lamb turned ram appears nowhere in John's visions. What he sees moves contrary to the representation found in *1 Enoch*, for in the Apocalypse the Lamb does not leave its old identity to become a ram, but *remains* (slain) Lamb. The association of this weak creature with the seven horns (again, symbol of governance and power) is thus paradoxical. If in *1 Enoch* the move is from vulnerable Lamb to powerful ram, in the Apocalypse the emphasis remains, as the twenty-eight references scattered throughout Revelation indicate, focused on the vulnerable Lamb. There is nothing in early Judaism's messianic expectations to parallel the Lamb that has horns and that *remains* the slain Lamb.

Even, as we shall see, the vision of Jesus as conquering warrior with a robe clad in blood (19:11-16) belongs to the Lamb's "rhetorical program."[30] The disjunction between the lion and the Lamb of Rev. 4:5, 6 remains a jarring one.[31] In an instant, it reconfigures the more predictable theological categories of Rev. 4:1—5:5 associated with divine power, especially from a Greco-Roman imperial perspective, and draws them into the oblique orbit of irony inscribed in Revelation's opening chapters.

The ironies in the first five chapters of Revelation are declarative. They center on incongruities of description. From chapter 6 onward they take on a more dramatic nature. I have already deployed the term *theatricality* to explore the way John "tells" through "showing." I argued in an earlier chapter that the warnings and promises to the seven churches are dramatically acted out in the events and characters that make up the Apocalypse's remaining chapters. One of Revelation's hortatory strategies is to offer impersonations of John's listeners that his audience is either to envy or resent. We can now expand this concept of theatricality to encompass what D. L. Muecke calls "dramatised irony."

Dramatized irony describes the ironist's function as "simply to present ironic situations or events to our sense of irony." "In this ironic mode," Muecke continues,

> the ironist does not appear either as an impersonal voice or in any disguise. He simply arranges that the characters of his play or novel, story, verse narrative, or dramatic monologue expose themselves in their ironic predicament directly to the audience or reader. He himself is the puppet-master and as such out of sight. This is the only way in which dramatists can be ironical (short of bringing themselves more or less identifiably on stage).[32]

The ironist as "puppet-master" is the one who looks down from on high and lets the ironies unfold and speak for themselves. John is not quite the aloof puppeteer of Muecke's dramatized irony. He is, as we saw in chapter 2, the kind of ironist who cannot resist the temptation to get in on the action. We saw that this happens either obliquely, through the interpolation of simile and metaphor to emphasize the intended meaning of apocalyptic symbolism, or by direct editorial asides. Just a moment ago we also saw John fall flat on his face, plummeting from his apocalyptic perch to prostrate himself before an angel, and so to burst onto the stage in an ironizing burlesque performance of idolatry.

More usually, however, John stays out of the way of what he sees and lets events speak for themselves. As the Apocalypse's plots unfold, ironies build on one another in dramatized form. I have been exploring the ways in which the opening five chapters function as a kind of "crash course" in Revelation's ironical view of the world. Reversals, application of laudatory imperial language to otherwise unlikely characters, and surprising juxtapositions teach listeners/readers to see the world with the self-reflexive distance of the ironist, which warns the observer not to take anything at face value and to be prepared for the most incongruous of outcomes.

John's "flat-landers," suffering their calamitous sequences from chapter 6 onward, carry on in an ignorant idolatry that is highly ironical. It is ironical because we "mountain dwellers," that is, we privileged hearers/readers who have had the benefit of John's training in the grammar of divine incongruity, can look down from on high with our puppet-master and chuckle. We as privileged insiders know from the outset that those who once pierced Jesus will soon wail (Rev. 1:7), that the faithful "poor" are in fact "rich" (2:9), that the self-satisfied wealthy are pitiably naked (3:17). By contrast, nothing prepares the idolatrous enemies of God for what is about to happen to them, or for the reversals of fortune to come.

Ignorance leads the idolatrous from the very outset to draw wrong conclusions from apocalyptic misfortune. At 6:5, John witnesses the opening of the third seal and the advent of the third rider of the Apocalypse, the black horse of famine. We the listeners know whence and to what end these riders gallop across the apocalyptic stage. Those on stage do not. At verse 6, the inflated price for wheat and barley expresses supply-and-demand economics. The additional suggestion not "to harm" the oil and wine moves this event from a straightforward description of inflated prices in terrible times toward an ironical play of ignorance in the face of the obvious. For what reason, we find ourselves asking, does this voice in the midst of the four living creatures urge that conservation? At 18:13, we have our answer: like the wheat and barley sold for an outrageous price, so oil and wine belong to the wheeling and dealing of those merchants profiteering from trade with Babylon/Rome. They may save their goods to sell them at a higher price when, as a consequence of tragedies that the riders on horseback unleash, supply is low and demand is high, but we listeners know their days are numbered. Rhetorically, the opening of the fifth seal (6:9-11), with its promise of vindication to the subaltern saints "slain for the word of God," returns us to the heavenly perspective and makes the incongruity of the preceding saving of luxury items more pronounced.

Later, when the parodically titled "Babylon the Great" (17:5; 18:2, 9, 16, 17, 19; 14:8) comes crashing down in just "one hour" (18:10, 17, 19) and the "smoke from her goes up for ever and ever" (19:3), listeners/readers are not nearly so shocked as those kings, merchants, and shippers of 18:9, 11, 17, who are surprised by the swiftness of her destruction. In fact, one is left wondering why they could not see Babylon's destruction coming.

Repeatedly, from chapters 6 to 18, insider listeners/readers look down at the dramatic ironies of characters who, apocalyptic plagues and woes notwithstanding, refuse to "repent of the works of their hands nor give up worshiping demons and idols of gold and silver and bronze and stone and wood, which cannot either see or hear or walk; nor did they repent of their murders or their sorceries or their immortality or their thefts" (9:20). Faced with Exodus-like plagues, they rather curse God (16:9, 11, 21), or more unbelievably still, worship the beast and ask, in high irony, "Who is like the beast, and who can fight against it?" (13:4). The listener/reader learned the answer to that question early on. The inability of the idolatrous to detect the counterfeit in the second beast's performances of God's power (13:12-15) serves to reinforce the dramatic irony.

Throughout these sequences, John repeatedly comes back to the heavenly perspective, either by returning as narrator to look into heaven for the unveiling of more mysteries (10:1—11:2; 15:5-8), or by interrupting visions of earthly mayhem with the liturgical repose of heavenly worship (7:4-17; 14:1-5). John fixes his audience's eyes downward onto the stage below and lets the ironies of nonrepentance speak for themselves.

IRONY DEMYSTIFYING

"Who is like the beast, and who can fight against it?" Nothing prepares the antagonists in the Apocalypse for John's answer. His response leads us to an appraisal of the political uses of Revelation's dramatic irony and begins to move us in the direction of parody. The question, as we have seen, drips with irony. But so does John's reply, that the one slain by the beast (Rev. 12:4-6) is up to the task. In the first place, the use of imperial slogans and political vocabulary borrowed from imperial and Hellenistic court ritual to celebrate the Lamb's identity literally makes the Lamb "like the beast." The consistent application of this terminology to the Lamb allows John to juxtapose slain Lamb and powerful beast, and thereby to offer a sharp critique of Roman imperial might and authority. Jarringly so, for there could not be a less likely candidate to fight against the beast. That he is a slain Lamb, the murdered victim of God's enemy, makes John's claim of the Lamb's power counterintuitive, if not laughable.

Linda Hutcheon coins the phrase "irony demystifying" to describe "critical, debunking, judging irony," and associates such irony with what she calls "irony oppositional," namely, "the subversive doubling within and against the dominant."[33] Revelation 12–13 and 17–18 are excellent examples of demystifying, oppositional irony. As we have seen, the question "who is like the beast" (13:4) expresses a dramatic irony arising out of a clever juxtaposition between what the reader knows and what the deceived idolaters do not. The audience knows that the beast deceives them with counterfeit signs and wonders because the narrator tells us so (13:13-15), but those guilty of false worship do not know, shut out as they are from the narrative commentary. Further, these characters are in no way prepared for the swift destruction of Babylon the Great, hence the pathos of their dirges in chapter 18. We, however, learn of its coming demise well in advance of the event; we even celebrate it earlier in Rev. 14:8. What is common to chapters 12–13 and 17–18 is a sharp socioeconomic and political irony, which cuts to the bone the ideology by which the Roman Empire legitimates its power.

John schools us in the true identity of the beast from 12:3 onward, where he offers us an exposé of the power behind the Roman emperor's throne. He thus arranges the apocalyptic stage for the debunking of "irony demystifying." This provides the basis for a further oppositional irony, when John portrays the slain Lamb as a subversive double of imperial power. Our narrator is careful to show the link between the dragon/serpent/devil of 12:3, 7, 9, 12, 14, 15, 16, 17 and the beasts of 13:1-10, 11-17. The former gives its authority to the latter (13:2); the beasts resemble the dragon (13:1, 11; 17:3). The reference to the whore of Babylon astride the red beast with seven heads and ten horns (17:3), repeating the image of the dragon from 12:3, asks that we assess the careers of

Babylon the whore/Babylon the Great and her supporters (chaps. 17–18) in the light of the earlier representation. The final destruction of the devil, beast, and false prophet (19:10) brings the motifs introduced earlier to their demystifying conclusion.

Revelation 12–13 and 17–18 offer a sustained political ironizing of Roman imperial ideology. Chapter 12 plays directly on imperial propaganda. The chapter replicates the narrative structure of a widely shared myth associated with Python, Leto, and Apollo, and with Seth, Isis, and Horus.[34] Broadly outlined, these myths recount a dragon/giant/monster (Python/Seth-Typhon) pursuing a female figure (Leto/Isis), the defeat of the antagonist by a combat figure (Apollo/Horus), and the restoration of order. Roman imperial propaganda used this combat myth as a political celebration of imperial order brought about through Jupiter's sons—successive Roman emperors—vanquishing anti-Roman challengers (the dragon, Seth-Typhon).[35] Imperial propaganda favored depictions of the emperor as Jupiter vanquishing the forces of chaos, restoring social order, and guaranteeing peace and concord.[36] Jovian ideology was a common motif on coins and imperial monuments of Asia Minor. The emperor's victories over enemies, as in Domitian's victory over the Chatti, were commemorated as a Jovian defeat of chaos's agents.[37]

The brute realities of imperial rule were, however, readily apparent, and it was easy to lampoon Jupiter's imperial descendant as a Typhon. Such a pillorying appears, for example, in Pseudo-Seneca's *Octavia*, which lampoons Nero as Typhon. The pro-Trajanic, second-century writer Dio Chrysostom similarly dispatched Domitian by depicting him as a Typhon-like tyrant.[38] Revelation 12–13 and 17–18 belong in this line of political resistance.

When John describes the beasts as agents of the dragon, or the whore of Babylon as riding a red beast (a scarlet animal being Seth-Typhon's signature), he positions his dramatic, demystifying irony on a stage of counter-imperial politics.[39] Jupiter is Typhon; the emperor is a tyrannical beast. Further, the reference to the counterfeit signs and wonders of the beast, especially creating fire that comes down from heaven, leading to false worship of the beast (Rev. 13:13-15), may similarly allude to Jovian thunder and lightning. Possibly John's vision of "the two wings of the great eagle," by means of which the woman pursued by the dragon flees into the wilderness (12:14), continues the political inversion.[40] John's point is that "Jupiter" is in fact the beast.[41]

Demystifying irony continues in Revelation's exposure of Rome's economic order. In chapters 17–18, sham Jupiter becomes a luxury-loving whore astride the scarlet beast/Seth Typhon (17:3). John's caricature of the whore of Babylon's paraded luxury also resembles concurrent criticism of Roman love of luxury, connected in satire with the economic prosperity of the Roman order.[42] It further echoes Second Temple apocalyptic critiques of Roman luxury.[43] Luxury and economics are the threads common to chapters 13 and 17–18. We learn in 13:17 that the precondition of the pursuit of wealth is the worship of the beast.

The whore's destruction signals the end of the trade in luxury goods listed in chapter 18. Again, the official ideology associated with the Jovian reign of Roman emperors was that the order established by the divine emperor flowered in economic prosperity. A supporter of imperial order like Aelius Aristides, for example, could celebrate that to the victor went the spoils. The Mediterranean Basin, he writes, provides Romans

> abundantly with whatever is in them. Produce is brought from every land and every sea, depending on what the seasons bring forth, and what is produced by all lands, rivers and lakes and the arts of Greeks and barbarians. If anyone wants to see it all he must either travel over the whole earth to see it in such a way or come to this city. For what grows and is produced among individual peoples is necessarily always here, and here in abundance.[44]

No wonder the merchants and shipmasters of Revelation 18 mourn the passing of Babylon! Courting the favor of Rome's divine "son of Jupiter" translated into economic blessings delivered via imperial patronage and favors. The imperial cult was a means of an occupying foreign ruler to exert influence in the networks of traditional elites.[45] It was also a means of the occupied, especially the "little guy"—traders and merchants and their social networks—to gain access to new spheres of socioeconomic power.[46] This helps to explain why in Asia Minor the imperial cult was popular among first-century *collegia* or associations of traders.[47]

However, just as Caesar, the divine son of Jupiter, had his Senecan *Octavia*, so Rome's much-celebrated prosperity had its satirists. Petronius depicts the Roman as a conqueror possessing "the whole world, sea and land and the course of sun and moon. But he was not satisfied." Roman greed leads to war, rape of land, and extinction of animals. Fortunes express themselves in drunkenness and gluttony.[48] For Petronius it is the best of times; it is the worst of times. John echoes Petronius's demystifying ironical celebration of Roman economic might when he states that among the luxury goods brought to an end by Babylon's untimely end are "slaves, that is, human souls" (Rev. 18:13) or that, amid the famine brought on by war, luxury goods are squandered (6:5). For John, the economic benefits derived from a fake peace built up by a counterfeit Jupiter are all part of the same demonic sham. The "critical, debunking, judging irony" could not be more acidic.

PARODIES IN THE CONTACT ZONE

John is not content to deploy ironical inversion here and there. His use of imperial titles, iconography, and court ritual is extensive. And this is what gets him in the most trouble with contemporary interpreters. For Robert M. Royalty, for example, John's Jesus is just one more emperor; his new creation, Jerusalem, is another Rome.[49] That is, *if* John is not being ironical. Here Linda Hutcheon's identification of oppositional irony as "subversive doubling within and against the dominant" is most instructive. The whole of the Apocalypse may be read as a parody in which one discourse, that of imperial might and power, is subverted by being applied to another, that of the slain Lamb.

Hutcheon outlines a theory of parody that is useful for exploring Revelation's sustained uses of irony. Parody, according to Hutcheon, involves ironic inversion through imitation. "Parody is . . . repetition with critical distance, which marks difference rather than similarity." It is "ironic playing with multiple conventions, . . . extended repetition with critical distance. . . ."[50] Hutcheon broadens parody beyond traditional formal definitions indicated, for example, in the *Oxford English Dictionary*'s definition of parody as "an imitation of a work more or less closely modeled on the original, but so turned as to produce a ridiculous effect." She accepts this formal definition, which parallels definitions from antiquity.[51] But she insists on broadening the discussion of parody to include an exploration of how parody works. This, too, parallels ancient usage. Ancient Mennipean parody similarly extended beyond mock aping of style to include satirical imitation of well-known themes and characters involved in highly ironical conversations and situations.[52] The relevance of Hutcheon's treatment to the ironies of the Book of Revelation are readily apparent when she speaks of parody as "an integrated structural modelling process of revising, replaying, inverting, and 'trans-contextualising' previous works of art."[53] Parody, she insists, is *"doubly coded* in political terms: it *both* legitimises and subverts that which it parodies."[54]

This is what makes the politics of parody such risky business. Parody imitates, but it does not merely quote. Parodic double-coding upsets routine meanings by inscribing distance and difference. "Replaying" conserves and reinforces; it can also be a first step toward revision and inversion. In a later study, Hutcheon deploys the phrase "irony's edge" to describe a critical space opened when one signifier works double-duty to mean two things without necessarily meaning either.[55] Parody is "repetition with critical difference."[56] Parody is "ironic repetition."[57] Parody has a "target," which is "always another form of art, or more generally, another discourse."[58] "Parodying," Mikail Bakhtin states, "is the creation of a *decrowning double;* it is that same 'world turned inside out.'"[59] Replaying, inverting, revising, turning the world inside out, decrowning—the iconoclastic side of parody—presume and create contact zones.

Mary Louis Pratt coins the phrase "contact zones" to describe "social spaces where cultures meet, clash, and grapple with each other, often in contexts of highly asymmetrical relations of power."[60] In asymmetrical power relations, as in colonialism, for example, difference and protest often take the form of parody and ironical playing out of the dominant discursive community.

Pratt illustrates by citing the example of a seventeenth-century letter composed by an indigenous Andean, Felipe Guamanan Poma de Ayala, and addressed to Philip III, king of Spain.[61] Guamanan Poma adopts the style and form of a Spanish chronicler of conquest and colonial history but offers a counterchronicle by recording a different history of his people and describing the customs of the colonized from the bottom up. His letter ends by inverting the roles of colonizer and colonized, in a mock question-answer interview in which the rapacious, violent king of Spain comes to Guamanan Poma with admiring observations of his indigenous Andean society, seeking information on how best to reform his empire. Guamanan Poma refutes a dominant political ideology through caricature, inversion, ironical reversal of roles, and a counterdiscursive reformulation of monarchical government, through the application of indigenous Andean institutions and values. In this contact zone of colonial domination, parody replays. It also inverts, revises, and overturns.

With these notions of parody, we are ready to return to the Apocalypse. Robert M. Royalty, investigating Revelation's developments of Older Testament motifs of wealth and power, together with its application of Roman imperial images to represent the book's visions of heavenly good fortune, argues that John replaces one empire with another. In support he thoroughly exegetes John's modulations of Older Testament texts dealing with the uses and abuses of wealth, and of God's judgments concerning wealth and rich cities or nations. He demonstrates that the Older Testament concern for social justice or the oppression of the poor, the widowed and the orphan are completely absent from the Apocalypse.

In the texts that John borrows or develops, judgment comes on wealthy powers for their neglect of justice and for oppression. Royalty notes that in the Apocalypse, however, the wealth of the oppressor power, Babylon/ Rome, is merely transferred from one account to that of theocratic Jerusalem's. There is no prophetic critique of injustice. Both Older Testament and Second Temple Jewish texts "include one notable feature that the Apocalypse of John lacks completely—a strong concern for the poor."[62] This leads to a sharp conclusion that Revelation "creates a new culture of power that mimics the dominant ideology; only the names and labels are changed. Revelation replaces Rome with the New Jerusalem and Caesar's court with God's, but the underlying power structures are essentially the same."[63] Revelation's theological "Achilles' heel" (Schüssler Fiorenza) could not be more dramatically exposed. John imitates and replays empire.

But does he not also invert it? Is the slain Lamb not a parodying double of Roman power and dominion? Does not the transfer of wealth from the whore of Babylon's account to the slain Lamb's trigger a crash in imperial fortunes? Are we not dealing here with a theological "Black Tuesday"? Like Guamanan Poma, John plays his Apocalypse out in an imperial contact zone. He adopts the categories of an imperial dominant discourse, but he inflects them in a way that we may describe as parody. John does not replace one empire with another; he turns empire inside out.

This is already indicated at the conclusion of the throne-room vision, in which John ironically juxtaposes power and weakness by applying the language of power and might, describing the one seated on the throne, Yahweh (Rev. 4:8-11), to the conquering seven-horned Lamb (5:5, 6, 9, 12-13). The drama of liturgical acclamation, as well as the terms of praise, closely imitates Roman imperial honor and worship of the emperor, as do the costume, the instruments, and the sounds and images associated with them. This is imperial imagery inverted to describe a counterimperial vision.

As the Apocalypse unfolds, John continues to parody Roman power and dominion. If he replays the structural logic of Roman domination, he turns its notions of power and glory inside out by drawing notions of might and violence into "the rhetorical programme of the Lamb" (Loren Johns). This continues to include Roman motifs as well as motifs from Second Temple Judaism. John inverts and reconfigures both. Thus, as the Apocalypse revolves toward its ending, John returns to the "throne" and the "Lamb" of chapters 4-5, mentioning both together (7:10-12, 17; 14:1, 4; 15:3; 21:22; 22:1, 3; see also 19:1-6, 7, 9). Thence issues the unfolding apocalyptic drama of John's visions. As we saw in chapter 5, the heavenly scenes interjected amid the cycles of earthly apocalyptic woes continue to return the audience to a heaven's-eye view of earthly calamity and to urge listeners to adopt this transcendent perspective. It is a perspective defined by the slain Lamb who stands before the throne of Yahweh, who provides the vanishing point for John's apocalyptic canvas. The slain Lamb is a kind of theological coefficient that qualifies and "transcontextualizes" all that follows, from chapter 5 onward.

These points are usually made by way of oxymoron. At 7:10-11, imperial and Older Testament language of acclamation, including the language of salvation, is ascribed to the Lamb. At 15:3, the song of exodus victory ("the song of Moses") is equally "the song of the Lamb." In 21:24, the bounty of the nations is brought in imperial-looking triumph (v. 26) to "the Lord God the Almighty and the Lamb" (21:22). By identifying slain Lamb and God in this way, the Apocalypse offers one of the Newer Testament's highest christologies. But the identification of *slain Lamb* and God destabilizes imperial notions of power *and* Older Testament and Second Temple Jewish theological categories concerning divine might and majesty. If John perches Christ on high, he brings God down to bloodied earth. John rehearses and subverts *both* contemporary politics and theology. His parodies accept the structural logic of the religio-political world he inherits, only to turn that world inside out.

Two passages in particular invert both political and theological notions of power and majesty—Rev. 6:12-17 and 19:11-21. The former does so more straightforwardly, the latter more subtly and parodically.

With the opening of the sixth seal (6:12-17), the Apocalypse modulates into burlesque. At first blush, the episode is a straightforward application of an Older Testament trope of the day of wrath/day of the Lord, depicting Yahweh's judgment as the advent of the day of punishment for sin (6:17; Zeph. 1:14-15; Jer. 30:7; Joel 1:15; 2:1-2, 11, 31; Mal. 4:5). The day of wrath comes to "the kings of the earth and the great men and the generals and the rich and the strong, and everyone, slave and free." The categorization expresses imperial hierarchy.[64] The kings and great men hide in caves and urge the mountains to fall on them to save them from "the face of him who is seated on the throne." John here replays the Older Testament military metaphor of conquering Yahweh. Their cry echoes the cry of despair of God's enemies in Hosea 10:8b, before the coming of the Lord. But when we witness them hiding, additionally, from "the wrath of the Lamb," the motif moves from an emphasis on Yahweh's righteous judgment of sin toward the parodic incongruity of mighty generals fleeing in terror from a Lamb. The introduction of this unlikely character to an otherwise traditional metaphor of a conquering God draws both the Older Testament motif and the response of the judged into an ironical play of incongruity that the Apocalypse nowhere attempts to resolve. John is not, after all, the systematic theologian attempting to harmonize notions of divine omnipotence with weakness, but, as we shall see below, to insist upon the power of faithful testimony (hence 6:9). His is a parody of power and might.

At 19:11-21, in the episode of the conqueror on the white horse, John develops a more formally military metaphor to describe divine victory over enemies. Again, he deploys both Older Testament and Roman imperial categories to describe the victory of Jesus. The passage draws on earlier descriptions of Jesus, now portraying him in a more integrated way as a warrior on a white horse going forth to battle the beast.[65] The image is consistent with Older Testament formulations of Yahweh as divine warrior.[66] Jesus, like the warring Yahweh/Israel of the Older Testament, vanquishes his enemies, assured of victory because of the rightness of his cause against the beast and against his idolatrous followers

(19:20-21). Further, the dramatic depiction of the conquering rider echoes the earlier reference (17:14) to the Lamb warring against the beast and his allies. John wants us to remember the warrior-Lamb acclaimed in 5:12 and depicted in battle at 6:12-17. He indicates this further by the way his list of enemies in 19:18 echoes that of 6:15.[67]

At this point the image grows unstable. On the one hand, John heavily inscribes the rhetorical tropes associated with divine holy war in the Apocalypse. These figures, so offensive to Western first-world sensibilities, must be interpreted in their rhetorical program. Elisabeth Schüssler Fiorenza's discussion of Revelation's gendered imagery demonstrates the importance of attention to the rhetorical framework of ancient texts. Resisting some interpreters' literal readings of John's gendered heroes and villains, she insists on attention to "a critical rhetorical multisystemic interpretation of that language in terms of socio-political and cultural-linguistic systems of domination."[68] John's language of war requires the same "critical rhetorical multisystemic interpretation."

Just as the Apocalypse's motif of the slain Lamb does not describe a literal animal, so the references to war and battle do not describe literal skirmishes. They belong to a rhetorical program inherited both from the Older Testament tradition of divine intolerance of idolatry and Yahweh's election and protection of Israel, and are typical of their apocalyptic genre. In particular, John wants his audience to configure itself as Israel being rescued by Yahweh from exile (18:4; see Isa. 48:20; 52:11; Jer. 50:8; 51:6, 9, 45), or as God's people witnessing the punishment of Egypt through plagues on account of idolatry (Rev. 11:4-6; 12:14; 16:1-21). This is John's "contact zone" with Hebrew Bible tradition.

If, on the one hand, John replays the cultural-linguistic code of domination, on the other hand he subverts it. He takes a reigning sociopolitical system that defines his daily existence and that of his audience and then teases it out of shape. The metaphor of a Lamb conquering a Beast is incongruous, shifting the Older Testament tradition of holy war in a new direction. At 19:13, the image of warring Yahweh is wholly inverted. The image of the rider's robe dipped in blood begs the question, with whose blood is it spattered?

Some exegetes, invoking Older Testament divine-warrior imagery, argue that John is drawing on Isa. 63:1-3, and that the blood belongs to the Lamb's enemies.[69] In Isaiah 63, the garments of Yahweh are red from the blood of his enemies, stained from the winepress of his wrath. Earlier, in Rev. 14:19-20, John also alludes to the Isaiah 63 image. So John must have this passage in mind when, shortly after the reference to the blood-stained robe, he goes on to refer to "the winepress of the fury of the wrath of God the Almighty" (19:15). The majority of the Palestinian Targums develop the metaphor similarly, using it to develop profiles of the coming Messiah.

John, however, is not merely replaying an Older Testament passage. He repeats, but with critical difference. That his is more probably an ironic, parodic repetition of the Older Testament theme is indicated by the foreshadowing passage, 17:14. The Lamb here conquers, but in Revelation he always does so as slain Lamb. And where there is reference in the Apocalypse to having garments covered in blood, it is always with the Lamb's blood. Similarly, John links the metaphor of fine linen—white and pure clothing of the army following the warrior in 19:14—to the blood of the Lamb (Rev. 7:13-14; 22:14; see 3:4-5, 18; 19:8). Finally, he connects conquering with the blood of the Lamb (12:11). All of this makes it probable that the blood covering the warrior's robe in 19:14 is the Lamb's blood. John thus destabilizes the Older Testament profile of a conquering divinity by insisting that, by the Lamb's own suffering, he vanquishes his enemies.

The further reference to the two-edged sword, by means of which God's enemies are slain, represents another inversion. Again, the metaphor belongs to the conquering-Yahweh portrait,[70] and, like Isaiah 63, found its way into messianic expectation (*Wis.* 18:15–16; *Pss. Sol.* 17:24; 4Q161; *4 Ezra* 13:10-11). The *Lamb's* sword, however, is his word of faithful testimony, a testimony that leads to death. Again, in Rev. 12:11, with reference to John's community, the dragon is conquered "by the word of their testimony." John repeatedly uses the term "testimony" (*martyria* and its cognates) to designate the faithfulness of Jesus (1:2, 5, 9; 3:14; 12:17; 19:10), and it has been rightly described as the most prominent motif of Revelation's Christology.[71]

Faithful testimony in Revelation involves testimony unto death, a form of testimony that conquers God's enemies. John dramatizes this in the story of the "two witnesses" of 11:3-12. Here John brings a martyr-vindication/exaltation motif together with a vision of destruction. As William Klassen has argued, John's wedding of holy-war language with testimony is shared in Maccabean and Qumran texts.[72] Jewish parallels show that Revelation shares a notion of holy war waged not with physical weapons, but by faithful testimony.[73] But the Apocalypse does not contain Maccabean and Qumran notions of atoning suffering for the sins of the impure.[74] Even the Apocalypse's picture of robes washed in the Lamb's blood belongs more to the language of conquest and victory through imitation of the cruciform Jesus' faithful testimony than it does to atoning sacrifice (Rev. 7:10, 14; 14:5; 19:14). Revelation uniquely replays a violent Older Testament or more apocalyptic messianic motif of conquering divine warrior by inverting it with its references to the blood of the suffering Lamb and the sword of Jesus' faithful testimony to death. Through ironic inversion and parody (conquering through defeat; slaying through testifying/dying), John turns the theological world he inherited inside out and initiates the most destabilizing of apocalyptic applications.

In addition to inverting theological notions of power and force inherited from Judaism, Revelation overturns imperial notions of military power and triumph. The white horse,[75] the crowned rider,[76] the inscription on the rider's thigh,[77] as well as the cavalcade of horses that follow him[78] and possibly the red robe all mirror imperial notions of power.[79] In particular, they echo iconography associated with Roman military triumph and/or imperial *adventus*, as well as pictures used to depict an emperor's apotheosis.[80] But again, John's white rider is a Lamb in emperor's clothing, and the former's aping of imperial power in this way well expresses the "transcendental buffoonery" of irony and parody. The white rider's many crowns parody those of the dragon (12:3). His violence replays that of the whore, the beast, and their allies (11:7; 12:17; 13:15; 17:6, 13), but with the inversion that not by slaying others, but by rather by being slain, do the Lamb and his white-robed followers triumph (Rev. 7:10, 14; 11:7, 11-13; 12:5, 7-11; 14:2-5). The white rider/slain Lamb as imperial *triumphator* continues the rhetorical playfulness with imperial ideology that the throne-room visions initiated, and continues to co-opt notions of domination and might to subvert them. The politics of John's parody unsettles the dominant colonizing discourse of empire. In his contact zone, the white rider/slain Lamb becomes emperor, but along the way toward his triumph he decrowns all prevailing notions of imperial might and military power.

In Rev. 6:12-17 and 19:11-21, John continues the parodying rhetorical program of the Lamb begun in chapter 5. These episodes take up traditional notions of divine power and vengeance, as well as contemporary political ideology, replay, and then subvert them. There is no denying that much in the Apocalypse expresses more traditional apocalyptic motifs. Nevertheless, however much John accepted those traditional conceptions, his own rhetorical program subverts them. John sweeps more traditional notions of divine vengeance and apocalyptic judgment into his parodic program, and so achieves a transformation of them that destabilizes even his own most straightforward visions of judgment and bliss.

The question remains whether John finally resolves the ironies these parodying visions initiate, whether he brings his ironies to a close, and whether he settles on a version of empire more ironical than the one he replaces, but nevertheless a place where an emperor can feel at home. There is also a question whether his Apocalypse leaves us unsettled by his destabilizing ironies, reaching for something secure to hold on to as he subverts prevailing notions of might and power, honor and prestige, victory and success, and so leaves the world turned inside out. Do the Apocalypse's parodies resolve into an allegorical replacement of one empire by another (thus, Royalty), or does Revelation refuse resolution and subvert even its own utopian vision?

A FOOL'S PARADISE

The last chapter showed that, at Revelation's conclusion, characters begin appearing who should not be showing up (21:24-26; 22:15). No one can say, given their apocalyptic history (Rev. 19:17-20; 20:7-10, 13; 21:8), where those kings and nations come from, or those impure dogs hanging about Jerusalem's gates. Their reintroduction destabilizes John's otherwise stable apocalyptic world. No wonder: once irony and parody surface, instability is never far behind. Wayne Booth distinguishes between stable and unstable ironies. Stable ironies are easily identifiable, with a clearly marked beginning and ending. Unstable ironies have indeterminate boundaries; their presence remains uncertain. In unstable irony, Booth argues, an author "refuses to declare himself . . . for *any* stable proposition, even the opposite of whatever proposition his irony vigorously denies. The only sure affirmation is that negation that begins all ironic play: '*this* affirmation must be rejected.'"[81] As we have seen, John's parodies in the contact zone of imperial Roman imagery result in ironies that deconstruct *both* politics and hallowed Older Testament notions of God's might. On this reading it is no longer clear where parody stops and straightforward description of theological beliefs and hopes begins. This is also the case in John's depictions of the new heaven and earth, where once again destabilizing ironies begin to rock what appear to be, or at least traditionally have been interpreted to mean, the most stable of theological expectations. John's final vision, like those we have been considering, reveals the Apocalypse situated precariously amid unstable ironies.

John's well-documented use of Older Testament and Second Temple motifs to represent the New Jerusalem (20:1—22:5) needs no rehearsal.[82] Less recognized is the degree to which his Jerusalem resembles Greco-Roman civic ideals and their philosophical underpinnings. In fact, many scholarly discussions ignore the politics of John's final vision altogether, arguing that Revelation's depiction of the heavenly Jerusalem is intended allegorically as a celebration of God's faithful people.[83] An overly swift allegorical translation, however, ignores the way John's vision of the heavenly Jerusalem plays within the contact zone of Greco-Roman utopian politics and imagery and results in an unstable ironical exposure of empire.

John's vision of the heavenly Jerusalem, spiritual as it undoubtedly was, nevertheless adopted the very down-to-earth terms of contemporary political ideals.[84] His careful contrasting of Jerusalem (21:1—22:5) with Babylon (17:1—18:24) shows him staying within the contact zone of civic imperial space. He moves beyond contrast and comparison, driving home the point that the heavenly Jerusalem is everything Babylon is *not*. His vision "is a specific protest against the tears and the sufferings of the oppressed, the cries and griefs of those who have been tortured and killed, caused by the rule of Rome."[85]

He signals his desire to compare the two cities by furnishing them with identical introductions (Rev. 17:1, 3; 21:9, 10). Squared-off characteristics follow. The whore Babylon clothes herself in Orientalizing luxury to seduce her paramours (17:4); Jerusalem, a chaste bride, is adorned and bejeweled for her husband (21:3, 9-11, 19). The whore Babylon makes the saints suffer (17:6); Jerusalem is a city of healing for the nations, where there is no more suffering (21:2; 22:2). The kings of the earth gather to war against Babylon (17:16), and traders mourn the loss of their commerce with her (18:9-19); the kings of the earth bring their "glory and honor" into Jerusalem's gates and so show their allegiance to the heavenly city (21:24, 26). Babylon herself is impure and gathers fornicators (later her murderers) about her (17:2, 4, 5, 16); those barred from entering Jerusalem include murderers, fornicators, and idolaters (21:8; 22:15). Babylon the "great/mighty city" (18:9, 16, 18, 19, 21) is outsized by giant Jerusalem (21:15-17). After Babylon's destruction, the city lies in darkness (18:23); night never falls in Jerusalem (21:23, 25; 22:5). The empty city Babylon, bereft of all sounds of weddings (18:23), contrasts with heavenly Jerusalem descending in wedding celebration (21:2, 9). In sum, John's depiction of Jerusalem resketches Babylon, but as a reversed image.

While these representations undoubtedly signify more than urban realities, John nevertheless constructs them from contemporary political ideology. Is the contrast, though, strictly one of type and anti-type, as Robert Royalty proposes? Is heavenly Jerusalem a Babylon with cleaner streets and safer neighborhoods? The rehearsal/reversal of parody makes the new heaven and earth of John's final vision unstable. If heavenly Jerusalem's streets are paved in gold, they also drip with irony. The political peace of heavenly Jerusalem, the Pax Jerusalem, comes not through the might of imperial terror, but through the suffering of the Lamb and those who bear his witness in suffering and endurance.

Let us look more closely at John's parodic reversal of the Roman imperial peace and see if there are limits to John's irony. John's vision of the heavenly Jerusalem both replays Jewish utopian ideals associated with Israel's fortunes and repeats pagan utopian notions as well. While Greco-Roman utopias are usually idyllic natural places, in one instance, that of Lucian's *Vera historia* (mid–second century c.e.), it includes a city. In a parody of utopian ideals, Lucian, newly arrived on the Island of the Blessed, comes to the city where the Blessed Ones live.

> The city itself is all of gold and the wall around it of emerald. It has seven gates, all of single planks of cinnamon. The foundations of the city and ground within its wall are ivory. There are temples of all the gods, built of beryl, and in them great monolithic altars of amethyst, on which they make their great burnt-offerings. Around the city runs a river of the finest myrrh, a hundred royal cubits wide and five deep, so that one can swim in it comfortably. For baths they have large houses of glass,

warmed by burning cinnamon; instead of water is hot dew in
the tubs. . . . Nobody grows old, but stays the same age as on
coming there. Again, it is neither night amongst them nor yet
very bright day, but the light which is on the country is like the
gray morning toward dawn, when the sun has not yet risen. . . .
The grape-vines yield twelve vintages a year, bearing every
month; the pomegranates, apples and other fruit-trees were said
to bear thirteen times a year.[86]

This quotation bears such a striking resemblance to John's vision of
heavenly Jerusalem (jewels, river, gates, fruit trees) that a later Christian
scholiast wondered if Lucian was copying from the Apocalypse.[87] Perhaps it was John doing the cribbing. The first step in parody is rehearsal.

Lucian capitalizes on ancient urban ideals. Even if daily reality did
not match with ideological imagination, dominant philosophical, religious, and political ideology idealized the ancient city as embodying law
and order, freedom, beauty, and moral purity—in other words, the best
of a culture believed to have been divinely bestowed.[88] Ancient philosophers were agreed that the hallmark of the ideal city was moral beauty;
the physical beauty of such states symbolized the well-ordered ethical
lives of their citizens.[89]

Lucian's beautiful utopia mirrors the good lives of its inhabitants. In
his speech to the citizens either of Alexandria or Rhodes, Dio Chrysostom praises them by saying that their moral virtues reflect the fairness of
their city.[90] The city symbolized for philosophers the best of humankind.
According to Aristotle, humans are "animals that are by nature (*physei*)
political," and so the city represents an ideal, divinely prescribed institution.[91] Civic government, more expressly monarchy, expresses Zeus's
governance over all humans.[92] Stoic cosmopolitanism was a natural
corollary of the idea of a single divine law governing all people, expressing itself in similarly organized city-states. For the Stoics Zeno and
Chryssipus, the banding together of people in ordered urban living
expresses the divine ordering of the cosmos in which all people are "one
community and one polity . . . and have a common life."[93]

Such ideals could be powerfully legitimating of imperial ambition.
Alexander the Great's spreading of Hellenistic culture through the foundation of city-states or the establishment of governing structures modeled on Greek cities could be justified politically as the extension of a

kind of divinely ordained natural civic law. Plutarch cites Alexander's empire as the expression of Zeno's stoic ideal. "It was Alexander who gave effect to the idea," he says. But in what follows, his most glowing report of empire, Plutarch finds it necessary to massage the facts to fit the political ideology. Alexander "conquered through force of arms, and he brought together into one body all people everywhere, uniting and mixing in one great loving-cup (*en kratēsi philotēsiō*), as it were, people's lives, their characters, their marriages, their very habits of life" (329C–D; revised trans. Frank Cole Babbit [LCL]). The conquered were brought into "one great loving-cup" through force?

Roman political philosophers and poets such as Cicero and Horace similarly celebrated the Roman republic as a divinely constituted urban reality.[94] Cicero was deeply suspicious of grand ideologies that promised to bring all of humankind into a divinely ordained political unity.[95] But those sympathetic to imperial notions could justify the spread of empire by claiming they were only establishing a divinely willed political-religious order. By representing himself as restorer of the republic, saving Rome from civil war and chaos, Augustus was able to bring imperial dynastic ambitions under the umbrella of traditional civic philosophies.[96] That civic-imperial ideology is celebrated in some of the most famous lines of Virgil's *Aeneid:* "O Roman, to rule the nations with thy sway—these shall be thy arts—to crown Peace with Law, to spare the humbled, and to tame in war the proud" (6:847–53; H. Rushton Fairclough [LCL]).[97] Further, successive emperors' claims to divine sonship, both as successors to the divinized Julius and as ancestors of Aeneas (who was grandchild of Jupiter through his mother Aphrodite), allowed for a renewed political philosophy wedding traditional political thinking concerning the divine ordering of the city-state with imperial ideals. Jupiter's ordering of chaos was erected over Rome and therefore the civilized world. Thus emperors continued the political program initiated under Alexander, and invoked the same Jovian justification for it.[98]

Thus, when the Stoic philosopher Epictetus portrayed the universe as a "single city" (*mia polis; Diss.* 3.24.10), he was reflecting the political philosophical ideas of his Stoic ancestors; he was also expressing an imperial ideology. And when Dio Chrysostom celebrated Trajan as modeled after Jupiter's beneficent rule of all people (*Or.* 1.65), he was describing the imperial justification for bringing far-lying city-states under the banner of single rule. The empire is the divinely ordered city of Rome writ large.

This is the urban ideological backdrop to John's vision of the heavenly Jerusalem. To even the least literate of Revelation's Greek audience, the political side of his depiction of the heavenly Jerusalem must have been obvious. The representation of Rome as Babylon, a luxuriating Oriental tyrant, and her political order dissolving into civil war following misbegotten alliances with kings (17:13, 16) is a thinly veiled description of Rome's unofficial, bellicose past, and continues the parody described earlier of "Jupiter" as "beast."

By the time John turns, in chapter 21, to depict Jerusalem as everything Babylon is not, he has prepared his audience to listen for political caricature. His portrait of life in the heavenly Jerusalem is immediately recognizable as a rehearsal of well-known imperial claims. The heavenly Jerusalem is a city any earthly Jupiter would be proud of. It offers a vision of a divinely established order in which those erstwhile warring kings of the earth (21:24) bring their glory and honor into a city gleaming with jewels and gold (21:18-21), with city gates forever opened (21:25) because of an abiding and eternal peace. Its walls and foundations, built of the same jewels paraded by Babylon and merchandised by her profiteering tradespeople, here express not greed but the beauty (read moral purity, hence 21:27; 22:15) of a divinely established political order. Possibly John's reference to the city as foursquare (21:16) replays the Roman tradition of Romulus having founded *Roma quadrata*.[99]

In a way always aspired to but never achieved by Greco-Roman city-states, Jerusalem brings city and country together; its walls enclose a green space, the Garden of Eden (22:1-2).[100] Its main street is not a forum lined by temples and civic monuments. It is the river of life. And absent from the city is any temple, "for its temple is the Lord God the Almighty and the Lamb." Even if listeners had never heard of Virgil's famous fourth *Eclogue* celebrating the idyllic harmony of the Augustan political order ("But for thee, child, shall the earth untilled pour forth, as her first pretty gifts, straggling ivy with foxglove everywhere, and the Egyptian bean with the smiling acanthus. . . . The serpent, too, shall perish, and the false poison-plant shall perish; Assyrian spice shall spring up on every soil" [ll. 18–20, 24–25]), John's garden city would have struck a resonating political chord, accustomed as Greek culture was to conceiving utopias as idyllic.[101]

What we find, then, in John's climactic vision is something like Lucian's utopia, or at least a picture of heaven that would have been recognizable as a pagan's ideal state. Yet John's vision differs in a way that challenges the most cherished ideals of imperial politics and their Greco-Roman philosophical justifications. His Jerusalem is part of a subversive counterpolitics. Playing on the civic loyalties of his ancient civic listeners, John in his final vision urges an urban audience already used to fierce interurban competition for imperial favor to redirect their allegiance away from the religio-socio-political order of Rome and its enterprising elites toward the Lamb.[102] For if at the heart of the Roman imperial order is a religious claim that legitimates rule by military might and domination (Virgil's "tame in war the proud"), at the center of John's heavenly Jerusalem is the slain Lamb (21:22, 23; 22:1, 3), the victim of such taming might. John's counter-politics critiques the politics of violence and cruelty. Throughout the Apocalypse, John foregrounds the Lamb, and so cross-examines all forms of violence, including forms issuing forth from the throne room of God. John rehearses an Older Testament and Roman imperial discourse to celebrate his Jerusalem, but he subverts that discourse by placing at its center this unlikely hero.

The stable political order envisioned by the heavenly Jerusalem does not come through a military commander bringing the forces of chaos to heel through military might, but by the faithful testimony of Jesus of Nazareth, the slain Lamb. The Book of Revelation entertains its listeners with many wars and battles, but military victory in the Apocalypse always returns to the death of the Lamb. His defeat is what delivers victory and thereby contests what we might mean when we speak of winners and losers. The Apocalypse does not build heavenly Jerusalem on the foundation of glorious military might, but on a glorious defeat, both of the Lamb and of those witnesses faithful unto death (21:14; see also 3:12). John's Revelation ends by keeping the promise that "Jesus Christ is the faithful witness, the firstborn of the dead, and the ruler of kings on earth" (1:5). But it does so through an ironizing parody of the politics of domination. It inscribes a deeply destabilizing irony into notions of power and might dominant among John's contemporaries.

The "rhetorical situation" standing behind the Apocalypse was probably a dispute triggered by Christians willing to participate in pagan civic festivities in order to preserve their economic livelihood. John's ironies destabilized his listeners' world by demanding they pay attention to the basis of the economic goods they pursued so enthusiastically, and by dressing up his prophetic competition as the beast's minions. His listeners were treated to an ending that turned their world inside out, exposing the politics of imperial domination, and inviting them to walk along a more costly way.

The rhetoric cast *in front of the text* is more universally destabilizing. John makes the unlikely figure of a slain Lamb, the cruciform, the focus of language of imperial might, the wielder of the sword against tyrants, and the center of a utopian political vision. By developing a sustained unstable irony John challenges any straightforward notion of what it means to be powerful, to fight, and to build the city of God. Finally, he even destabilizes his own Apocalypse, by bringing the nations who once warred against the Lamb into Jerusalem's city gates (21:24), and by planting a tree there for "the healing of the nations" (22:2).

This is a juxtaposition John nowhere seeks to resolve, just one more in a series that we have encountered both in this and in previous chapters. His is an irony "all the way down"—an irony he never concludes in a manifesto or blueprint for achieving a utopian order. The Apocalypse's ending (Rev. 22:8ff.), we remember, is no ending at all. John at the conclusion of his Apocalypse rather returns his listeners to their present, but with the sounds of costly testimony ringing in their ears. Revelation wagers that an old world is ended and a new one begun in testifying to and emulating the cruciform Jesus. To borrow a phrase from Bertram Stubenrauch, the Apocalypse offers "endtime instead of the destruction of the world."[103] It uses narrative time to turn the world inside out. It retells the world in order to subvert it with new ways of seeing and behaving.

John's Apocalypse brings a world to an end. But it is not so clear, after the dust of the promised new heaven and earth have settled, how all the things it promises can exist. It is not clear how things are going to turn out in a narrative world in which unsavory characters show up again (22:15), hanging around Jerusalem's unlocked doors (21:25)—this time *after* death and Hades have been destroyed (Rev. 20:13-14)—safe from the threat of disposal (contrary to 21:8). His vision leaves us with instability on all sides, save this—the promise of life through faithful testimony to the slain Lamb, and the power that conquers through dying. The Apocalypse asks us to believe, with Emmanuel Lévinas, that "Living dangerously is not despair, but the positive generosity of Uncertainty."[104] Revelation's promised utopia is a fool's paradise.

7

Remembering Apocalypse

The little narrative remains the quintessential form of
imaginative invention.

> —Jean-François Lyotard,
> *The Postmodern Condition: A Report on Knowledge*

In 1972, John Howard Yoder concluded *The Politics of Jesus* with
these words:

Perhaps Christians in our age are being made ready for a new
awareness of the continuing relevance of the message of the
Apocalypse. There is a widespread recognition that Western
society is moving toward the collapse of the mentality that has
been identified with Christendom. Christians must recognize
that they are a minority globally and locally in the midst of the
followers of non-Christian and post-Christian faiths. Perhaps
this will prepare us to see how inappropriate and preposterous
was the prevailing assumption, from the time of Constantine
until yesterday, that the fundamental responsibility of the church
for society is to manage it.

And might it be, if we could be freed from the compulsiveness of the vision of ourselves as the guardians of history, that
we could receive again the gift of being able to see ourselves as
participants in the loving nature of God as revealed in Christ?
Perhaps the songs of the earliest church might restore this to us

if the apostolic argument cannot. A church once freed from compulsiveness and from the urge to manage the world might then find ways and words to suggest as well to men outside her bounds the invitation to a servant stance in society.[1]

For Yoder, "the continuing relevance of the message of the Apocalypse" is its call to the church to interrupt society's favorite ways of doing business with a subversive public witness—what I have been calling "costly testimony." Yoder's Mennonite heritage made him justifiably distrustful of Christian strategies for the transformation of society by means of allegiance with the state. Such cooperation had resulted historically in the persecution of Anabaptists by the Christian establishment—one in a series of botched attempts "to build Jerusalem in this our green and pleasant land" (William Blake). More important for Yoder, however, is that such alliances result in what Jacques Ellul, in a similar argument, named the "political perversion" of Christian faith—the subversion of Christianity by exchanging the potent metaphors and narratives of a faith community for the overpowering, universal secular metaphors and narratives of the Enlightenment and the liberal state.[2] Both Yoder and Ellul insisted instead on Christian witness whose business was *not* to care for or transform the secular, but to trouble it by urging faithful Christians to live out public lives formed by, steeped in, and nurtured by the potent religious stories of the biblical witness.

To borrow a category from postmodern biblical exegesis, Yoder and Ellul called for the decolonization of Christendom. Theirs was, *in fine,* an appeal to Christian counterpolitics, and a recovery of reading biblical texts that destabilized interpretations—interpretations that preserved a socioeconomic status quo, making contemporary Christian communities largely uncritical or, worse, enthusiastic beneficiaries of a first-world military-industrial social order. For Yoder, the Apocalypse outlined a counterpolitics whose time had come.

The argument of the preceding chapter indicates how correct Yoder was to look to Revelation for the content of that counterimperial vision. Rehearsing in order to reverse, enthroning so as to decrown, setting up only to knock down, Revelation unmasks the masquerade of tyrannical political power and urges its hearers to walk a more costly way.

It urges through hearing. Yoder hears in "the songs of the earliest church" the troubling public witness that the church may yet recover.

The songs to which he refers are, of course, from Revelation, recording praise to the crucified Lamb of God—the parodically doubling emperor who goes forth to conquer by being conquered. In the mainstream church, the possibility of hearing the parody of the Apocalypse is eliminated in the Revised Common Lectionary's expurgation of John's Revelation. Nevertheless, the parody slips in through the mainstream church's backdoor, surviving in its hymnody, and thereby remains a potent source of apocalypse-styled public witness steeped in the irony of God's self-revelation in the crucified victim of imperial power and might. In its hymnody, perhaps now in tongues strange to interpret, the church discovers itself read by the Apocalypse's witness. It proclaims itself as that singing, worshiping collection of dispersed peoples on whose beauty God looks with longing and joy. It overhears itself praising, beseeching, lamenting, hoping in the peculiar often strained metaphor of theological poetry. Apocalypse survives in the church's music, speaking into being a community of troubling public witness.

Or at least it may do so still. Perhaps the first-world church, once it gives up its palliative care of the Social Gospel mission to transform society, may yet recover the power of parody and discover the potency of subversive speech. An earlier chapter explored the sense of the *unheimlich* arising from overhearing the strained syntax of poorly spoken English and incorrect German. My grandmother found pleasure in exotic grammar, speaking the world into being on her terms rather than those of the world around her. Greek Canadian literary critic Smaro Kamboureli discovers in such border language the rich seedbed of irony when she writes, "My immigrant culture affords me the (perverse?) pleasure of a doubled view. My language is the window that looks onto my home and into my homelessness."[3]

My grandmother's perverse pleasure of a doubled view found expression in words, endings, and fragments of speech migrating from one language to another, sentences and words begun in English, ended in German, and vice versa. Her language was a "house of being," a final refuge no one could steal.[4] Certainly, her language preserved difference; it addressed the world around her and created social identity on her own terms, not those of the dominant culture pressuring her to assimilate. She nursed an idiosyncratic grammar—playing ironically in a contact zone of dominant culture, purposely destabilizing, even mocking, received English grammar through unorthodox syntax and nonsense words.

As a child, overhearing the world spoken into existence on the most incorrect of grammatical terms was to be spoken into a world imitated and overturned, revered and criticized, embraced and kept at arm's length. Whatever the motivation, the doubled view arising from strained syntax and consciousness of cultural imitation was perversely pleasurable, destabilizing the firmest of cultural constructs, even those of our own much-touted German identity. We spoke and heard ourselves into being.

As retrospective apocalyptic narrative couched in the most ironic of theological and political terms, does not the Apocalypse similarly offer a window to look onto the Christian home and onto the homelessness of contemporary secular culture? It too speaks into existence a richly mixed house of being for faithful Christians to inhabit and respeak the world.

Richard Rorty, in a book on irony and public life, describes the social power of the ironist's doubled view. Those, he argues, seeking to find reasons to be kinder, less cruel, more courageous, less cowardly human beings need to surround themselves with other like-minded people and to tell each other the stories to convince themselves that these are the best ways to be human. They need to hear themselves spoken into being. For Rorty the doubled view of irony arises from the observation that there are often as many compelling reasons to be cruel as to be kind, to be selfish as to be giving, to be exploiters of the earth as to be its stewards. A sense of the ironic is what you get in the absence of extralinguistic courts of appeal—uncontestable sources of moral authority written on the human heart within or the starry heaven above.

Rorty is convinced that such extralinguistic moorings do not exist for the ethical life. There are no "final vocabularies"—final appeals to God, the Good, Beauty, Truth, and so on—but the vocabularies we settle on in our own storying of the world around us. What Rorty calls "liberal ironists" live in society *as though* their vocabularies were more final than the plurality of vocabularies furnished to support moral decision making around them. But in the absence of any extralinguistic appeal—a "knock 'em down" final vocabulary—they know theirs is not the only one.

One may wish to argue with this relativism. It remains a fact, however, that whatever the sources of our moral persuasion, they come to us mediated by language; if language is not the irreducible bedrock on which our moral lives are built, without it there could be no ethical house of being. Thus thrown into language as we are, being equally compelled in the manifold subcultures in which we find ourselves to be more cruel and more kind, we only have each other to convince ourselves to be one or the other. So it is that

> the person who has doubts about his own final vocabulary, his own moral identity, and perhaps his own sanity—*desperately needs to talk to other people, needs this with the same urgency as people need to make love, he needs to do so because only conversation enables him to handle these doubts, to keep himself together, to keep his web of beliefs and desires coherent enough to enable him to act.*[5]

Rorty later argues for the importance of a socially shared *focus imaginarius*, a focus for the imagination, in winning allegiance to competing goods in a pluralistic society.[6]

The emphasis the Apocalypse places on the power of testimony invites us to extend Rorty's argument by insisting that *foci imaginarii* need *voces imaginariae:* voices to sound the imagination. We humans need voices to speak and ears to listen ourselves into shared story, to compel ourselves into becoming kinder, more gentle, and loving creatures. We need to "make noise" and to throw dissonant voices into the public square of conversations at a time when some stories, especially harmful ones, threaten to drown out others and to make us more brutal human beings.

The decolonizing doubled view of the Book of Revelation, rehearsing empire so as to expose it, replaying exploitative tyranny to dethrone it, offers first-world Christian communities of faith precisely such a *focus imaginarius* articulated in the ironical praise of the crucified Jesus of Nazareth. Its preposterous hymning of a slain Lamb as the right object of imperial praise and ceremony furnishes listeners with the *voces imaginariae* to sound themselves into new possibilities of human existence. To speak and overhear oneself hymning this Lamb, when placed in the subversive counterimperial politics of John's prophetic witness, disenchants other persuasive stories competing for attention, stories urging people to mistreat one another and creation. To speak and overhear oneself praising the crucified Lamb of God is to find voices and ears to tell and hear (Rev. 2:7, 11, 17, 29; 3:6, 13, 22) the story of God's claim on us and our world.

The Apocalypse inspired Yoder to conceive of a church that gives up the management and transformation of society and that attends, instead, to public witness. Yoder's vision, like Rorty's, is a vision that champions irony—the irony of the cross. Yoder's irony is not born, however, from a wry acknowledgment that there are no final courts of appeal for grounding the moral life. His irony is born out of the Apocalypse's wager that the Christian grounding for such a life is found in God's siding with the faithful witness Jesus Christ, the victim of empire, the one who witnesses to God's rule even at the cost of his life. Let us call this "cruciform irony," a *focus imaginarius* expressing and calling forth a particular form of communal self-storying at the end of Christendom—indeed, exhorting the church to a renewed theatricality on the multiple and complicated stages of contemporary secular society.

Cruciform irony pays attention, first, to public performance and to the ways a subculture constructs itself through idiosyncratic speech and enacted roles. It recognizes that speech and theatricality take place in the contacts zones of contemporary culture, and in its idioms. The cruciform expresses what Dietrich Bonhoeffer called "the this-worldliness of Christianity."[7] That is, it calls for full immersion in secular life, a "deep this-worldliness" in the daily struggles and problems that beset us all, especially among the disenfranchised, whoever or wherever they may be. The cruciform seeks God not in an otherworldly flight from society, or journey within, but in the intercourse of daily life. Its God is not a philosophical or theological abstraction, but comes clothed in the highly evocative metaphors of a community's sacred texts. In Revelation, God is known in the narrative of the slain Lamb and in the performance of costly testimony in the life of the daily and the mundane. Such a Christianity invites us to conceive of time renewed with possibility in each human encounter. This is a "worldly Christianity."[8] It discovers in the story of the incarnation an insistence that, in daily society, God is fully present and the resurrected Jesus Christ is discovered. It thus rejects quietism, and discovers in costly testimony genuine political engagement.

Such a worldly Christianity cultivates ironical distance. If it discovers in its stories of the slain Lamb the mediation of time and social identity, it does not insist that its vocabulary is final, or ultimate. It nurtures a cultural position allowing it to look at its own small story as well as the larger stories to which citizens give their allegiance, with enough distance to allow self-critique. We might say, borrowing a motif from Dietrich

Bonhoeffer, that its irony arises from the conviction that all vocabularies, including its own, are "penultimate" (*Vorletzte*),[9] that no vocabulary or witness is final. Its vocabulary is always in a process of reform and revision as a result of its brushing up against the other vocabularies and witnesses constitutive of a pluralistic society. Christianity is an irony centered in the humility that "now we see in a mirror dimly" (1 Cor. 13:12). Nevertheless, it invites full commitment to its vision of human existence and creation, convinced that the slain Lamb reveals a life-affirming pattern of a "face-to-face" relationship grounded in the love of neighbor and of God. This irony witnesses to the world with the "(perverse?) pleasure of a doubled view," knowing that without final vocabularies the language of any subculture is a "window that looks onto my home and into my homelessness."

Cruciform irony is a paradoxically elevated perspective—the view of things from the cross of Jesus of Nazareth—in which those who live in praise of his witness and in obedience to his call have learned of the *basileia* of God's surprise. It is an irony cultivated by the Gospels' celebration of the resurrection of the crucified criminal as "a condition of affairs or events of a character opposite to what was, or might naturally be, expected; a contradictory outcome of events as if in mockery of the promise and fitness of things" (Oxford English Dictionary). It recognizes in the cross the enduring challenge to any culture or subculture that becomes too certain of its social privilege, whether it be that of political empires, a "Christian society," technological manipulation of human desire, or "the end of history" via democratic capitalism. Cruciform irony is an irony dedicated to costly testimony, to naming the Seth-Typhons of our age that offer the promise of a Jovian peace and make the world a desert, masking its idolatrous lies by ordering the world through threat and misbegotten desire.

In many parts of the world cruciform ironists are imprisoned and murdered. In societies where its proclamation is tolerated, its preachers work in their small gatherings to encourage costly testimony to the Lamb. They try to find the words to help listeners poke fun, unmask, reverse, challenge, and contest ways of seeing and interpreting the world that make for crueler neighbors. It makes use of culturally dominant *foci imaginarii* that urge us to be greedier, more idolatrous, more self-centered neighbors as contact zones to express the irony of the cross. Its preachers are duplicitous double-agents, immersed in the world but speaking a new world into existence with peculiarly accented tonalities and startling words of the cross and resurrection—enchanting *voces imaginariae*. They give their listeners ears to hear what costly testimony might sound like in their everyday lives. Their assembly halls are *Mundhäuser* (Luther)—houses of proclamation ringing out with the ironical proclamation of the Lamb who conquers, filled with news strange to the status quo's ways of doing business.[10] They trouble their listeners into trouble-making discipleship.

Cruciform ironists are content with the little story of God's little one from Nazareth and his fate. They have given up on controlling or writing the script for the metanarrative of secular culture. For they know that this has always led to the transformation of the church from *Mundhaus* into *Kaiserhof* (court of Caesar). They have given up on triumphalist attempts to Christianize the globe, on revolutionizing society through the application of Christian socialism or conservatism, on filling pews with ever more converts, on measuring the success of its witness by the size of its buildings and the strength of its offerings. They remain aloof from models promising church growth. Cruciform ironists are deeply suspicious of megachurch success stories. They know that the way of costly testimony is narrow, difficult, and small.

Cruciform irony does not hope for a new evangelical awakening. It does not pray for Christian revival. It suspects such hoped-for transformations as temptations to unbelief and faithlessness. Rather, it is confident that it already possesses all the growth, revival, and awakening it needs, certain that the proclamation of the gospel suffices to awaken trust in God, to revive hearers and to call them to life. Practically, cruciform ironists know how often in Christendom's history "awakenings" have led to the supplanting of the ironical power of the slain Lamb and to the supplanting of costly testimony to him with the power of Caesar's sword and the translation of the gospel into political organizations, moral orders, and institutional arrangements. Cruciform irony knows that in the *basileia* (kingdom, realm, dominion, commonweal) of God, as with mustard seeds, less is more.

As does Douglas John Hall, cruciform irony insists on the disestablishment of the church and warns followers of the Lamb when they speak of a "Christian society," or a transformation of contemporary culture through Christian values, of the danger of converting the slain Lamb into a pantocrator ruling alongside or through Caesar.[11] Cruciform ironists insist on nonconformity in practicing the nonconformity of the protagonist of its little story. Such irony celebrates that, to those oppressed and suffering injustice, the Book of Revelation is a comfort. But to those possessing wealth or accustomed to walking in the halls of power, the Apocalypse is an earthquake. Against such a backdrop, the cross is the revelation of imperial violence—whether the violence of an ancient Roman Empire or a contemporary empire. Amid the appeals to become ever more greedy and to hoard even more of the world's riches, cruciform irony is satisfied with the abundance that comes from loving God and one's neighbor as oneself.

With exiled Guatemalan poet and social activist Julia Esquivel, Christianity's little story finds us, at its ending, whether with the female witnesses before the Easter tomb (Mark 16:1-8), or standing before the Lamb's opened book of life (Rev. 20:12), "threatened with resurrection." The story proclaims that God's way is never a closed book, for the gates to the city are forever open. It proclaims that death does not have the last word, for the stone is rolled away, and that the future is always open to God's surprise and awaiting possibility. Christianity looks for the resurrected Jesus not in heaven after death, but in this world *before* the grave, "on the open road to Galilee" (Mark 16:7), known and recognized in the living out of God's commonweal on and for earth.[12] Its demands are therefore invitations.

> Join us in this vigil
> and you will know what it is to dream!
> Then you will know how marvellous it is
> to live threatened with Resurrection!
>
> To dream awake,
> to keep watch asleep,
> to live while dying,
> and to know ourselves already
> resurrected![13]

Cruciform irony affirms the contingencies of history and remains skeptical of grand appeals to the providential arrangements of history and time, to the nature and destiny of humankind, to recipes for utopian social reform. Instead it settles down to live out a little story of God's presence in the world, knowing that to do so is already to begin to make trouble. "Anyone," Emmanuel Lévinas writes, "who reveals himself as humble, on the side of the defeated, the poor, or the persecuted . . . is precisely not conforming to the social order. . . . To present oneself in this poverty of the exile is to interrupt the coherence of the universe. To pierce immanence without thereby taking one's place within it."[14] To pierce immanence is to contest and challenge the order of things—especially orders of domination, brutality, and terror practiced by a so-called godly state, legitimated by reference to an allegedly Christian God. It is to rupture and interrupt coherence and to live out a renewed ordering of the world on terms foreign to the final vocabularies of global security and prosperity that make slaves of us all. It is to pierce this violent world order without thereby taking one's place in it. This is cruciform irony.

On Good Friday they gather, near the Anglican Cathedral in downtown Vancouver, a monument from another age, nestled between high-rise apartment buildings, exclusive shops, and corporate centers of commerce. Just a few of them, never very many, but enough for passersby to notice the youngsters and seniors, the moms and dads, the singles and couples dressed for the march—some in suits and dresses as though for church, others casually. From all corners of the city they come, usually the same ones, but each year there are a few new faces. Lately TV cameras and newspaper reporters have been showing up. One or two curious ones stop to see what is going on; others, embarrassed, hurry by. One of the organizers calls the gathering to attention, welcomes them and explains the route. She and a couple of others pick up the heavy wooden cross constructed for the "crosswalk" and lead the group across the street to their first stop, the headquarters of a national bank. They pray for wisdom in the uses of the world's resources, for forgiveness for greed, for courage to speak up for those who pay for the beauty and majesty of the shining buildings in whose shadows they stand. Their route takes them to the Vancouver Stock Exchange, the city's courts, the jail, to trendy shopping streets—wherever decision and image makers gather. Along the way a few are singing, "Worthy, worthy, worthy is the Lamb." The notes rise, blending with the sounds of traffic and streets coming alive below. The sun reflects gold off the glass towering above. Steel shakes off the cold from the night and sparkles. As though these girders and glass reflected a Jerusalem. As though city walls were warming themselves with song.

Abbreviations

ABD	*Anchor Bible Dictionary. Edited by D. N. Freedman. 6 vols. New York, 1992*
ANF	*Ante-Nicene Fathers*
ANRW	*Aufstieg und Niedergang der römischen Welt: Geschichte und Kultur Roms im Spiegel der neueren Forschung.* Edited by H. Temporini and W. Haase. Berlin, 1972–
BETL	Bibliotheca ephemeridum theologicarum lovaniensium
BZNW	Beihefte zur Zeitschrift für die neutestamentliche Wissenschaft
CBQ	*Catholic Biblical Quarterly*
CNT	Commentaise du Nouveau Testament
ConBNT	Coniectanea neotestamentica
ET	English translation
FRLANT	Forschungen zur Religion und Literatur des Alten und Neuen Testaments
HDR	Harvard Dissertations in Religion
HNT	Handbuch zum Neuen Testament
HTR	*Harvard Theological Review*
ICC	International Critical Commentary
JBL	*Journal of Biblical Literature*
JSNT	*Journal for the Study of the New Testament*
JSNTSup	Journal for the Study of the New Testament: Supplement Series

LCL	Loeb Classical Library
NICNT	New International Commentary on the New Testament
NovTSup	Novum Testamentum Supplements
NTS	*New Testament Studies*
ÖTK	Ökumenischer Taschenbuch-Kommentar
PW	Pauly, A. F. *Paulys Realencyclopädie der classischen Altertumswissenschaft.* New edition G. Wissowa. 49 vols. Munich, 1980
SBM	Stuttgarter biblische Monographien
SC	Sources chrétiennes. Paris: Cerf, 1943–
SNTSMS	Society for New Testament Studies Monograph Series
TDNT	*Theological Dictionary of the New Testament.* Edited by G. Kittel and G. Friedrich. Translated by G. W. Bromiley. 10 vols. Grand Rapids, 1964–1976.
TTZ	*Trierer theologische Zeitschrift*
TWNT	*Theologische Wörterbuch zum Neuen Testament.* Edited by G. Kittel and G. Friedrich. Stuttgart, 1932–79
WA	*Weimarer Ausgabe.* Martin Luther. *Werke.* Kritische Versamtaufgabe. Weimar: Böhlau, 1883–
WUNT	Wissenschaftliche Untersuchungen zum Neuen Testament
ZBNT	Zürcher Bibelkommentar: Neues Testament
ZNW	*Zeitschrift für die neutestamentliche Wissenschaft und die Kunde der älteren Kirche*

[N.B.: Abbreviations for ancient sources follow *The Oxford Classical Dictionary,* second edition, ed. N. G. L. Hammon and H. H. Scullard (Oxford:Clarendon, 1970), ix–xxii.]

Notes

Preface

1. For studies that take up this promising avenue of investigation, see Philip A. Harland, *Claiming a Place in Polis and Empire: The Significance of Imperial Cults and Connections among Associations, Synagogues, and Christian Groups in Roman Asia* (c. 27 B.C.E.– 138 C.E.) Ph.D. dissertation, University of Toronto 1999 (Ann Arbor, Mich.: UMI, 1999); Steven J. Friesen, *Imperial Cults and the Apocalypse of John: Reading Revelation in the Ruins* (Oxford: Oxford University Press, 2001).

1. Apocalypse Troubles

1. See Bernard McGinn, *Visions of the End: Apocalyptic Traditions in the Middle Ages* (New York: Columbia University Press, 1979): the Crusades, 149–54; Savonarola, 277–83; Hussites and German apocalypticists, 259–69; Ernst Bloch, *Thomas Münzer als Theologe der Revolution* (Frankfurt am Main: Suhrkamp, 1998): Columbus, 284–85; and Catherine Keller, *Apocalypse Now and Then: A Feminist Guide to the End of the World* (Boston: Beacon, 1996), 151–80.

2. For historical Christian acceptance of and resistance to Revelation, see Gerhard Maier, *Die Johannesoffenbarung und die Kirche,* WUNT 25 (Tübingen: Mohr, 1981).

3. Luther's apocalyptic expectations were highly detailed. In the Roman Catholic rejection of reform, the military sack of Rome of 1527/28, and the Muslim invasion of Western Europe he saw signs of the last days. The Great Whore of Babylon (the Roman Catholic Church) would persecute the saints (the

Reformers), be defeated by erstwhile European allies (Rev. 17:6, 15-17), and trigger the Battle at Armageddon (Rev. 16:16)—the final Christian-Muslim showdown. See, for example, *WA* 7:47, 53, 152f., 417, 404f., 447, 590f., more fully discussed by Peter Martin, "Martin Luther und die Bilder zur Apokalypse," *Vistigia Bibliae: Jahrbuch des Deutschen Bibel-Archivs* 5 (1983): 129ff.; and Hans Ulrich Hofmann, "Luther und die Johannes-Apokalypse: Dargestellt im Rahmen der Auslegungsgeschichte des letzten Buches der Bibel und im Zusammenhang der theologischen Entwicklung des Reformators," *Beiträge zur Geschichte der biblischen Exegese* 24 (1982).

4.   *WA* 7:417-21.

5.   For a survey with further literature, see Eugen Weber, *Apocalypses: Prophecies, Cults, and Millennial Beliefs through the Ages* (Toronto: Random House, 1999).

6.   Linda Hutcheon, *A Poetics of Postmodernism: History, Theory, Fiction* (New York: Routledge, 1988).

7.   Trans. John P. Leavey, *Semeia* 23 (1982): 63–97.

8.   For surveys of the Apocalypse's influence and further literature, see Norman Cohn, *The Pursuit of the Millennium,* 2d ed. (Oxford and New York: Oxford University Press, 1970); Weber, *Apocalypses;* Ernst Bloch, *Prinzip der Hoffnung,* 5th ed. (Frankfurt am Main: Suhrkamp, 1998); ET=*The Principle of Hope,* trans. Melville Plaice et al. (Oxford: Basil Blackwell, 1986).

9.   Quoted by Hal Schuster, *The Unauthorized Guide to the X-Files: Conspiracies Probed, Secrets Revealed, Subterfuges Exposed, Plus! The FBI Infiltrated* (Rocklin, Calif.: Prima, 1997), 27.

10.   Thus Mark Kingwell, *Dreams of Millennium: Report from a Culture on the Brink* (Toronto: Viking, 1996), 270.

11.   Wes Howard-Brook and Anthony Gwyther, *Unveiling Empire: Reading Revelation Then and Now* (New York: Orbis, 1999), 19–39.

12.   Keller, *Apocalypse Now and Then*, 12.

13.   Stephen O'Leary, *Arguing the Apocalypse: A Theory of Millennial Rhetoric* (Oxford and New York: Oxford University Press, 1994), 86–89.

14.   Aside from the critical "letters" of chapters 2 and 3 and the war of chapter 12, the Revised Common Lectionary offers churchgoers selective protection from the characteristic elements of John's Apocalypse. In year A, Revelation appears only once (Rev. 7:9-17); in year B, twice (Rev. 21:1-6a and 1:4b-8). Year C prescribes six readings from the second to the seventh week of Easter (1:4-8; 5:11-14; 7:9-17; 21:1-6; 21:10 and 21:22—22:5; and 22:12-14, 16-17, 20-21). Notably, the last reading from chapter 22 expunges from the text all warning and admonition, including, ironically, the warning against adding to or taking away from Revelation's text (vv. 18-19).

15.   Ernest Becker, *The Denial of Death* (New York: Free Press, 1973).

16. Thus, for example, William Stringfellow, *Conscience and Obedience: The Politics of Romans 13 and Revelation 13 in Light of the Second Coming* (Waco, Tex.: Word, 1977); Daniel Berrigan, *Beside the Sea of Glass: The Song of the Lamb* (New York: Seabury, 1978); Walter Wink, *Naming the Powers* (Philadelphia: Fortress Press, 1984); Howard-Brook and Gwyther, *Unveiling Empire*.

17. David E. Aune, *Revelation,* Word Biblical Commentary (Dallas: Word, 1997). For a bibliography, see Robert L. Muse, ed., *The Book of Revelation: An Annotated Bibliography,* Books of the Bible 2, Garland Reference Library of the Humanities 1387 (New York: Garland, 1996); although it is 352 pages in length, its editor laments that time constraints permitted him only to be "somewhat comprehensive" (xi).

18. Aune, *Revelation,* cviii, cxix.

19. David L. Barr, *Tales of the End: A Narrative Commentary on the Book of Revelation* (Santa Rose, Calif.: Polebridge, 1998), 1.

20. Tina Pippin, *Apocalyptic Bodies: The Biblical End of the World in Text and Image* (New York: Routledge, 1999), 117.

21. Elisabeth Schüssler Fiorenza, *The Book of Revelation: Justice and Judgment,* 2d ed. (Philadelphia: Fortress Press, 1998), 218.

22. Alan Boesak, *Comfort and Protest: The Apocalypse from a South African Perspective* (Philadelphia: Westminster, 1987), 38.

23. Pablo Richard, *Apocalypse: A People's Commentary on the Book of Revleation* (New York: Orbis, 1995), 3.

24. Adela Yarbro Collins, *Crisis and Catharsis: The Power of the Apocalypse* (Philadelphia: Westminster, 1984), 156–57.

25. John G. Gager, *Kingdom and Community: The Social World of Early Christianity* (Englewood Cliffs, N.J.: Prentice-Hall, 1975), 51.

26. Leonard L. Thompson, *The Book of Revelation: Apocalypse and Empire* (New York: Oxford University Press, 1990), 197.

27. David A. DeSilva, "The Social Setting of the Revelation to John: Conflicts within, Fears Without," *Westminster Theological Journal* 54 (1992): 273–302, here 301.

28. Christopher Rowland, *Revelation* (London: Epworth, 1993), 135–36.

29. Ron Farmer, "Divine Power in the Apocalypse to John: Revelation 4–5 in Process Hermeneutic," *SBL Seminar Papers* 133 (1997): 85–100, here 97.

30. Richard Bauckham, *The Theology of the Book of Revelation* (Cambridge: Cambridge University Press, 1993), 149–50.

31. Stephen Moore, "The Beatific Vision as a Posing Exhibition: Revelation's Hypermasculine Deity," *JSNT* 60 (1995): 27–55, here 49.

32. Robert M. Royalty Jr., *The Streets of Heaven: The Ideology of Wealth in the Apocalypse of John* (Macon, Ga.: Mercer University Press, 1998), 246.

33. Philip F. Esler, *The First Christians in Their Social Worlds: Social-Sci-*

entific Approaches to New Testament Interpretation (New York: Routledge, 1994), 145, 146.

34. Bruce Malina, *On the Genre and Message of Revelation: Star Visions and Sky Journeys* (Peabody, Mass.: Hendrickson, 1995), 1, 2, 12, 19, 25, 266.

35. Fernando F. Segovia, "Cultural Studies and Contemporary Biblical Criticism: Ideological Criticism as a Mode of Discourse," in *Reading from This Place*, vol. 2: *Social Location and Biblical Interpretation in Global Perspective*, ed. Fernando F. Segovia and Mary Ann Tolbert (Minneapolis: Fortress Press, 1995), 1.

36. Pippin, *Apocalyptic Bodies*, 9.

37. Umberto Eco, *The Role of the Reader: Explorations in the Semiotics of Texts* (Bloomington: Indiana University Press, 1984), 49.

38. Of the growing literature on the genesis of autobiography in literary criticism and its development in biblical study, I cite only representative works, in which fuller biographies may be found: Ingrid Rosa Kitzberger, ed., *The Personal Voice in Biblical Interpretation* (New York: Routledge, 1999); Jeffrey L. Staley, *Reading with a Passion: Rhetoric, Autobiography, and the American West in the Gospel of John* (New York: Continuum, 1995); Janice Capel Anderson and Jeffrey L. Staley, eds., "Taking It Personally: Autobiographical Biblical Criticism," *Semeia* 72 (1995); Daniel Patte, *Ethics of Biblical Interpretation: A Reevaluation* (Louisville: Westminster John Knox, 1995). For autobiography and the Apocalypse, see T. M. S. Long, "A Real Reader Reading Revelation," *Neotestamentica* 28, no. 2 (1994): 395–411.

39. Segovia and Tolbert, *Reading from This Place*.

40. Roland Barthes, *The Pleasure of the Text*, trans. Richard Miller (New York: Hill & Wang, 1996), 14.

41. For interpretation as conversation, see H.-G. Gadamer, *Wahrheit und Methode: Grundzüge einer philosophischen Hermeneutik*, 6th ed. (Tübingen: J. C. B. Mohr, 1990), 387–494 (ET: *Truth and Method*, trans. Garrett Barden and John Cumming [New York: Seabury, 1975]).

42. Alfred M. de Zayas, *Nemesis at Potsdam: The Expulsion of the Germans from the East*, 3d ed. (Lincoln: University of Nebraska Press, 1989), xix, places the number of expellees at fifteen million. For a fuller account, see Theodor Schieder, *Dokumentation der Vertreibung der Deutschen aus Ost-Mitteleuropa*, in *Verbindung mit Adolf Diestelkamp, Rudolf Laun, Peter Rassow, Hans Rothfels*, 5 vols. (Bonn: Bundesministerium für Vertriebene, Flüchtlinge und Kriegsgeschädigte, 1953–62).

43. For the military history of the Soviet invasion and German defense of West Poland, see Wolfgang Schumann and Olaf Groehler, eds., *Deutschland im zweiten Weltkrieg*, vol. 6: *Die Zerschlagung des Hitlerfaschismus und die Befreiung des deutschen Volkes (Juni 1944 bis zum 8. Mai 1945)* (Cologne: Paul-Rugenstein, 1985), 498–522.

44. Johannes Kaps, ed., *The Tragedy of Silesia,* trans. Gladys Hartinger (Munich: "Christ Unterwegs," 1952/53); Marco Picone Chiodo, *"Sie werden die Stunde verfluchen . . .": Sterben und Vertreibung der Deutschen im Osten, 1944–1949* (Munich: Herbig, 1990). Wolfgang Benz, ed., *Die Vertreibung der Deutschen aus dem Osten: Ursachen, Ereignisse, Folgen* (Frankfurt am Main: Fischer, 1996), provides a critical analysis of these accounts, especially in the essays of Josef Henke, "Exodus aus Ostpreussen und Schlesien: Vier Erlebnisberichte," 114–21, and Alois Harasko, "Die Vertreibung der Sudetendeutsch: Sechs Erlebnisberichte," 132–47.

45. James Berger, *After the End: Representations of Post-Apocalypse* (Minneapolis: University of Minnesota Press, 1999), 34; cataclysm and revelation, 38.

46. Ursula Hegi, *Tearing the Silence: On Being German in America* (New York: Touchstone, 1998), especially her concluding reflections, 287–302.

47. Maurice Halbwachs, *Les cadres sociaux de la mémoire: The Social Framework of Memory* (New York: Arno, 1971), 35–39, 98–145; idem, *The Collective Memory,* trans. Francis J. Ditter and Vida Yazdi Ditter (New York: Harper & Row, 1980).

48. For a chronicle and analysis of post–World War II European immigration to Canada, see Modris Eksteins, *Walking since Daybreak: A Story of Eastern Europe, World War II, and the Heart of Our Century* (Toronto: Key Porter Books, 1999); Irving Arabella and Harold Troper, *None Is Too Many: Canada and the Jews of Europe, 1933–48* (New York: Random House, 1982); Jean Bruce, *After the War* (Don Mills, Ont.: Fitzhenry and Whiteside, 1982); David C. Corbett, *Canada's Immigration Policy* (Toronto: University of Toronto Press, 1957); Mark Wyman, *DP: Europe's Displaced Persons, 1945–1951* (Philadelphia: Balch Institute; Cranbury, N.J.: Associated University Presses, 1989); Donald H. Avery, *Reluctant Host: Canada's Response to Immigrant Workers, 1896–1994* (Toronto: McClelland and Stewart, 1995); Harold Troper, "Canada's Immigration Policy since 1945," *International Journal* 48 (1993): 255–81; Michael R. Marrus, *The Unwanted: European Refugees in the Twentieth Century* (New York: Oxford University Press, 1985).

49. Frank Kermode, *The Sense of an Ending: Studies in the Theory of Fiction* (Oxford: Oxford University Press, 1968), 45.

50. Jacques Ellul, *Apocalypse: The Book of Revelation,* trans. George W. Schreiner (New York: Seabury, 1977).

51. Recently, see Margaret Barker, *The Revelation of Jesus Christ* (Edinburgh: T. & T. Clark, 2000); and John W. Marshall, *Parables of War: Reading John's Jewish Apocalypse,* Studies in Christianity and Judaism 10 (Waterloo, Ont.: Wilfred Laurier University Press, 2001), who have resurrected a version of an older theory (for example, J. B. Lightfoot, *Biblical Essays* [New York: Macmillan, 1893], 52) that the Apocalypse contains an allegorically coded mem-

ory of the Jewish War (66–70 C.E.) and of Nero's persecution of the church (ca. 64 C.E.). If true, such studies indicate further the degree to which John looks backward as much as forward.

52. Thus Thompson, *Revelation*, 172. Thompson notes that in the Greek text the preposition *en* ("in") and definite article (*tē*) modify the entire phrase (*en tē thlipsei kai basileia kai hypomonē Iēsou*). This is only cumbersomely translatable into English as "in the tribulation-and-kingdom-and-endurance-of/from Jesus." On this reading, John's "in Jesus" would be analogous to Paul's "in Christ" (e.g., Rom. 6:5-11).

53. Bruce Malina, "Christ and Time: Swiss or Mediterranean?" *CBQ* 51 (1989): 1–31.

54. Gerd Theissen, "Tradition und Entscheidung: Der Beitrag des biblischen Glaubens zum kulturellen Gedächtnis," in *Kultur und Gedächtnis*, ed. Jan Assmann and Tonio Hölscher (Frankfurt am Main: Suhrkamp, 1988), 170–98, here 174.

55. For a full discussion, see S. R. F. Price, *Rituals and Power: The Roman Imperial Cult in Asia Minor* (Cambridge: Cambridge University Press, 1984); Fergus Millar, *The Emperor and the Roman World* (Ithaca, N.Y.: Cornell University Press, 1977); and Daniel N. Schowalter, *The Emperor and the Gods: Images from the Time of Trajan*, Harvard Dissertations in Religion 28 (Minneapolis: Fortress Press, 1993).

56. Friedrich Nietzsche, *Unzeitgemässe Betrachtungen zweites Stück. Vom Nutzen und Nachteil der Historie für das Leben*, §§1–5 (= Giorgio Colli and Mazzino Montinari, eds., *Friedrich Nietzsche Sämtliche Werke: Kritische Gesamtausgabe*, 50 vols. [Berlin: Walter de Gruyter, 1969], 3.1:244–330, here §1, 244–53; for monumental, antiquarian, and critical history, see §§2–3, 254–66; ET=*Unfashionable Observations*, trans. Richard T. Gray [Stanford: Stanford University Press, 1995]).

57. Thus, Plato, *Phaedros* 275D.

58. Paradoxically, just at the time of its cultural eclipse, memory has become the topic of renewed scholarly interest. I cite here representative studies that furnish more complete bibliographies: Aleida Assmann, *Erinnerungsräume: Formen und Wandlungen des kulturellen Gedächtnisses* (Munich: C. H. Beck, 1999); Jan Assmann, *Das kulturelle Gedächtnis: Schrift, Erinnerung und politische Identität in frühen Hochkulturen* (Munich: C. H. Beck, 1999)—pages 14–166 furnish a fine overview before turning to ancient Egypt in the second half of the study. Patrick H. Hutton, *History as an Art of Memory* (Hanover, N.H.: University Press of New England, 1993), reviews the cultural currents of memory from the Renaissance to postmodernity; Mieke Bal, Jonathan Crewe, and Leo Spitzer, eds., *Acts of Memory: Cultural Recall in the Present* (Hanover, N.H.: University Press of New England, 1999), offer state-of-the-art studies in

the politics and cultural criticism of memory. See also Frances Yates, *The Art of Memory* (Chicago: University of Chicago Press, 1966), for a classic study.

59. Anselm Kiefer, "Zweistromland: Späte Plastik im Zweistromland" (Cologne, Dumont 1989); for further discussion see Assmann, *Erinnerungsräume*, 360–64, and for an appraisal of Kiefer as cultural troublemaker see Simon Schama, *Landscape and Memory* (Toronto: Random House, 1995), 120–34. For *National Geographic* as manufacturer of nature, see Sallie McFague, *Super, Natural Christians* (Philadelphia: Fortress Press, 1997), 82–87.

60. Friedrich Nietzsche, "Zarathustra's Vorrede," in *Also Sprach Zarathustra: Ein Buch für Alle und Keine*, §§ 4–5 (= Colli and Montinari, *Friedrich Nietzsche Sämtliche Werke*, 6.1:10–15; ET=*Thus Spake Zarathustra: A Book for All and None*, trans. Thomas Common [Mineola, N.Y.: Dover, 1999]).

61. Francis Fukuyama, *The End of History and the Last Man* (New York: Avon, 1992), esp. 287–339.

62. Jean Baudrillard, *The Illusion of the End*, trans. Christ Turner (Stanford, Calif.: Stanford University Press, 1994), 1–9, here 9.

63. For the place of nostalgia in postmodern architecture, see Peter Anselm Riedl, "Nostalgie und Postmoderne," in *Kultur und Gedächtnis*, ed. Jan Assmann and Tonio Hölscher (Frankfurt am Main: Suhrkamp, 1988), 340–67.

64. Douglas Coupland, *Life after God* (New York: Pocket Books, 1994).

65. Jean-François Lyotard, *The Postmodern Condition: A Report on Knowledge*, trans. Geoff Bennington and Brian Massumi, Theory and History of Literature 10 (Minneapolis: University of Minnesota Press, 1999), esp. 3–6, 14–41.

66. Theodor W. Adorno, "Was bedeutet: Aufarbeitung der Vergangenheit," in *Bericht über die Erzieherkonferenz am 6 und 7. November in Wiesbaden* (Frankfurt: Suhrkamp, 1960), 14 = *Gesammelte Schriften 10.2* (Frankfurt am Main: Suhrkamp, 1977), 555–72; see similarly, Jürgen Habermas, *Vergangenheit als Zukunft*, ed. Michael Haller (Zürich: Pendo Verlag, 1990), 45–96 (ET: *The Past as Future*, trans. Max Pensky [Lincoln: University of Nebraska Press, 1994]), though in a characteristically more optimistic vein.

67. Frederic Jameson, "Postmodernism and Consumer Society," in *The Anti-Aesthetic: Essays on Postmodern Culture*, ed. Hal Foster (New York: New Press, 1998), 111–25, esp. 115–18.

68. Jean Baudrillard, *Simulacra and Simulations*, trans. Sheila Faria Glaser (Ann Arbor: University of Michigan Press, 1994), 12; for discussion of the simulacra, see pp. 1–42.

69. In public conversation at Vancouver School of Theology's Peter Kaye Lectures, 1995; see also Stanley Hauerwas, *After Christendom: How the Church Is to Behave if Freedom, Justice, and a Christian Nation Are Bad Ideas* (Nashville: Abingdon, 1991), 93–112, esp. 109.

70. For a discussion of the Social Gospel Movement in North America, with

particular attention to the Canadian reality, as well as its roots especially in British Protestantism, see Phyllis D. Airhart, *Serving the Present Age: Revivalism, Progressivism, and the Methodist Tradition* (Montreal and Kingston, Ont.: McGill-Queen's University Press, 1992); Phyllis D. Airhart and Roger C. Hutchinson, eds. "Christianizing the Social Order: A Founding Vision of the United Church of Canada," *Toronto Journal of Theology* 12, no. 2 (1996). Ernest Lee Tuveson, *Millennium and Utopia: A Study in the Background of the Idea of Progress* (Berkeley: University of California Press, 1949), remains an indispensable introduction to the American Social Gospel. Walter Rauschenbusch, *A Theology for the Social Gospel* (Philadelphia: Westminster John Knox, 1997), first published in 1917, outlines its manifesto.

71. See Alexis de Tocqueville, *De la démocratie en Amérique*, 3 vols. (Paris: Charles Gosselin, 1836), here 2:208–34, esp. 215–22, and 3:232 39 (ET=Democracy in America, trans. Henry Reeve [New York: Bantam, 2000], pp. 345–63, and 650–81, esp. 652–58) for the relationship between religion and the enjoyment of economic goods in the United States. De Tocqueville's observations have been repeated by more recent observers of American religiosity: Peter Berger, *The Noise of Solemn Assemblies: Christian Commitment and the Religious Establishment in America* (Garden City, N.Y.: Doubleday, 1961); similarly Martin E. Marty, *Righteous Empire: The Protestant Experience in America* (New York: Harper Torchbooks, 1970); Sidney E. Mead, *The Lively Experiment: The Shaping of Christianity in America* (New York: Harper & Row, 1963); William Stringfellow, *A Private and Public Faith* (Grand Rapids: Eerdmans, 1962).

72. Thus, most recently, Jean-Marie Guéhenno, *The End of the Nation-State*, trans. Victoria Elliott (Minneapolis: University of Minnesota Press, 2000); Michael Hardt and Antonio Negri, *Empire* (Cambridge: Harvard University Press, 2001); similarly, Lyotard, *Postmodern Condition*, 14–17.

73. Robert N. Bellah et al., *Habits of the Heart: Individualism and Commitment in American Life* (New York: Harper & Row, 1985), here 271. I am more skeptical than these authors about the importance of recovering a notion of the "citizen," in the traditional sense of that term, since the understanding of the "state" to which the term belongs is defunct.

74. The success of nongovernmental organizations in shaping and monitoring corporate conduct internationally is a recent development. For a description of their growing influence, see Margaret Keck and Kathrun Sikking, *Activists beyond Borders: Advocacy Networks in International Politics* (Ithaca, N.Y.: Cornell University Press, 1998); and Naomi Klein, *No Logo: Taking Aim at the Brand Bullies* (New York: Picador, 2000). Garry Gereffi, Ronie Garcia-Johnson, and Erica Sasser, "The NGO-Industrial Complex," *Foreign Policy* 125 (July/August 2001): 56–65, offer a journalistic retrospective from a liberal economic bias and an annotated bibliography.

75. John Howard Yoder, *The Politics of Jesus* (Grand Rapids: Eerdmans, 1972), 248.

76. H. Richard Niebuhr, *Christ and Culture* (New Haven: Yale University Press, 1951), 190–229. Niebuhr's book offers a typology of responses of the church to culture ("Christ against culture," "Christ of culture," "Christ above culture," "Christ and culture in paradox," and "Christ the transformer of culture"), insisting that he is not promoting any single typology (230–34). But that claim seems disingenuous when one discovers that his study offers a sustained critique of each option *except* the "Christ the transformer of culture" type (see pp. 190–96 and compare pp. 76–82, 108–16, 185–89, and 141–49).

77. Mark Kingwell, *The World We Want: Virtue, Vice, and the Good Citizen* (Toronto: Viking, 2000), 120. Kingwell's appraisal is on secular terms heavily indebted to Alisdair MacIntyre's *After Virtue: A Study in Moral Theory,* 2d ed. (Notre Dame, Ind.: University of Notre Dame Press, 1997).

78. Thus, especially, John G. Gager, *Kingdom and Community: The Social World of Early Christianity* (Englewood Cliffs, N.J.: Prentice-Hall, 1975), 49–65; Paul D. Hanson, *The Dawn of Apocalyptic* (Philadelphia: Fortress Press, 1975), 158–61; John J. Collins, *Daniel, First Maccabees, Second Maccabees with an Excursus on the Apocalyptic Genre* (Wilmington, Del.: Glazier, 1981), 145.

79. Boesak, *Comfort and Protest,* 38.

80. See, for example, Colin J. Hemer, *The Letters to the Seven Churches of Asia Minor in Their Local Setting,* JSNTSup 11 (Sheffield: JSOT Press, 1986); W. M. Ramsay, *The Seven Letters to the Seven Churches of Asia and Their Place in the Plan of the Apocalypse* (London: Hodder & Stoughton, 1904).

81. I build here on the reconstruction of M. Hubert, "L'architecture des lettres aux sept églises," *Revue biblique* 67 (1960): 349–53. For the seven messages as preparation for what follows, see Wiard Popkes, "Die Funktion der Sendschreiben in der Johannes-Apocalypse: Zugleich ein Beitrag zur Spätgeschichte der neutestamentlichen Gleichnisse," *ZNW* 74 (1983): 90–107, here 106.

82. Thompson, *Book of Revelation,* 116–32, 171–201. See also David A. DeSilva, "The 'Image of the Beast' and the Christians in Asia Minor: Escalation of Sectarian Tension in Revelation 13," *Trinity Journal* 12 (1991): 185–208; idem, "The Revelation to John: A Case Study in Apocalyptic Propaganda and the Maintenance of Sectarian Identity," *Sociological Analysis* 53 (1992): 375–95; idem, "Social Setting of the Revelation to John"; idem, "The Persuasive Strategy of the Apocalypse: A Socio-rhetorical Investigation of Revelation 14:6–13," *SBL Seminar Papers* 37, no. 1 (1998): 785–806. Paul B. Duff, *Who Rides the Beast? Prophetic Rivalry and the Rhetoric of Crisis in the Churches of the Apocalypse* (Oxford: Oxford University Press, 2001), adopts a perspective similar to Thompson's and William Royalty's (see below). Duff presents a reading of Revelation very close to my own: John's Apocalypse challenges those among his

audience who "took a more liberal stance toward the larger pagan society than did John and his audience" (14). While I agree that the seven messages reflect factionalism among John's listeners, I am persuaded by Elisabeth Schüssler Fiorenza's critique of this position, including the similar position that I articulated in an earlier work, that John's criticisms extend beyond ecclesial to more sectarian interests and include structures of domination and tyranny governing the Roman Empire as a whole. I am grateful to Professor Schüssler Fiorenza for showing the weaknesses of my own overly sectarian reading (see her epilogue in *The Book of Revelation*) and the importance of a wider concern. In the chapters that follow I either presume or argue for a preoccupation on John's part not only with the church but with the Roman Empire more generally.

83. Gerd Theissen, *The Social Setting of Pauline Christianity*, trans. John H. Schütz (Philadelphia: Fortress Press, 1982), 121–43.

84. More ambitiously, Ugo Vanni, "Paolinismo o antipaolinismo nell'Apocalisse?" in *Antipaolinismo: Reazioni a Paolo tra il I e il II secolo*, ed. Roma Penna, Atti del II convegno nazionale di studi neotestamentari, Bressanone, 10–12 settembre 1987 (Bologna: Edizioni Dehoniane Bologna, 1988), 65–74, argues that the Apocalypse is a direct rebuttal of the Pauline teaching of 1 Corinthians 8–10.

85. Richard Bauckham, *The Climax of Prophecy: Studies on the Book of Revelation* (Edinburgh: T. & T. Clark, 1998), 338–83; J. Nelson Kraybill, *Imperial Cult and Commerce in John's Apocalypse*, JSNTSup 132 (Sheffield: Sheffield Academic Press, 1996).

86. Schüssler Fiorenza, *Book of Revelation*, 187–203; see also idem, "Die Worte der Prophetie: Die Apokalypse des Johannes theologisch lesen," *Jahrbuch für Biblische Theologie* 14 (1999): 71–94.

87. Royalty, *Streets of Heaven*, 10–11.

88. Royalty's study represents a strong corrective to earlier scholarship that tends to interpret economic references in the Apocalypse as metaphors for arrogance or spiritual corruption (thus, for example, Jürgen Roloff, *Die Offenbarung des Johannes*, ZBNT 18 [Zürich: Theologischer Verlag, 1984), 177; P. Prigent, *L'Apocalypse de Saint Jean*, CNT 14 [Geneva: Labor et Fides, 1988], 267–68).

89. David L. Barr, "The Apocalypse as a Symbolic Transformation of the World: A Literary Analysis," *Interpretation* 38 (1984): 39–50.

90. Edith McEwan Humphrey, "The Sweet and the Sour: Epics of Wrath and Return in the Apocalypse," *SBL Seminar Papers* 30 (1991): 451–60; idem, *The Ladies and the Cities: Transformation and Apocalyptic Identity in "Joseph and Asenath," 4 Ezra, the Apocalypse, and the Shepherd of Hermas*, Journal for the Study of the Pseudepigrapha Supplements 17 (Sheffield: Sheffield Academic Press, 1995).

91. Barbara R. Rossing, *The Choice between Two Cities: Whore, Bride, and Empire in the Apocalypse,* Harvard Theological Studies (Harrisburg, Pa.: Trinity Press International, 1999). My own reading, while agreeing with Rossing that Revelation offers an overarching development of a two-city motif, focuses more on the dynamic development of the characters associated with either city as the Apocalypse unfolds. My interest is less in static structures than in dynamic interplay between contrasting motifs—especially in chapter 5, in which I take up contrasting narrative temporalities associated with each.

92. Daniel Berrigan, *The Nightmare of God* (Portland: Sunburst, 1983), 107.

93. Royalty, *Streets of Heaven,* 246.

94. William Blake, "With Happiness Stretched across the Hills," l. 88, from *William Blake: A Critical Edition of Major Works,* ed. Michael Mason (Oxford: Oxford University Press, 1988), p. 27.

2. I, John

1. William S. Bowles, *St. John in Patmos* (London: Murray, 1832), 3–4, ll. 14ff.

2. For a thorough discussion of early Christian profiles, see R. Alan Cullpepper, *John, the Son of Zebedee: The Life of a Legend* (Minneapolis: Fortress Press, 2000), 139–86.

3. For reproductions of the works cited here, see Gertrude Schiller, *Ikonographie der christlichen Kunst,* vol. 5: *Die Apokalypse des Johannes* (Gütersloh: Gütersloher, 1991); Frits Van Der Meer, *Apokalypse: Die Visionen des Johannes in der europäischen Kunst* (Antwerp: Mercatorfonds, 1978); Gilles Quispel, *The Secret Book of Revelation: The Last Book of the Bible,* trans. Peter Staples (New York: McGraw-Hill, 1979). Reproductions are also found on the Internet: Hans Memling, *Saint John the Evangelist on Patmos* (right panel of tryptich, Saint John altarpiece): http://www.kfki.hu/~arthp/html/m/memling/2middle2/13john.html; Hans Burgkmair, *St. John the Evangelist in Patmos:* http://www.kfki.hu/~arthp/html/b/burgkmai/patmos.html; Hieronymus Bosch, *St. John the Evangelist on Patmos:* http://www.abcgallery.com/B/bosch/bosch67.html; Titian, *St. John the Evangelist on Patmos:* http://www.nga.gov/cgi-bin/pinfo?Object=43441+0+none.

4. Remarkably, apocalyptic/Apocalypse iconography is largely absent from artistic representation until the end of the nineteenth and the beginning of the twentieth century; see Max Peter Maass, *Das Apokalyptische in der modernen Kunst: Endzeit oder Neuzeit—Versuch einer Deutung* (Munich: Bruckmann, 1965); Richard W. Glassen and Bernhard Holeczek, eds., *Apokalypse: Ein Prinzip Hoffnung? Ernst Bloch zum 100. Geburtstag* (Heidelberg: Braus, 1985); Angela Jurkat, *Apokalypse: Endzeitstimmung in der Kunst und Literatur des Expressionismus* (Alfer: VDG, 1993); Gregory Fuller, *Endzeitstimmung: Düstere*

Bilder in goldener Zeit (Cologne: Dumont, 1994); Justin Hoffmann, *Dekonstruktionskunst: Der Mythos der Zerstörung in der Kunst der frühen sechziger Jahre* (Munich: Schreiber, 1995); Karlheinz Stierle and Rainer Warning, eds., *Das Ende: Figuren einer Denkform*, Poetik und Hermeneutik 6 (Munich: Fink, 1996); Marie-Luis Syring, ed., *"Happy End": Zukunfts- und Endzeitvisionen der 90er Jahre* (Kunsthalle Düsselfdorf, 1996); Rita Burrichter, "Der Blick in den Abgrund—Die Proklamation einer erneuerten Welt: 'Ende' und 'Wende' als bildliches Phänomen," in *Jüngste Tage: Die Gegenwart der Apokalyptik*, ed. Michael N. Ebertz and Reinhold Zwick (Freiburg im Breisgau: Herder, 2000).

5. Michel Foucault, *Madness and Civilization: A History of Insanity in the Age of Reason*, trans. Richard Howard (New York: Vintage, 1988), 38–64.

6. D. H. Lawrence, *Apocalypse and the Writings on Revelation*, ed. Mara Kalnins, 2d ed. (London: Penguin, 1995), 81–82. Subsequent page citations in the text are to Lawrence's work.

7. J. J. Collins, "Introduction: Towards the Morphology of a Genre," *Semeia* 14 (1979): 14–15. For an excellent critique, see Klaus Berger, *Formgeschichte des Neuen Testaments* (Heidelberg: Quelle & Meyer, 1984), 295–305, esp. 295: apocalypse morphologies are "not without a hint of arbitrariness."

8. Jung's archetypal interpretation was anticipated earlier in the twentieth century and builds on nineteenth-century theosophist readings; see Mara Kalnins's introduction to Lawrence's *Apocalypse*, 11–31, for a brief overview and references.

9. C. G. Jung, "Answer to Job," in *The Collected Works of C. G. Jung*, vol. 11: *Psychology and Religion: West and East*, trans. R. F. C. Hull, 2d ed. (London: Routledge, 1968), 450. Subsequent page citations in the text are to Jung's work.

10. Michel Foucault, *The Birth of the Clinic: An Archaeology of Medical Perception*, trans. A. M. Sheridan Smith (New York: Vintage, 1988), 108.

11. Ibid., 114.

12. C. A. Meier, *Persönlichkeit: Der Individuationsprozess im Lichte der Typologie* (Breisgau: Walter, 1977), 73–75.

13. B. Grunberger, *Vom Narzissmus zum Objekt* (Frankfurt am Main: Suhrkamp, 1976), 25–39; and idem, *Narziss und Anubis* (Munich and Vienna: Verlag Internationale Psychoanalyse, 1988), 2.76ff., 142ff.

14. J. Chasseguet-Smirgel, *Anatomie der menschlichen Perversion*, trans. Elke vom Scheidt, 2d ed. (Stuttgart: Deutsche Verlagsanstalt, 1989), 169–94, esp. 169–71; see also idem, *Das Ichideal: Psychoanalytischer Essay über die "Krankheit der Idealität,"* trans. Jeannette Friedeberg (Frankfurt am Main: Suhrkamp, 1987), 18–32.

15. Eugen Drewermann, *Tiefenpsychologie und Exegese*, vol. 2: *Wunder, Vision, Weissagung Apokalypse, Geschichte, Gleichnis* (Freiburg im Breisgau: Walter, 1987), 508. I cite here only this aspect of Drewermann's extensive Jungian discussion of the Apocalypse (pp. 436–591), summarized nicely by Hartmut Raguse, *Psychoanalyse und biblische Interpretation: Eine Auseinander-*

setzung mit Eugen Drewermanns Auslegung der Johannes-Apokalypse (Stuttgart: W. Kohlhammer, 1993), 130–42.

16. Raguse borrows the phrase "depressive position" from Melanie Klein, "A Contribution to the Psychogenesis of Manic-Depressive States," in *Love, Guilt, and Reparation and Other Works, 1921–1945* (London: Hogarth, 1985).

17. Raguse, *Psychoanalyse*, 165ff., 198ff., 230–31; see also idem, "Das zeitenende im Lichte der Offenbarung des Johannes: Versuch einer pschoanalytischen Interpretation," in Ebertz and Zwick, *Jüngste Tag*, 340–59.

18. Paul de Man, *Allegories of Reading: Figural Language in Rousseau, Nietzsche, Rilke, and Proust* (New Haven: Yale University Press, 1979), 188–245.

19. John G. Gager, *Kingdom and Community: The Social World of Early Christianity* (Englewood Cliffs, N.J.: Prentice-Hall, 1975), 49–57.

20. Adela Yarbro Collins, *Crisis and Catharsis: The Power of the Apocalypse* (Philadelphia: Westminster, 1984), 141–63.

21. Tina Pippin, *Death and Desire: The Rhetoric of Gender in the Apocalypse of John* (Louisville: Westminster John Knox, 1992), 72–73 (Apocalypse as product of the male unconscious); 84 (a phallocentrism); 98–103 (women's ways of nonviolence and knowing). See also the more developed comments in idem, *Apocalyptic Bodies: The Biblical End of the World in Text and Image* (New York: Routledge, 1999), 92–99, 117–27; Adela Yarbro Collins, "Feminine Symbolism in the Book of Revelation," *Biblical Interpretation* 1 (1993): 20–33; and Quispel, *Secret Book*, esp. "The Apocalypse as a Process of Individuation," 129–35.

22. Stephen Moore, "Revolting Revelations," in *The Personal Voice in Biblical Interpretation*, ed. Ingrid Rosa Kitzberger (New York: Routledge, 1999), 183–200, esp. 193–94; idem, "The Beatific Vision as a Posing Exhibition: Revelation's Hypermasculine Deity," *JSNT* 60 (1995): 27–55, esp. 52–53. See also, similarly and as gingerly, Catherine Keller, *Apocalypse Now and Then: A Feminist Guide to the End of the World* (Boston: Beacon, 1996), 44–46.

23. Raguse, *Psychoanalyse*, 87–89, 106–29.

24. Susan Sontag, *Against Interpretation and Other Essays* (New York: Anchor/Doubleday, 1990), 2–14, here 6–7.

25. H.-G. Gadamer, *Wahrheit und Methode: Grundzüge einer philosophischen Hermeneutik*, 6th ed. (Tübingen: J. C. B. Mohr, 1990), 387–494.

26. Ibid., 311.

27. Sontag, *Against Interpretation*, 7; Gadamer, *Wahrheit und Methode*, 270–312, esp. 305–12. (See p. 213, n. 41 for ET details.)

28. Gadamer converses with this critique of his *oeuvre* in the essays collected in part four of *Wahrheit und Methode: Ergänzungen Register*, 2d ed. (Tübingen: J. C. B. Mohr, 1993), 219–372, esp. 232–75 and 361–72. For a self-assessment of his career (until 1973), the relationship of his intellectual development to Romanticism, the interpretation of classical philosophy, and his migration to Heidelberg, see pp. 479–508.

29. Paul Ricoeur, *Husserl: An Analysis of His Phenomenology*, trans. Edward G. Ballard and Lester E. Embree (Evanston, Ill.: Northwestern University Press, 1967), 228, 232; idem, "Existence et hermeneutique," *Dialogue* 4, no. 1 (1965): 25.

30. Wayne Booth, *The Rhetoric of Fiction* (Chicago: University of Chicago Press, 1961), 139.

31. See, for example, the thorough discussion by David E. Aune, *Revelation 1–5*, Word Biblical Commentary (Dallas: Word, 1997), xlvii–lvi, with bibliography.

32. Thus, for example, Quintillian 6.2.7–12, 20–36.

33. For Asiatic rhetoric as decadent, see Quintillian 8.pref.17; Eduard Norden, *Die antike Kunstprosa vom VI. Jahrhundert v. Chr. bis in die Zeit der Renaissance* (Leipzig: J. B. Teubner, 1909), 263ff. John also invites us to participate in the emotions of his characters (for example, 6:12-17; note the appended theological interpretation, 18:1—19:9).

34. See the useful discussions of J. Ramsey Michaels, "Revelation 1.19 and the Narrative Voices of the Apocalypse," *NTS* 37 (1991): 604-20; and M. Eugene Boring, "The Voice of Jesus in the Apocalypse of John," *Novum Testamentum* 34 (1992): 334-59. These are the only sustained exegetical discussions of narrative voice in the Apocalypse.

35. See 17:9 for a similar call for wisdom and interpretation but this time mediated through an angel.

36. Examples of this use of relative clauses include Rev. 4:5d; 5:8e; 9:20; 10:6b; 11:8b; 14:4-5; 20:8d, 12f. See also 9:11b-c; 12:17; 16:14; 20:5b; 20:2c, 12; 21:22b, 23b-c for narrative descriptions that carry out an analogous narrative function embedded amid vision sequences.

37. The Greek text offers a more sophisticated connection by tonally and rhythmically linking the relative clause with the vision (accepting the reading of *Sinaiticus*): *echōn kerata hepta kai opthalmous hepta* **hoi eisin ta hepta pneumata tou theou apestalmenoi eis pasan tēn gēn** (the relative clause is boldface).

38. Boring, "Voice of Jesus," 357.

39. See similarly David L. Barr's accessible treatment in *Tales of the End: A Narrative Commentary on the Book of Revelation* (Santa Rosa, Calif.: Polebridge, 1998), 3-5, 26-29. My reading differs from Barr's in my insistence on a degree of mischief in the blending of voices. Barr detects a "telescoping" perspective (privileging the voice of Jesus/the divine over that of John, the faithful mouthpiece [29]). I discover a blending of voices that destabilizes any easy identification and thus insists on the audience's attention as it attempts to follow the unfolding narrative.

40. Ugo Vanni, "The Ecclesial Assembly 'Interpreting Subject' of the Apocalypse," *Religious Studies Bulletin* 4 (1984): 79-85, offers a similar interpretation: "The reader will read through what the author has written, and this [*sic*] from this moment will be literarily put in the mouth of John. From this point

onwards the 'I' of the author, of the reader, and of John coincide" (81). Vanni in this quotation privileges the reader, but here as in other studies he insists that the Apocalypse is more a score for liturgical performance than one for private reading. He argues that communal responses to the Apocalypse's public recitation (for example, according to Vanni, the "Amen" of Rev. 1:7 is a liturgical cue for antiphonal response to the lector's greeting) convert passive listeners into active participants in Revelation's drama.

3. Seeing Things

1. For further discussion, see Michel Foucault, *Discipline and Punish: The Birth of the Prison* (New York: Vintage, 1979), 195–228.

2. For a full set of Christian and Jewish examples of the all-seeing eye of God in ancient apocalyptic literature, see Harry O. Maier, "Staging the Gaze: Early Christian Apocalypses and Narrative Self-Representation," *Harvard Theological Review* 90 (1997): 131–54, here 141 n. 40.

3. Foucault, *Discipline and Punish*, 170–71.

4. For the honor-shame code of the ancient Mediterranean world, see Bruce Malina, *The New Testament World: Insights from Cultural Anthropology* (Louisville: Westminster John Knox, 1993), in which further literature is cited. For the function of public monuments in winning honor in ancient cities, see G. Sjoberg, *The Preindustrial City, Past and Present* (Glencoe, Ill.: Free Press, 1960), and for visibility in imperial society more particularly, see Ramsay MacMullen, *Roman Social Relations, 50 B.C. to A.D. 284* (New Haven: Yale University Press, 1974). The most accessible (and thorough) description of social expectations of dress, gait, and so on can be found in Clement of Alexandria's *Paedagogos*, bks. 2–3 (*ANF* 2.209–95), a state-of-the-art compendium of the dominant ethos. See Iseltraut Hadot, *Seneca und die griechische-römische Tradition der Seelenleitung* (Berlin: de Gruyter, 1969); and P. Hadot, *Exercises spirituel et philosophie antique* (Paris: Études augustiniennes, 1981), for the philosophical backdrop. The proverb appears in Aeschylus, *Agamemnon* 788: *to dokein einai* ("To be is better than to seem"); similarly, Plato, *Gorgias* 527b.

5. In what follows I am extending the conclusions of David Hellholm, *Das Visionbuch des Hermas als Apokalypse: Formgeschichtliche und texttheoretische Studien zu einer literarischen Gattung*, vol. 1: *Methodologische Vorüberlegungen und makrostrukturelle Textanalyse,* ConBNT 13/1 (Lund: Gleerup, 1980), concerning the apocalyptic genre of *The Shepherd of Hermas.*

6. For a fuller discussion with citations of major studies concerning the date, authorship, social setting, genre, and purpose of *The Shepherd,* see Carolyn Osiek, *The Shepherd of Hermas,* Hermeneia (Minneapolis: Fortress Press, 1999).

7. All quotations are from the translation of Kirsopp Lake, *The Apostolic Fathers*, vol. 2, LCL (Cambridge: Harvard University Press, 1976), which I sometimes slightly revise.

8. See similarly Patricia Cox Miller, *Dreams in Late Antiquity: Studies in the Imagination of a Culture* (Princeton: Princeton University Press, 1994), 142.

9. Minucius Felix, *Octavius* 10.3–5 (Rendall, LCL [slightly revised]). For cannibalism and orgies, see chapter 9.

10. Justin, *Apology* 1.12 (Coxe, *ANF* [slightly revised]).

11. This sense of invigilation, in contemporary studies an overly neglected aspect of ancient apocalyptic literature, provides further support for those readings of the Apocalypse of John as a text centered in exhortation and admonition. See, for example, the discussions of Philipp Vielhauer, "Introduction," in Edgar Hennecke and Wilhelm Schneemelcher, eds., *New Testament Apocrypha*, trans. R. McL. Wilson, vol. 2 (Philadelphia: Westminster, 1964), 587; Christoph Münchow, *Ethik und Eschatologie: Ein Beitrag zum Verständnis der frühjüdischen Apokalyptik* (Göttingen: Vandenhoeck & Ruprecht, 1982); David Aune, *Prophecy in Early Christianity and the Ancient Mediterranean World* (Grand Rapids: Eerdmans, 1983), 19, 274–78, 299–304; Ulrich B. Müller, *Prophetie und Predigt im Neuen Testament: Formgeschichtliche Untersuchungen zur urchristlichen Prophetie* (Gütersloh: Mohn, 1975), 45–108; and Ferdinand Hahn, "Die Sendschreiben der Johannesapokalypse: Ein Beitrag zur Bestimmung prophetischer Redeformen," in *Tradition und Glaube*, ed. Gert Jeremias, Heinz-Wolfgang Kuhn, and Hartmut Stegemann (Göttingen: Vandenhoeck & Ruprect, 1971), 357–94.

12. Edward Gibbon, *The History of the Decline and Fall of the Roman Empire*, 7 vols. (London: Methuen, 1896), 2:27.

13. For a (highly conjectural) pre-Montanist dating, see Marie Turcan, *Tertullien: Les spectacles*, SC 332 (Paris: du Cerf, 1986), 37–46.

14. Tertullian, *De Spectaculis* 29.3 (Glover, LCL [slightly revised]). For God's watching of shows, 20.2–6.

15. Barbara Freedman, *Staging the Gaze: Post-modernism, Psychoanalysis, and Shakespearean Comedy* (Ithaca, N.Y.: Cornell University Press, 1991), 1.

16. Erving Goffman, *The Presentation of Self in Everyday Life* (New York: Doubleday, 1959), 19, quoting Robert Ezra Park.

17. Jacques Lacan, *The Four Fundamental Concepts of Psycho-Analysis*, trans. Alan Sheridan (New York: W. W. Norton, 1981), 73.

18. Ibid., 83.

19. Freedman, *Staging the Gaze*, 1.

20. Ibid., 7–46.

21. See Shadi Bartsch, *Actors in the Audience: Theatricality and Double-speak from Nero to Hadrian* (Cambridge: Harvard University Press, 1994), for another application of these notions to ancient society.

22. *Poetics* 1452a10–11; 1454b16; "A discovery is, as the very word implies, a change from ignorance to knowledge, and thus to either love or hate, in the personages marked for good or evil fortune" (1452a11, 30–32). In the "discovery of persons," Aristotle continues, "it may be that of one party only to the other, the latter being already known; or both the parties may have to discover themselves" (1452b11, 4–5). Reversal ("peripety") "is the change of the kind described from one state of things within the play to its opposite . . ." (1452a11, 21–23). "The finest form of Discovery is one attended by Peripeties . . ." (1452a11, 33–34).

23. Homer, *Odyssey* 19.386–475; 21.205–25.

24. See, for example, the so-called *cena* episode of Petronius's *Satyricon*, 15.26–78, with the commentary of W. Martin Bloomer, *Latinity and Literary Society at Rome* (Philadelphia: University of Pennsylvania Press, 1997), 205–24; and of Niall Slater, *Reading Petronius* (Baltimore: Johns Hopkins University Press), 85–86, both of whom note the theatrical performances of Trimalchio. See also the satires of Juvenal (*Sat.* 2, 3), Ovid (*Am. amor.* 1.506), and Horace (*E4*), in which such performances are similarly pilloried.

25. For example, *Philosophies for Sale, Cynics, Ikaromenippos*, and *Peregrinus* (the career of a masquerading ascetic who takes advantage of naive Christians).

26. B. P. Reardon, ed., *Collected Ancient Greek Novels* (Berkeley: University of California Press, 1989).

27. In the *Acts of Paul and Thecla*, for example, a text whose sources may well be contemporary with the Apocalypse, Thecla becomes the master of heroic asceticism, dresses as a male disciple of Paul, and so calls into question reigning cultural gender constructions. See Edgar Hennecke and Wilhelm Schneemelcher, eds., *New Testament Apocrypha*, trans. R. McL. Wilson, vol. 2 (Philadelphia: Westminster, 1964), 363–64; *Clem. Recog.* 7.8–37; 8.1, 33–38, again a text with second-century origins.

28. Edith McEwan Humphrey, *The Ladies and the Cities: Transformation and Apocalyptic Identity in "Joseph and Asenath," 4 Ezra, the Apocalypse, and the Shepherd of Hermas,* Journal for the Study of the Pseudepigrapha Supplements 17 (Sheffield: Sheffield Academic Press, 1995), 20–23, 85–118.

29. For example, the Joseph cycle of Genesis 37ff. offers Joseph a change of costume at each stage of the tale; similarly, Esther 4:1-4; 8:2, 15; Dan. 5:16, 29. The motif of clothing and stripping is a standard prophetic theme (e.g., Hosea 2; Isa. 61:10).

30. Reversals of fortune, positive or negative, threatened or predicted, are as follows: 1:7 (former crucifiers will wail); 1:18 (Jesus was dead but is alive); 2:5 (Ephesians are to repent or have their lampstand removed); 2:7 (those who conquer will eat in paradise—similarly, 2:9, 17, 26; 3:5, 12, 21); 2:10 (be faithful unto death and you will have the crown of life); 2:13 (repent of the Nicolaitans or suffer coming punishment); 2:22 (Jezebel's destruction), 23 (vindication of those

who resist her); 3:2-3 (church of Sardis to wake up and no longer sleep); 3:10 (persecuted Philadelphians to be kept from coming punishment); 3:17 (rich, prosperous, self-sufficient Laodiceans will be poor and naked). In many of these instances, John's Greek enacts the reversals it expresses; for example, 2:9, translated clause by clause and as literally as possible, reads, "I know your tribulation and poverty, *but rich you are*, and the blasphemy from those saying that they are Jews and are not but a synagogue of Satan." Ancient listeners would have not only heard a reversal, they would have experienced one.

31. I borrow metaphors from Susan Sontag, *On Photography* (New York: Anchor/Doubleday, 1977), 3–5.

32. Martin Jay, "Scopic Regimes of Modernity," in *Vision and Visuality*, ed. Hal Foster, Dia Art Foundation Discussions in Contemporary Culture 2 (Seattle: Bay Press, 1988), 3–23.

33. *De poet.* 1452b11, 1.

34. For an encyclopedic discussion of alleged sources and stages of construction as well as the more important studies over the past hundred years, see David E. Aune, *Revelation 1–5*, Word Biblical Commentary (Dallas: Word, 1997), cv–cxxxiii.

35. For example, Richard Bauckham, *The Climax of Prophecy: Studies on the Book of Revelation* (Edinburgh: T. & T. Clark, 1993), 1ff.; F. D. Mazzaferri, *The Genre of the Book of Revelation from a Source-Critical Perspective*, BZNW 54 (Berlin and New York: de Gruyter, 1989), 37ff.; Leonard L. Thompson, *The Book of Revelation: Apocalypse and Empire* (New York: Oxford University Press, 1990), 37–91; David L. Barr, *Tales of the End: A Narrative Commentary on the Book of Revelation* (Santa Rosa, Calif.: Polebridge, 1998).

36. As indeed the epexegetical 2:15 already suggests. See James Moffatt, "Revelation," in *The Expositor's Greek New Testament*, ed. W. Robertson Nicoll, 5 vols. (Grand Rapids: Eerdmans, 1990), 5:352.

37. Elisabeth Schüssler Fiorenza, *Justice and Judgment* (Philadelphia: Fortress Press, 1985), 170–77.

38. Edith Humphrey, "The Sweet and the Sour: Epics of Wrath and Return in the Apocalypse," in *SBL Seminar Papers*, ed. Eugene H. Lovering Jr. (Atlanta: Scholars Press, 1991), 457–60. This extends the acute observations of Adela Yarbo Collins concerning the similar hermeneutical function of chapter 12, at the very center of the intercalation (*The Combat Myth in the Book of Revelation*, Harvard Dissertations in Religion 9 [Missoula, Mont.: Scholars, 1976]).

39. For arrogation of the title Lord and God (*dominus et deus*) by the Roman emperor Domitian, see Suetonius, *Domitian* 4.4; 13.2; Dio Cassius 67.7.

40. Robert M. Royalty Jr., *The Streets of Heaven: The Ideology of Wealth in the Apocalypse of John* (Macon, Ga.: Mercer University Press, 1998), 246.

41. Ibid., 177–210.

42. Ibid., 246.

43. "Publicity is always about the future buyer. It offers him an image of himself made glamorous by the product or opportunity it is trying to sell. The image then makes him envious of himself as he might be. Yet what makes this self-which-might-be enviable? The envy of others" (John Berger, *Ways of Seeing* [London: BBC/Penguin, 1977], 132, whose use of masculine language is intentional). Advertising is usually addressed to the male or reflects a male gaze. Thus, the Apocalypse inscribes an idealized male identity (14:4), or at least a male desire (21:2, 9).

44. *The Globe and Mail,* June 28, 1947, quoted in Jean Bruce, *After the War* (Don Mills, Ont.: Fitzhenry and Whiteside, 1982), 96.

45. Modris Ecksteins, *Walking since Daybreak: A Story of Eastern Europe, World War II, and the Heart of Our Century* (Toronto: Key Porter Books, 1999), 92–93.

46. Guy Debord, *The Society of the Spectacle,* trans. Donald Nicholson-Smith, 3d ed. (New York: Zone, 1995), 12.

47. Ibid., 10, 154; see also Debord, *Comments on the Society of the Spectacle,* trans. Malcolm Imrie (New York: Verso, 1990), 8–10.

48. J. Baudrillard, *For a Critique of the Political Economy of the Sign* (St. Louis, 1981); see also idem, *L'Amerique* (Paris, 1986), for a critique of American society as the production of signs. The analysis applies equally to Canadian society; see also Chris Jenks, ed., *Visual Culture* (New York: Routledge, 1995), 3.

49. David Harvey, *The Condition of Postmodernity: An Enquiry into the Origins of Cultural Change* (Cambridge, England: Blackwell, 1990), 327–59; see, similarly, Frederic Jameson, *Postmodernism, or, the Cultural Logic of Late Capitalism,* 7th ed. (Durham, N.C.: Duke University Press, 1997), 154–80, 260–78.

50. Similarly, Ecksteins, *Walking since Daybreak,* 82.

4. Hearing Voices

1. Hanna Roose, "'Das Zeugnis Jesu': Seine Bedeutung für die Christologie, Eschatologie und Prophetie in der Offenbarung" (Ph.D. diss., University of Saarland, 1997), 156–242.

2. Franz Joseph Dölger, "Theou phonē," *Antike und Christentum: Kultur- und religionsgeschichtliche Studien* 5 (1933): 218–23.

3. Bruce M. Metzger, *Breaking the Code: Understanding the Book of Revelation* (Nashville: Abingdon, 1993).

4. Ibid., 13.

5. Ibid., 14.

6. For discussion and critical text, see F. C. Burkitt, *The Book of Rules of Tyconius,* Texts and Studies 3, pt. 1 (Cambridge: Cambridge University Press,

1894); F. Lo Bue, *The Turin Fragments of Tyconius' Commentary on Revelation,* Text and Studies, n.s., 7 (Cambridge: Cambridge University Press, 1963).

7. Thus *De Genesi ad litteram* 12; *De doctrina christiana* 1–3; *De magistro* 11.36—14.46.

8. Thus, David L. Barr, "The Apocalypse of John as Oral Enactment," *Interpretation* 40 (1986): 243–56; John E. Hurtgen, *Anti-language in the Apocalypse of John* (Lewiston, N.Y.: Mellen Biblical Press, 1993); Allen Dwight Callahan, "The Language of the Apocalypse," *HTR* 88 (1995): 453–70; J. A. Du Rand, "A Socio-psychological View of the Effect of the Language (Parole) of the Apocalypse of John," *Neotestamentica* 24 (1990): 351–65.

9. For a survey of the history of scholarly attention to oral culture in antiquity and representative cross-cultural studies, see Walter J. Ong, *Orality and Literacy: The Technologizing of the Word* (New York: Routledge, 1993), 16–30. For a further survey with particular attention to orality in biblical studies, see Paul J. Achtemeier, *"Omne verbum sonat:* The New Testament and the Oral Environment of Late Western Antiquity," *JBL* 109 (1990): 3–27; *Semeia* 39 (1987), an issue edited by Lou H. Silberman on the theme "Orality, Aurality, and Biblical Narrative"; and *Semeia* 65 (1995), an issue edited by Joanna Dewey on the theme "Orality and Textuality in Early Christian Literature." See also Werner H. Kelber, *The Oral and the Written Gospel: The Hermeneutics of Speaking and Writing in the Synoptic Tradition, Mark, Paul, and Q* (Philadelphia: Fortress Press, 1983); Vernon K. Robbins, "Rhetoric and Culture: Exploring Types of Cultural Rhetoric in a Text," in *Rhetoric and the New Testament: Essays from the 1992 Heidelberg Conference,* ed. Stanley E. Porter and Thomas H. Olbricht, JSNTSup 90 (Sheffield: Sheffield Academic Press, 1993), 443–63; and Robert W. Funk, *Parables and Presence: Forms of the New Testament Tradition* (Philadelphia: Fortress Press, 1982), esp. "The Apostolic Presence: Paul," 81–102, and "The Apostolic Presence: John the Elder," 103–10.

10. Classically, Marshall McLuhan, *The Gutenberg Galaxy* (Toronto: University of Toronto Press, 1962).

11. Walter J. Ong, *The Presence of the Word: Some Prolegomena for Cultural and Religious History* (Minneapolis and Oxford: University of Minnesota Press, 1967), 1–110.

12. For "oral literature" and the function of writing in hybrid cultures, see ibid., 10–15; and Achtemeier, *"Omne verbum sonat,"* 9–19.

13. George Bernard Shaw, *The Adventures of the Black Girl in Her Search for God* (New York: Dodd, Mead, 1933), 73, cited by Callahan, "Language of the Apocalypse," 453.

14. Ong, *Orality and Literacy,* 36–57. Ong's typology, sometimes contrasting oral and print-based cultures, contains the following dimensions: "additive rather than subordinative" (37); "aggregative rather than analytic" (38); "redun-

dant or 'copious'" (39); "conservative or traditionalist" (41); "close to the human lifeworld" (42); "agonistically toned" (43); "empathetic and participatory rather than objectively distanced" (45); "homeostatic" (46); "situational rather than abstract" (49).

15. M. Eugene Boring, *Revelation,* Interpretation (Louisville: John Knox, 1989), 130.

16. F. Blass and A. Debrunner, *A Greek Grammar of the New Testament and Other Early Christian Literature,* trans. Robert W. Funk (Cambridge: Cambridge University Press, 1961), 258. See also verse 4, *kai ēkousa ton arithmon ton esphragismenōn heauton tesserakonta tessares chiliades, esphragismenoi ek pasēs phōles huiōn Israēl,* in which *arithmon . . . heauton* forms homoioteleuton, and *tesserakonta tessares* a further instance of paronomasia.

17. For a striking example combining alliteration, parechesis, paronomasia, and homoioteleuton, see 14:6: *kai eidon allon angelon petomenon en mesouranēmati, echonta euangelon aiōnion euaggelisai epi tous kathēmenous epi tēs gēs kai epi pan ethnos kai phylēn kai glōssan kai laon.* For onomatopoeia, see the climactic set of expressed woes of those lamenting Babylon's fall (*ouai, ouai,* 18:10, 15, 19), with the added weight of epanadiplosis (repetition of significant words), as well as a parallelism with the epanadiplosis of 18:2 (*epesen epesen;* "fallen, fallen").

18. Ong, *Orality and Literacy,* 39–41.

19. Ibid., 37–38.

20. Ibid., 42–43.

21. Ibid., 42.

22. Ibid., 45–46 ("empathetic and participatory rather than objectively distanced"); 49–57 ("situational rather than abstract").

23. Thus, for example, David E. Aune, "The Influence of Roman Imperial Court Ceremonial on the Apocalypse of John," *Papers of the Chicago Society of Biblical Research* 28 (1983): 5–26.

24. Friedrich Engels, "Das Buch der Offenbarung," in *Friedrich Engels über Religion und Freiheit,* ed. Klaus Peters (Gütersloh: Gütersloher Verlagshaus Mohn, 1978), 239–44 (=Ludwig Arnold, ed., *Karl Marx Friedrich Engels Werke,* 5th ed. [Berlin: Dietz Verlag, 1973], 21:9–15; ET="The Book of Revelation," in *Karl Marx and Friedrich Engels on Religion,* no editor given [New York: Shocken, 1974], 205–12).

25. Ong, *Orality and Literacy,* 43–45.

26. Ibid., 43–44.

27. Ibid., 44.

28. Ibid., 45.

29. Ibid., 41–42, 38–39, and 46–49, respectively.

30. Ibid., 42.

31. For citations and further literature, see David E. Aune, *Revelation 1–5,* Word Biblical Commentary (Dallas: Word, 1997), 60–108, 266–86, probably the most exhaustive treatment to date.

32. For a discussion of time and verb tenses in the Apocalypse, see chapter 5 below.

33. R. H. Charles, *A Critical and Exegetical Commentary on the Revelation of St. John,* 2 vols., ICC (New York: Scribner's, 1920) 1:cxvii–clix; Charles's guide was later complemented by E. B. Allo, *L'Apocalypse du Saint Jean* (Paris: Gabalda, 1933), cxliv–clxx. See also E. C. A. Dougherty, "The Syntax of the Apocalypse" (Ph.D. diss., Catholic University of America, 1990), "the only complete analysis of the syntax of Revelation known to me" (Aune, *Revelation,* clxiii; Dougherty's dissertation was unavailable to me).

34. Charles, *Critical and Exegetical Commentary,* cxliii.

35. For a good overview, see Stanley E. Porter, "The Language of the Apocalypse in Recent Discussion," *NTS* 35 (1989): 582–603.

36. Thus, R. B. Y. Scott, *The Original Language of the Apocalypse* (Toronto: University of Toronto Press, 1928); C. C. Torrey, *The Apocalypse of John* (New Haven: Yale University Press, 1958), 13–48.

37. Also, J. H. Moulton, *A Grammar of New Testament Greek,* vol. 1: *Prolegomena* (Edinburgh: T. & T. Clark, 1908), 8–9; G. Mussies, *The Morphology of Koine Greek as Used in the Apocalypse of St. John: A Study in Bilingualism* NovTSup 27 (Leiden: E. J. Brill, 1971).

38. Thus, Steven Thompson, *The Apocalypse and Semitic Syntax,* SNTSMS 52 (Cambridge: Cambridge University Press, 1986).

39. Thus, C. G. Ozanne, "The Language of the Apocalypse," *Tyndale House Bulletin* 16 (1965): 3–9; F. C. Burney, *The Aramaic Origin of the Fourth Gospel* (Oxford: Clarendon, 1922), 15–20; and Austin Farrer, *A Rebirth of Images* (Glasgow: Glasgow University Press, 1949), 24.

40. H. B. Swete, *The Apocalypse of St. John* (New York: MacMillan, 1906), cxvii–cxxi; P. M. Bretscher, "Syntactical Peculiarities in Revelation," *Concordia Theological Monthly* 16 (1945): 95–105; Eduard Lohse, "Die altestamentliche Sprache des Sehers Johannes: Textkritische Bemerkungen zur Apokalypse," *ZNW* 52 (1961): 122–26; Angelo Lancellotti, *Sintas ebraica nel greco dell' Apocalypsealisse,* vol. 1: *Uso dell forme verbali* (Assisi, Italy: Studio Teologico Portiuncola, 1964); Heinrich Kraft, *Die Offenbarung des Johannes,* HNT 16A (Tübingen: Mohr [Siebeck], 1974), 16; Gregory K. Beale, "Revelation," in *It Is Written: Scripture Citing Scripture (Essays in Honor of Barnabas Lindars, S.S.F.),* ed. D. A. Carson and Hugh Godfrey Maturin Williamson (Cambridge: Cambridge University Press, 1988), 332; Daryl D. Schmidt, "Semitisms and Septuagintalisms in the Book of Revelation," *NTS* 37 (1991): 592–603; Callahan, "Language of the Apocalypse."

41. Hurtgen, *Anti-language*, 90; M. A. K. Halliday, *Language as Social Semiotic* (Baltimore: University Park Press, 1978), 154–93.

42. In particular, he explores instances of wordplay, re-, and overlexicalization with reference to Rev. 11:19—15:4 (Hurtgen, *Anti-language*, 89–140).

43. Callahan, "Language of the Apocalypse," 463.

44. Ibid., 464.

45. Ibid., 465.

46. Charles, *Critical and Exegetical Commentary,* clii–cliii.

47. Callahan, "Language of the Apocalypse," 467; other examples cited by Callahan include 2:13, *Antipas ho martys mou ho pistos mou; 1:13: homoion huion tou anthrōpou (huion* here in the accusative rather than the proper dative).

48. Ibid., 468.

49. Jacques Attali, *Noise: The Political Economy of Music,* trans. Brian Massumi, Theory and History of Literature 16 (Minneapolis: University of Minnesota Press, 1999), 26.

50. Ibid., 33.

51. Ibid., 60.

52. Callahan, "Language of the Apocalypse," 463.

53. N. K. Chadwick, *Poetry and Prophecy* (Cambridge: Cambridge University Press, 1942), 14, 27–28, 41–72.

54. Ruth Finnegan, *Oral Poetry: Its Nature, Significance, and Social Context* (Cambridge: Cambridge University Press, 1977), 214–71.

55. Dieter Georgi, "Who Is the True Prophet?" *HTR* 79 (1986): 100–126, here 123.

56. Julia Kristeva, *Revolution in Poetic Language,* trans. Margaret Waller (New York: Columbia University Press, 1984), reprinted in Kelly Oliver, ed., *The Portable Kristeva* (New York: Columbia University Press, 1997), 27–92, here 54.

57. Jürgen Habermas, "Modernity—An Incomplete Project," in *The Anti-Aesthetic: Essays on Postmodern Culture,* ed. Hal Foster (New York: New Press, 1990), 3–15.

58. Jürgen Habermas, *Theorie des kommunikativen Handelns,* 3d ed., 2 vols. (Frankfurt am Main: Suhrkamp, 1999; ET=*The Theory of Communicative Action,* trans. Thomas McCarthy [Boston: Beacon, 1984]); the exposition alternates between *Zwischenbetrachtungen* ("interim observations") and detailed expositions of the European intellectual heritage from Kant onward.

59. Ibid., 1:41–42.

60. Charles Taylor, "Sprache und Gesellschaft," in *Kommunikatives Handeln: Beiträge zu Jürgen Habermas' "Theorie des kommunikativen Handelns,"* ed. Axel Honneth and Hans Joas (Frankfurt am Main: Suhrkamp, 1986), 35–52.

61. Ingeborg Breuer, "Subjekt und Soziales: Das politische Denken des kanadischen Philosophen Charles Taylor," *Deutschlandradio* (February 3, 1995).

62. Julia Kristeva, *New Maladies of the Soul,* trans. Ross Guberman (New York: Columbia University Press, 1994), in Oliver, *Portable Kristeva,* 211.

63. Oliver, *Portable Kristeva,* 208–9.

64. Ibid., 206.

65. Ibid., 208.

66. The *unheimlich* received full development in 1920, in Sigmund Freud, "Jenseits des Lustprinzips," in *Sigmund Freud: Studienausgabe,* vol. 3: *Psychologie des Unbewußten,* ed. Thure von Uexküll and Ilse Grubisch-Simitix (Frankfurt am Main: Fischer, 1974; ET= "Beyond the Pleasure Principle," trans. and ed. James Strachey, *The Standard Edition of the Complete Psychological Works of Sigmund Freud* [London: Hogarth Press and the Institute of Psycho-Analysis, 1955], vol. 18:7–64), chaps. 2 and 3, pp. 222–33. Earlier treatments were developed in 1912/13, in "Totem und Tabu (einige Übereinstimmungen im Seelenleben der Wilden und der Neurotiker)," in Uexküll and Grubisch-Simitix, *Sigmund Freud,* 9:311 (ET=*Totem and Taboo: Resemblances between the Mental Lives of Savages and Neurotics,* trans. Strachey), and in Freud's 1919 essay "Das Unheimliche," in Uexküll and Grubisch-Simitix, *Sigmund Freud,* 4:241–74 (ET="The Uncanny," trans. Strachey, 17:210–50).

67. Julia Kristeva, *Strangers to Ourselves,* trans. Leon S. Roudiez (New York: Columbia University Press, 1991), 192. The emphasis is Kristeva's.

5. Games with Time

1. For the Apocalypse as epistle, see Martin Karrer, *Die Johannesoffenbarung als Brief: Studien zu ihrem literarischen, historischen und theologischen Ort,* FRLANT 140 (Göttingen: Vandenhoeck & Ruprecht, 1986).

2. Jacques Derrida, *The Post Card: From Socrates to Freud and Beyond,* trans. Alan Bass (Chicago: University of Chicago Press, 1987), 29.

3. Other anticipations and, hence, deferrals of an ending appear at Rev. 1:3; 2:16, 25; 3:11 (cf. v. 20); 10:6; 12:12; 17:10; 22:6, 7, 10, 12, 20.

4. Northrop Frye, *The Great Code: The Bible and Literature* (Toronto: Academic Press Canada, 1982), 137.

5. See Frank Kermode, *The Sense of an Ending: Studies in the Theory of Fiction* (Oxford: Oxford University Press, 1968), 7, 181n. 7, quoting Sir Philip Sidney, "a Poet thrusteth into the middest, euen where it most concerneth him, and there recoursing to the thinges forepaste, and diuining of thinges to come, maketh a pleasing analysis of all."

6. See Norman Cohn, *The Pursuit of the Millennium: Revolutionary Millenarians and Mystical Anarchists of the Middle Ages* (Oxford: Oxford University Press, 1980); Eugen Weber, *Apocalypses: Prophecies, Cults, and Millennial Beliefs*

through the Ages (Toronto: Random House, 1999); and Ernst Bloch, *Prinzip der Hoffnung,* 5th ed. (Frankfurt am Main: Suhrkamp, 1998), 2:575–614 (ET=*The Principle of Hope,* trans. Neville Plaice, Stephen Plaice, and Paul Knight [Cambridge, Mass.: MIT Press, 1986]).

7. Augustine had help from the third-century Donatist interpreter of the Apocalypse, Tyconius, whose *Rules* furnished Augustine with the exegetical means to resist the literal readings of his contemporaries.

8. For Revelation commentary in *City of God,* bks. 18–22, see Harry O. Maier, "The End of the City and the City without End: Augustine's *City of God* as Revelation," *Augustinian Studies* 30, no. 2 (1999): 153–64, an issue edited by Mark Vessey and Karla Pohlman, titled "History, Apocalypse, and the Secular Imagination: New Essays on Augustine's *City of God.*"

9. See *City of God* 20.30, in which Augustine cites Acts 1:6 ("It is not for you to know the times or seasons which the Father has fixed by his own authority") to counter millennial speculation.

10. Robert Markus, *Saeculum: History and Society in the Theology of St. Augustine* (Cambridge: Cambridge University Press, 1970), 14–15, 45–71.

11. I follow the translation of Marcus Dods in *Nicene and Post-Nicene Fathers of the Christian Church,* ed. Philip Schaff, vol. 2 (Grand Rapids: Eerdmans, 1977).

12. Markus, *Saeculum,* 70.

13. Catherine Keller, *Apocalypse Now and Then: A Feminist Guide to the End of the World* (Boston: Beacon Press, 1996), 102 (Keller's emphasis).

14. Thus, Rebecca Alban Hoffberger, foreword to *The End Is Near! Visions of Apocalypse, Millennium, and Utopia,* ed. Robert Manley (Los Angeles: Dilettante Press, 1998), 6: "61 percent of adults and 71 percent of teenagers believe the world will come to an end or be destroyed." See also *Time,* July 1, 2002.

15. Micahel Ortiz Hill, *Dreaming the End of the World: Apocalypse as a Rite of Passage* (Dallas: Spring Publications, 1994); see pp. 24–37 for a Jungian reading; 169–208 for the apocalyptic oneirocriticon; pp. 159–65 for a rite of passage.

16. Keller, *Apocalypse Now and Then,* 19.

17. Ibid., 87–88.

18. Ibid., 89.

19. James Berger, *After the End: Representations of Post-Apocalypse* (Minneapolis: University of Minnesota Press, 1999), 19; see p. 6 for the *Terminator II* quotation.

20. Ibid., 5–6.

21. See, for example, 11:1-13 (the two-witnesses episode), in which the narrative moves from future tense (11:2d-3), to present (v. 4), to conditional future/present (v. 5), to present (v. 6), to future (vv. 7-8), back to present (v. 9), then to future (v. 10a), and ends in the past tense (vv. 10b-13), a tangled skein of

time made even more complex by alternative tenses furnished by manuscript variants. A different form of achronicity appears when John disrupts the flow of events by injecting scenes that more properly belong later (e.g., 7:1-17, the vision of the white-robed saints who have come out of the great tribulation not in fact represented until chapters 11 and 13), or the announcement of the fall of Babylon at 14:8, followed immediately by a warning to anyone who worships the beast (the fall does not come, however, until chapter 18, with the laments over the destruction of Babylon). A. J. P. Garrow, *Revelation* (New York: Routledge, 1997), 15–65, misleadingly uses the term "foreshadowing" to describe similar passages in his insistence on the linearity of the plot of the Apocalypse. The achronicity of 11:1-13 is enough to make suspect the simplistic treatment of time in the Apocalypse as a straightforward recitation of past, present, and future (thus, G. K. Beale, "The Interpretive Problem of Rev. 1:19," *Novum Testamentum* 34 [1992]: 360–87; J. Ramsay Michaels, "Revelation 1:19 and the Narrative Voices of the Apocalypse," *NTS* 37 [1991]: 604–20).

22. Phillip Vielhauer, "Apocalyptic in Early Christianity: Introduction," in *New Testament Apocrypha*, vol. 2: *Writings Relating to the Apostles, Apocalypses, and other Related Subjects,* ed. Edgar Hennecke and Wilhelm Schneemelcher, trans. R. McLean Wilson (Philadelphia: Westminster, 1965), 621–22, citing the structural analysis of Günther Bornkamm, "Die Komposition der apokalyptischen Visionen in der Offenbarung Johannis," in *Studien zu Antike und Urchristentum* (München: Kaiser, 1959), 204–22.

23. I borrow the phrase from Umberto Eco, *Apocalypse Postponed* (Bloomington and Indianapolis: Indiana University Press, 1994).

24. "The Lamb slain since the foundation of time" (13:8) is a translation in keeping with the way John makes the fictive time of his Apocalypse spiral around Jesus' crucifixion; the other references to the Lamb that directly invoke the crucifixion are 5:6, 12; 7:14; 12:11. There are twenty-two other references to the Lamb that do not directly invoke the crucifixion but which imply it by the use of the title; the death of Jesus is invoked as a heading to Apocalypse: 1:5, 7. The connection of the blood of the Lamb and faithful testimony (*martyria*) is most explicit at 12:11 and is implied at 12:17, where the dragon battles those who "bear the testimony of Jesus" (*echontōn tēn martyrion Iēsou*). John also equates *martyria Iēsou Christou* with prophecy (19:10), and it is in this sense that *tēn martyrian Iēsou Christou* is to be interpreted at 1:2, 9. The triad testimony-prophecy-death forms an inseparable whole in the Apocalypse as the episode of the martyred two witnesses of 11:4-13 indicates. The episode anticipates the drama of 12:11 and 12:17 (testimony and war by the dragon), but defines testimony as prophecy. The two witnesses' testimony *is* prophecy as the parallel 11:6 (*tas hēmeras tēs prophēteias autōn*—"the days of their prophesying"), 11:7a (*tēn martyrion autōn*—"their testimony") indicate, and leads to their murder by the

beast in verses 7b-c. Thus, when John speaks of *tēn martyrion Iēsou Christou* at 1:2, 9, it is in this more multivalent sense of prophecy/testimony/death that *martyria* is to be understood (see also 20:4). The triad is also intended as polemical contrast to the alleged false prophecy of Balaam/the Nicolaitans/Jezebel (2:14, 20). False prophecy misleads one toward an idolatrous bearing of the mark of the beast (13:13-18; 19:20), which in turn keeps one from suffering, like Jesus, faithfully unto death (cf. 13:15; 20:4). False prophecy disrupts John's triad and, for this reason, is counterfeit testimony. The story of the cruciform Jesus of Nazareth, "who is the faithful witness, the firstborn from the dead" (1:5), is the pivot around which all of John's stories revolve.

25. See K-P. Jörns, *Das hymnsiche Evangelium: Untersuchungen zu Aufbau, Funktion und Herkunft der hymnische Stöcke in der Johannesoffenbarung* (Gütersloh: Mohr, 1971), esp. 167-70, for the hymns' narrative function. See also Jan A. du Rand, "'Now the Salvation of Our God Has Come . . .': A Narrative Perspective on the Hymns in Revelation 12-15," *Neotestamentica* 27 (1993): 313-30.

26. For Wisdom figures in the Apocalypse, see Adela Yarbro Collins, *The Combat Myth in the Book of Revelation* (Missoula, Mont.: Scholars Press, 1976), 65; Keller, *Apocalypse Now and Then*, 64-73.

27. Thus, for example, Hal Lindsey, *The Late Great Planet Earth* (Grand Rapids: Zondervan, 1970); idem, *There's A New World Coming: "A Prophetic Odyssey"* (Santa Ana, Calif.: Vision House, 1973).

28. John J. Collins, "Introduction: Towards the Morphology of a Genre," *Semeia* 14 (1979): 1-19, here pp. 6-7 and 14.

29. David Hellholm, "The Problem of Apocalyptic Genre and the Apocalypse of John," *Semeia* 36 (1986): 13-64.

30. Ibid., 47-52.

31. Elisabeth Schüssler Fiorenza, *Revelation: Justice and Judgment* (Philadelphia: Fortress Press, 1985), 46.

32. Elisabeth Schüssler Fiorenza, "Composition and Structure of the Book of Revelation," *CBQ* 39 (1977): 344-66, here 358 = Schüssler Fiorenza, *Revelation*, 174; see similarly, idem, "A Structuration of Revelation 4, 1-22, 5," in *L'Apocalypse dans le Nouveau Testament*, ed. J. Lambrecht (Gembloux, Belgium: Duculot, 1980), 77-104, though Lambrecht discovers "recapitulation which at the same time manifests intensification . . . yet does not exclude progress" (80). Frederick David Mazzaferri, *The Genre of the Book of Revelation from a Source-Critical Perspective*, BZNW 54 (Berlin and New York: de Gruyter, 1989), 330-78, reviews and critiques representative architectonic arrangements.

33. Yarbro Collins, *Combat Myth*, 5-55.

34. Adela Yarbro Collins, *Crisis and Catharsis: The Power of the Apocalypse* (Philadelphia: Westminster, 1984), 141-63.

35. Schüssler Fiorenza, *Revelation*, 174.

36. Paul Ricoeur, *The Rule of Metaphor: Multidisciplinary Studies of the Creation of Meaning in Language*, trans. Robert Czerny, Kathleen McLaughlin, and John Costello (Toronto: University of Toronto Press, 1997), esp. 101–33, 216–56; idem, *Time and Narrative*, trans. Kathleen McLaughlin and David Pellauer, vol. 2 (Chicago: University of Chicago Press, 1985).

37. The attentive reader will recognize in what follows my debt to Ricoeur, *Time and Narrative*, especially volumes 2 and 3, and his identification of a threefold dialectical mimesis among the worlds of the author, the text, and the reader, outlined in volume 1. The discussion builds in particular on the narrative treatments of David L. Barr, *Tales of the End: A Narrative Commentary on the Book of Revelation* (Santa Rosa, Calif.: Polebridge, 1998), in which the interested reader will find a fuller bibliography. Barr's attention to narrated time and the time of narration is a clear advance over the other two monograph-length studies of narrative in the Apocalypse—Garrow, *Revelation;* and James L. Resseguie, *Revelation Unsealed: A Narrative-Critical Approach to John's Apocalypse,* Biblical Interpretation Series 32 (Leiden: Brill, 1998)—both of which obliterate temporal achronicities in the Apocalypse in favor of a more linear plot progression, the former by attempting to isolate "the story in the text" (14–65), and the latter by reducing narrative time to a subset of point of view (45–47).

38. Kermode, *Sense of an Ending*, 44–45.

39. In fact, it may be the most playful ancient apocalypse, temporally speaking, that we possess. Its temporal variety contrasts sharply, for example, with the consistent temporal orientations of roughly contemporary apocalypses. *The Sybilline Oracles, 1 Enoch 1–36* and the *Apocalypse of Peter* offer linear futurist representations; narrative time is consistently *ex eventu* in Older Testament Daniel (chaps. 7–12); *Jubilees* 23; *1 Enoch* 83–90, 91–10; the *Ascension of Isaiah*; and *2 Baruch*. In *The Shepherd of Hermas*, narrative time frames allegorical exposition; in *4 Ezra*, serialized visions are framed by *ex eventu* prophecy; in *2 Enoch*, a tour of heaven and a retrospective account of creation give way to an account of coming judgment. In all of these apocalypses, past, present, and future follow in disciplined succession.

40. A. A. Mendilow, *Time and the Novel* (New York: P. Nevill, 1952), 106–7.

41. The command "write!" (*grapson*) is an aorist imperative. Here it indicates a command of limited duration, namely that of the time of the visions.

42. Käte Hamburger, *Die Logik der Dichtung*, 3d ed. (Vienna: Ullstein, 1980), 60–120. Hamburger's treatment of the preterit is complemented by a systematic analysis of all aspects of fictive time in Harald Weinrich, *Tempus. Besprochene und erzählte Welt*, Sprache und Literatur 16 (Stuttgart: W. Kohlhammer, 1964), esp. 7–105. Roland Barthes, *Writing Degree Zero*, trans. Annette Lavers and Colin Smith (New York: Hill & Wang, 1998), treats the preterit more polemically as a bourgeois monumentalization of time, and

238   Notes

proposes the phrase "zero degree of writing" (5) as a description of this ideological alliance (further, pp. 29–40).

43. Gérard Genette, *Nouveau discours du récit*, Collection Poétique (Paris:
Seuil, 1983), 53–55.

44. "The rounding wizard . . ." = H. T. Lowe's translation of "der raunende
Beschwörer des Imperfekts" in Thomas Mann, *Der Zauberberg* (Frankfurt am
Main: Fischer, 1982), 5 (ET=*The Magic Mountain* [London: Vintage, 1999], 1).

45. August Wilhelm Schlegel, *Die Kunstlehre: Kritische Schriften und Briefe
II,* ed. Edgar Lohner, Sprache und Literatur 5 (Stuttgart: W. Kohlhammer,
1963), 306–16; "die ruhige Besonnenheit des Erzählers."

46. For a detailed discussion of narrative distance and the way quotation
overcomes it, see Gérard Genette, *Narrative Discourse: An Essay in Method,*
trans. Jane E. Lewin (Ithaca, N.Y.: Cornell University Press, 1983) = *Figures III,*
Collection Poétique (Paris: Seuil, 1972), 162–85, and the discussion in *Nouveau
discours du récit*, 55–99.

47. See also the two-witnesses episode (11:1-13) and the commentary above.

48. Barr, *Tales of the End*, 119–21; Garrow, *Revelation*, 31.

49. For the aorist imperative as punctiliar, see F. Blass and A. Debrunner, *A
Greek Grammar of the New Testament and Other Early Christian Literature,*
trans. Robert W. Funk (Chicago: University of Chicago Press, 1961), 172.

50. Earth dwellers fornicate with the whore of Babylon (17:2); they go to
perdition (17:8). Revelation uses other synonyms to express the earthly domain,
and these too connote opposition to God and/or allegiance to the beast: "the
whole world" (12:9; 13:3; 16:14); "[all] the nations" (11:18; 14:8; 15:4; 18:3, 23;
19:15; 20:3, 8); "peoples and tribes and tongues and nations" (in varying order)
(11:9; 13:7; 17:15); "the kings of the earth" (6:15; 16:14; 17:2, 18).

51. For arguments against a universal soteriological scheme, see Ulrich B.
Müller, *Die Offenbarung des Johannes,* ÖTK zum Neuen Testament 19
(Würzburg: Echter, 1984), 216–17; and J. Webb Mealy, *After the Thousand Years:
Resurrection and Judgment in Revelation 20,* JSNTSup 70 (Sheffield: JSOT
Press, 1992), 228–30. Arguing for a universal inclusion of the nations, see Bauck-
ham, *Climax of Prophecy*, 238–337; Mathias Rissi, *Die Zukunft der Welt: Eine
exegetische Studie über Johannesoffenbarung 19,11 bis 22,15* (Basel: Friedrich
Reinhardt, n.d.), 96–100; Zeit und Geschichte (Zürich: Zwingli, 1952, 59–65);
and G. B. Caird, *A Commentary on the Revelation of St. John the Divine,* Black's
New Testament Commentaries (London: Adam & Charles Black, 1966),
298–301.

52. Kermode, *Sense of an Ending*, 47.

53. Thus, for example, Michael Harris, "The Literary Function of the
Hymns in the Apocalypse" (Ph.D. diss., Southern Baptist Theological Semi-
nary, 1989), and Jörns, *Das hymnsiche Evangelium*, 167–70, who write on the

hymns' narrative function. See also Garrow, *Revelation*, 15–16; Barr, *Tales of the End*, 77.

54. See also 12:10; 15:2-4; and 16:4-7 for other shorter examples.

55. Examples of grammatical structures include the sustained use of result clauses (vv. 3, 5, 7, 8); verses 2-8, 14, 16-17 are instances of parallelism; formulaic expression arises from the culling of these texts from biblical tradition, especially in Ezekiel 27 and Jeremiah 51.

56. Thus, especially, Günther Müller, "Die Bedeutung der Zeit in der Erzählkunst," 247–68; "Erzählzeit und Erzählte Zeit," 269–86; and "Über das Zeitgerüst des Erzählens (Am Beispiel des *Jürg Jenatsch*)," 388–418, in *Morphologische Poetik: Gesammelte Aufsätze,* ed. Elena Müller (Darmstadt: Wissenschaftliche Buchgesellschaft, 1974); Eberhard Lämmert, *Bauformen des Erzählens* (Stuttgart: J. B. Metzlersche Verlag, 1955), 73–94, 192–94; and Erich Auerbach, *Mimesis: The Representation of Reality in Western Literature,* trans. Willard R. Trask (Princeton: Princeton University Press, 1953). In Auerbach, see "The Brown Stocking," 525–53, and the observations on pp. 549–50.

57. See, similarly, Barr, *Tales of the End*, 147–48.

58. Thus William Blake, "Auguries of Innocence": "To see a world in a grain of sand, / And a heaven in a wild flower— / Hold infinity in the palm of your hand, / And eternity in an hour" (ll. 1–4), from *William Blake: A Critical Edition of Major Works,* ed. Michael Mason (Oxford: Oxford University Press, 1988), p. 27.

59. A detailed chronicle of the collapse of the southern wing of the eastern German front, including the slaughter at Tarnopol, can be found in Wolfgang Schumann, ed., *Deutschland im zweiten Weltkrieg,* vol. 5: *Der Zusammenbruch der defensivstrategie des Hitlersfaschismus an allen Fronten (Januar bis August 1944)* (Cologne: Pahl-Rugenstein, 1984), 78–103.

60. For looking into the eyes of the past, see Roland Barthes, *Camera Lucida,* trans. Richard Howard (New York: Noonday, 1981), 1–5.

61. John Berger, "The Suit and the Photograph," in *About Looking* (New York: Vintage, 1980), 31–40.

62. In 1929, Richard Walther Darrè penned a National Socialist manifesto, *Das Bauerntum als Lebensquell der Nordischen Rasse,* 2d ed. (Munich: J. F. Lehmanns: 1933), outlining the ideals of German agrarianism, the relationship of the German "race" to the land, and the need to reverse urbanization and "Proletarianismus" brought on by the Industrial Revolution. He later coined the Nazi slogan "Blood and Soil." For an overview of these concepts, their background, and related works, see Frank-Lothar Kroll, *Utopie als Ideologie: Geschichtsdenken und politisches Handeln im Dritten Reich* (Paderborn, Germany: Ferdinand Schöningh, 1998), 160–97. Readily accessible English introductions can be found in Simon Schama, *Landscape and Memory* (Toronto: Vintage Canada,

1996), 75–134; and Anna Bramwell, *Blood and Soil: Richard Walther Darrè and Hitler's "Green Party"* (Abbotsbrook, England: Kensal, 1985).

6. The Praise of Folly

1.   Elizabeth Cady Stanton, *The Woman's Bible* (New York: European Publishing, 1895–98), 179.

2.   Elizabeth Cady Stanton, "An Expurgated Edition of the Bible," *Free Thought Magazine,* no. 20 (December 1902): 704.

3.   Jack T. Sanders, *Ethics of the New Testament: Change and Development* (Philadelphia: Fortress Press, 1975), 115.

4.   David E. Aune, "The Influence of Roman Imperial Court Ceremonial on the Apocalypse of John," *Papers of the Chicago Society of Biblical Research* 28 (1983): 5–26, here p. 5.

5.   David E. Aune, "The Form and Function of the Proclamations to the Seven Churches (Revelation 2–3)," *NTS* 36 (1990): 182–204.

6.   Sophie Laws, *In the Light of the Lamb: Imagery, Parody, and Theology in the Apocalypse of John* (Wilmintgton, Del.: Michael Glazier, 1988), esp. 41–43.

7.   M. Eugene Boring, *Revelation,* Interpretation (Louisville: John Knox, 1989), 154.

8.   Tina Pippin, *Apocalyptic Bodies: The Biblical End of the World in Text and Image* (New York: Routledge, 1999), 117.

9.   Elisabeth Schüssler Fiorenza, *The Book of Revelation: Justice and Judgement,* 2d ed. (Philadelphia: Fortress Press, 1998), 9, 214.

10. Robert M. Royalty Jr., *The Streets of Heaven: The Ideology of Wealth in the Apocalypse of John* (Macon, Ga.: Mercer University Press, 1998).

11. Stephen D. Moore, "The Beatific Vision as a Posing Exhibition: Revelation's Hypermasculine Deity," *JSNT* 60 (1995): 27–55; see also idem, *God's Gym: Divine Male Bodies of the Bible* (New York: Routledge, 1996). Moore builds on the imperial titles of praise cited by Dominique Cuss, *Imperial Cult and Honorary Terms in the New Testament,* Paradosis 23 (Fribourg, Switzerland: University Press Fribourg, 1974); and the numismatic study of Ernest P. Janzen, "The Jesus of the Apocalypse Wears the Emperor's Clothes," *SBL Seminar Papers* 130 (1994): 637–61.

12. Friedrich Nietzsche, *The Birth of Tragedy and the Genealogy of Morals,* trans. Francis Golffing (Garden City, N.Y.: Doubleday, 1956), 185.

13. Laws, *In the Light of the Lamb,* 77.

14. Cited in D. C. Muecke, *The Compass of Irony* (London: Methuen, 1969), 198, without reference.

15. Anaximenes, *Rhet.* 21, 1: *Eironeia de esti legein ti mē prospoioumenon*

legein ē tois enantiois onomsi ta pragmata prosagoreuein ("Irony is saying what one pretends not to say or naming things by using opposite terms").

16. Theophrastus, *Characters* 1.

17. Aristotle, *Eudemian Ethics* 4.1221a.6; *Nicomachean Ethics* 13.1127a.22; 13.1127b.22; 7.1108a.21.

18. For example, *Gorg.* 489e; *Statesman* 1.337a; *Apol.* 38a. Plato also uses the term to describe dissembling in *Soph.* 268a; *Crat.* 384a; *Euthyd.* 302b.

19. Muecke, *Compass of Irony*, 42.

20. Quintillian 8.6.1, for irony generally; the situational is implicit when he remarks that irony "is made evident to the understanding either by the delivery, the character of the speaker or the nature of the subject. For if any one of these three is out of keeping with the words, it at once becomes clear that the intention of the speaker is other than what he actually says" (8.6.54; *The Institutio Oratoria of Quintillian*, Butler [LCL]). His reference to "the nature of the subject" broadens the verbal into the situational.

21. Thus Wiard Propkes, "Die Funktion der Sendschreiben in der Johannes-Apokalypse: Zugleich ein Beitrag zur Spätgeschichte der neutestamentlichen Gleichnisse," *ZNW* 74 (1983): 90–107.

22. Linda Hutcheon, *Irony's Edge: The Theory and Politics of Irony* (New York: Routledge, 1995), 52.

23. Franz Sauter, *Der römische Kaiserkult bei Martial und Statius* (Stuttgart and Berlin: W. Kohlhammer, 1934), remains the best sourcebook for the abundant parallels. See also Andreas Alföldi, *Die monarchische Repräsentation im römischen Kaiserreiche* (Darmstadt: Wissentschaftliche Buchgesellschaft, 1970), 1–118; Theodor Mommsen, *Römisches Staatsrecht*, 3d ed. (Leipzig: S. Hirzel, 1887), 1:355–79; David E. Aune, *Revelation 1–5*, Word Biblical Commentary (Dallas: Word, 1997), 1:287–314; and Aune, "Influence," 5–26. Both of Aune's writings remain the best studies for exploring Revelation's parallels with imperial politics.

24. The thunderbolt and lightning are Jupiter's emblems; see Statius (*Silv.* 1.praef.; 4.4.58) and Martial (6.10; 7.56; 14.1) for Domitian as *Iuppiter Noster* and *Tonans Noster*. For numismatic evidence of the Jovian thunderbolt applied to Domitian, see H. Mattingly and R. A. G. Carson, *Coins of the Roman Empire in the British Museum*, 6 vols. (London: Trustees of the British Museum, 1976), 2:381, no. 381; 389, no. 410; 399, no. 443. For Jovian theology and the cult of the emperor under the Flavians, see J. Rufus Fears, Princeps a diis electus: *The Divine Election of the Emperor as a Political Concept at Rome*, Papers and Monographs of the American Academy in Rome 26 (Rome: American Academy in Rome, 1977), 220–22; idem., "The Cult of Jupiter and Roman Imperial Ideology," *ANRW* 2/17.1 (1981): 3–141, here 79; K. Scott, *The Imperial Cult under the Flavians* (Stuttgart: Kohlhammer, 1936). For ancient associations of

Roman rulers with Jupiter, see Lily Ross Taylor, *The Divinity of the Roman Emperor,* Philological Monographs 1 (Middleton, Conn.: American Philological Association, 1931), 44–57. For the Apocalypse's uses of political language reserved for the praise of emperors, see Cuss, *Imperial Cult,* 53–88, as well as Sauter's more thorough study of honorific titles in imperial-court ideology, *Kaiserkult,* though without direct reference to Revelation.

25. Simon Price, "From Noble Funerals to Divine Cult: The Consecration of Roman Emperors," in *Rituals of Royalty: Power and Ceremonial in Traditional Societies,* ed. David Cannadine and Simon Price (Cambridge: Cambridge University Press, 1987), 56–105, here 82–91. Seneca's *Apocolocyntosis* as well as Lucian's *Council of the Gods, Icaromennipus,* and *Nero* indicate the linking of political merit and apotheosis throughout the period contemporary with the Apocalypse.

26. Thus, Suetonius, *Domitian* 13.2; Dio Cassius 67.4.7; 67.13.4; Martial *Epigr.* 5.5, 8; 7.2, 5, 34; 8.2, 82; 9.2, 66. The references from Martial, Domitian's contemporary, reveal how much Thompson, *Apocalypse,* 97–101, overstates the case that representations of Domitian as Lord and God reflect anti-Flavian propaganda under Trajan; see the discussion of Aune, *Revelation,* 1:310–11, 316–17, and the fuller citations of P. Touilleux, *L'Apocalypse et les cultes de Domitien et de Cybele* (Paris: Librairie Orientaliste Paul Geunther, 1935), 100–103. See also Sauter, *Kaiserkult,* 105–16, where he offers an excursus on *sanctus* as a title of imperial adulation.

27. Thus, Friedrich Spitta, "Christus das Lamm," in *Streitfragen der Geschichte Jesus* (Göttingen: Vandenhoeck & Ruprecht, 1907), 172–223; R. H. Charles, *A Critical and Exegetical Commentary on the Revelation of St. John,* The International Commentary (Edinburgh: T. & T. Clark, 1920), 1:141; Ernst Lohmeyer, *Die Offenbarung Johannes,* HNT 16 (Tübingen: J. C. B. Mohr, 1953), 51–55; Robert H. Mounce, *The Book of Revelation,* NICNT (Grand Rapids: Eerdmans, 1977), 145; Etienne Trocmé, "Lamb of God," in *The Oxford Companion to the Bible,* ed. Bruce M. Metzger and Michael D. Coogan (New York: Oxford University Press, 1993), 418–19; Bruce J. Malina, *On the Genre and Message of Revelation: Star Visions and Sky Journeys* (Peabody, Mass.: Hendrickson, 1995), 101.

28. For discussion, see C. Burchard, "Das Lamm in der Waagschale," *ZNW* 57 (1966): 219–28; and N. Hohnjec, *"Das Lamm—to arnion" in der Offenbarung Johannes* (Rome: Herder, 1980).

29. Laws, *In the Light of the Lamb,* 27–28.

30. Thus, Loren H. Johns, "The Lamb in the Rhetorical Program of the Apocalypse of John," *SBL Seminar Papers* 134 (1998): 762–84.

31. Similarly, Joachim Jeremias, *"amnos, arēn, arnion,"* *TDNT* 1:338–41; Traugott Holtz, "Die Christologie der Apokalypse des Johannes," *Texte und*

Untersuchungen, 2d ser., 85 (1971): 48–50; Aune, *Revelation,* 1:353; Johns, "Rhetorical Program," 778–79; David L. Barr, *Tales of the End: A Narrative Commentary on the Book of Revelation* (Santa Rosa, Calif.: Polebridge, 1998), 69–70.

32. Muecke, *Compass of Irony,* 92–93.

33. Linda Hutcheon, *Splitting Images: Contemporary Canadian Ironies* (Toronto: Oxford University Press, 1991), 8.

34. Adela Yarbro Collins, *The Combat Myth in the Book of Revelation,* HDR 9 (Missoula, Mont.: Scholars Press, 1976). Her study builds on earlier treatments: A. Dietrich, *Abraxas: Studien zur Religionsgeschichte des späteren Altertums* (Leipzig: Teubner, 1891), 111–26; H. Gunkel, *Schöpfung und Chaos in Urzeit und Endzeit: Eine religionsgeschichtliche Untersuchung über Gen 1 und Ap Joh 12* (Göttingen: Vandenhoeck & Ruprecht, 1895); W. Bousset, *Die Offenbarung Johannis* (Göttingen: Vandenhoeck & Ruprecht, 1906), 351–56. Independently, the following argue similarly: A. Vögtle, "Mythos und Botschaft in Apokalypse 12," in *Tradition und Glaube: Das frühe Christentum in seiner Umwelt (Festschrift K. G. Kuhn),* ed. G. Jeremias, H.-W. Kuhn, and H. Stegemann (Göttingen: Vandenhoeck & Ruprecht, 1971), 395–415; H. Gollinger, *Das "grosse Zeichen" von Apokalypse 12,* SBM 11 (Würzburg and Stuttgart: Echter Verlag, 1971), 127–33; H. D. Saffrey, "Relire l'Apocalypse à Patmos," *Revue biblique* 82 (1975): 385–417; J. Fontenrose, *Python: A Study of Delphic Myth and Its Origins* (Berkeley: University of California Press, 1980), 46–69; R. Bergmeier, "Altes und Neues zur 'Sonnenfrau am Himmel' (Apk 12)," *ZNW* 73 (1982): 97–109.

35. See similarly Jan Willem van Henten, "Dragon Myth and Imperial Ideology in Revelation 12–13," *SBL Seminar Papers* 130 (1994): 496–515, here 508–9.

36. See Klaus Wengst, *Pax Romana and the Peace of Jesus Christ,* trans. John Bowden (London: SCM, 1987), 19–26, for discussion and literature.

37. Thus, van Henten, "Dragon Myth," 512. See also J. Rufus Fears, "The Theology of Victory at Rome: Approaches and Problems," *ANRW* II 17/2 (1981): 736–826, here 816–18; and idem, "Cult of Jupiter," 79, with particular reference to the depiction on Trajan's column as Jupiter defeating the Dacians.

38. Thus, *Octavia* 237–41; Dio Chrysostom *Or.* 1 contrast the benevolent reign of "order" (*eunomia*), "peace" (*eirēnē*), and "law" (*nomos*) under Heracles, the first son of Zeus (1.67–84), allegorically representing "kingship" (*basileia*) with its home on the royal peak sacred to Zeus, and "tyranny" (*tyrannis*) with its house on a peak named after Typhon.

39. For Seth-Typhon as red animal or those associated with it as red, see Fontenrose, *Python,* 81; and Jan Willem van Henten, "Antiochus IV as a Typhonic Figure in Daniel 7," in *The Book of Daniel in the Light of New Findings,* ed. A. S. van der Woude, BETL 106 (Louvain: Peeters, 1993), 228–38, here 236–38.

40. For the eagle in imperial propaganda, see O. Keller, *Thiere des classischen Altertums in culturgeschichtliche Beziehung* (Innsbruck, 1887), 236–76; and Fears, *Divine Election*, 115. For the use of the eagle as symbol of apotheosis, see Taylor, *Divinity of the Roman Emperor*, 165. See Dio 4.2–5.5 for the apotheosis ritual of the emperor Pertinax (5.5 for an eagle released from Pertinax's funeral pyre). For Domitian's celebration of Jupiter's protection of him during his war with the Chatti—he issued coins of an eagle standing on a thunderbolt—see Fears, *Divine Election*, 195; and Mattingly, *Coins of the Roman Empire*, vol. 2: nn. 51–53. The eagle also has associations with the exodus tradition (Exod. 19:4).

41. For thunder and lightning machines in the first and second centuries, their possible use in imperial Jovian ideology, and their relation to Rev. 13:13-15, see Steven J. Scherrer, "Signs and Wonders in the Imperial Cult: A New Look at a Roman Religious Institution in the Light of Rev 13:13-15," *JBL* 103 (1984): 599–610.

42. In depicting Roman authority as *Babylonian* tyranny, John was not only investing his Apocalypse with Older Testament narratives of liberation from exile. His depiction of the whore of Babylon in Oriental finery imitates pervasive Greek and Roman satire and philosophical criticism of Oriental luxury—thus, for example, Livy 34.4; 39.6–7; Polybius 31.25; Vellus, *Hist.* 2.1.1; Sallust, *Cat.* 10.1–13.5; Juvenal, *Sat.* 3.180–81; 6.290–97, 457-59, 501-9. See A. Alföldi, *Monarchische Repräsentation*, 9–25, for the influence of Persian costume on Roman imperial insignia. The descriptions also echo Older Testament treatment (2 Kings 9:30-31; Prov. 7:10-20; Isa. 3:16—4:1; Jer. 4:30; Ezek. 16:15-18; 23:1-10, 11-19, 26-27 ; Hosea 2:13).

43. Thus, for example, *Sib. Or.* 3.350-80; 4.145-48; 5.155-78.

44. Aristides, *Eulogy of Rome* 11.

45. Thus, S. R. F. Price, *Rituals and Power: The Roman Imperial Cult in Asia Minor* (Cambridge: Cambridge University Press, 1984); S. Friesen, *Twice Neokoros: Ephesus, Asia, and the Cult of the Flavian Imperial Family,* Religions in the Greco-Roman World 116 (Leiden: Brill, 1993); Arnoldo Momigliano, "How Roman Emperors Became Gods," *The American Scholar* 55 (1986): 181–93. David Magie, *Roman Rule in Asia Minor to the End of the Third Century after Christ* (Princeton: Princeton University Press, 1950), remains a solid introduction to the economic and sociopolitical backdrop of the imperial cult in Asia Minor.

46. Richard Bauckham, *The Climax of Prophecy: Studies on the Book of Revelation* (Edinburgh: T. & T. Clark, 1998), 338–83; J. Nelson Kraybill, *Imperial Cult and Commerce in John's Apocalypse,* JSNTSup 132 (Sheffield: Sheffield Academic Press, 1996); also, Heinz Geisen, "Das römische Reich im Spiegel der Johannes-Apokalypse," *ANRW* 2/26.3 (1996): 2502–614, here 2503–22.

47. For inscriptions and discussion, see Philip A. Harland, *Claiming a Place in Polis and Empire: The Significance of Imperial Cults and Connections*

among Associations, Synagogues, and Christian Groups in Roman Asia (27 B.C.E.–138 C.E.) (Ann Arbor, Mich.: UMI Dissertation Services, 2001), 121–93; with direct reference to Revelation, see pp. 243–313.

48. Petronius, *Satyricon* 119.1–36.

49. Royalty, *Streets of Heaven,* 211–40.

50. Linda Hutcheon, *A Theory of Parody: The Teachings of Twentieth-Century Art Forms* (New York: Routledge, 1991), 6, 7.

51. See, for example, Quintillian 9.2.35: parody as "a name drawn from songs sung in imitation of others, but employed by an abuse of language to designate imitation in verse or prose."

52. Lucian's Menippean satires and treatises—for example, *The Downward Journey; Menippus; Council of the Gods; Zeus Catechized; Icaromenippus*—include ridiculing exposés of ideas, gestures, mock performances, dialogues, otherworldly journeys, reversals of fortune, and debates, as does Seneca's parody *Apocolocyntosis divi Claudii* (The pumpkinificaton of the divine Claudius). For the Mennipean, see Joel C. Relhan, *Ancient Menippean Satire* (Baltimore: Johns Hopkins University Press, 1993); H. K. Riikonen, *Menippean Satire as a Literary Genre with Special Reference to Seneca's "Apocolocyntosis,"* Commentarius humanarum litterarum 83 (Helsinki: Finnish Society of Sciences and Letters, 1987); Mikhail Bakhtin, *Problems of Dostoevsky's Poetics,* ed. and trans. Caryl Emerson, Theory and History of Literature 8 (Minneapolis: University of Minnesota Press, 1984), 101–80; and Northrop Frye, *Anatomy of Criticism: Four Essays* (Princeton: Princeton University Press, 1973), 309–14.

53. Hutcheon, *Theory of Parody,* 11.

54. Linda Hutcheon, *The Politics of Post-Modernism* (New York: Routledge, 1989), 101 (my emphasis).

55. Linda Hutcheon, *Irony's Edge: The Theory and Politics of Irony* (New York: Routledge, 1994), 64.

56. Hutcheon, *Theory of Parody,* 20.

57. Hutcheon, *Irony's Edge,* 64.

58. Hutcheon, *Theory of Parody,* 16.

59. Bakhtin, *Problems of Dostoevsky's Poetics,* 127.

60. Mary Louis Pratt, "Arts of the Contact Zone," *Profession (MLA)* (1991): 33–40, here 34.

61. Felipe Guamanan Poma de Ayala, "El primer nueva corónica y buen gobierno," *Siglo* (Mexico) 21 (1980), an issue edited by John Murra and Rolena Adorno.

62. Royalty, *Streets of Heaven,* 71, and more generally, 39–80.

63. Ibid., 246.

64. Kraybill, *Imperial Cult,* 72 78.

65. Thus, "faithful and true," and possessing eyes "like a flame of fire," 19:11,

12; foreshadowed by 1:14; 2:18; 3:7, 14; ruling with a "rod of iron," 19:15; 2:27; the two-edged sword, 19:15, 21; 1:15; 2:16.

66. Thus, Exod. 14:4, 14, 18; 15:1-18; 17:14-16; Num. 21:14-15; Deut. 7:16-26; 9:4-7; 20:10-18; 33:27-28; Josh. 1:1-18; 3:7-13; chapters 6–7; 10:14, 42; 11:6; Judges 5; 1 Sam. 14:23; 2 Sam. 5:17-25; Psalm 68; 78:53-55; Isa. 26:16—27:6; 52:7-12; 59:15-20; 63:1-6; Amos 2:9; Habakkuk 3; Zech. 14:1-21. For the Older Testament and Yahweh and/or Israel engaging in holy war, see Gerhard von Rad, *Der heilige Krieg im alten Israel* (Göttingen: Vandenhoeck & Ruprecht, 1958); and P. D. Miller Jr., *The Divine Warrior in Early Israel* (Cambridge: Harvard University Press, 1973).

67. Thus, 19:18: "kings, . . . captains, . . . mighty men, . . . all men, both free and slave, both small and great"; 6:15: "kings of the earth and the great men and the generals and the rich and the strong, and every one, slave and free. . . ."

68. Schüssler Fiorenza, *Revelation*, 215–26, here 218.

69. Thus, E. B. Allo, *L'Apocalypse du Saint John* (Paris: Gabalda, 1933), 304–5; Aune, *Revelation*, 3:1057.

70. Thus, Isa. 11:4; Ps. 2:9. See Deut. 32:41; Isa. 34:5-6; Jer. 12:12; 47:6; Ezek. 21:3-5; 30:24; 32:10; Zech. 13:7; Ps. 17:13; 1 Chron. 21:12.

71. Thus, Mitchell G. Reddish, "Martyr Christology in the Apocalypse," *JSNT* 33 (1988): 85–95, here 87.

72. W. Klassen, "Jesus and Phinehas: A Rejected Role Model," *SBL Seminar Papers* (1986): 490–500. See further idem, "Vengeance in the Apocalypse," *CBQ* 28 (1966): 300–311; and idem, "War in the NT," *ABD* 6:867-75.

73. See, for example, *4 Macc.* 16.14-15.

74. Thus, *4 Macc.* 17.22; 18.14; 1QS8.10.

75. For the political image of the rider on a white horse as military "savior" delivering his followers from adversity, see S. I. Johnston, "Riders in the Sky: Cavalier Gods and Theurgic Salvation in the Second Century," *Classical Philology* 87 (1992): 303–21; for the use of horses in military triumph, see Plutarch, *Aem.* 34.4.

76. For political victors as crowned, see 1 Macc. 11:13 and Josephus, *Jewish War* 13.113 (Ptolemy VI in triumphal procession enters Antioch with two diadems). Dio Chrysostom, *Or.* 1.78–82, represents Tyranny allegorically as bearing many diadems and scepters; see also Diodorus Siculus 1.47.5.

77. For a statue of Zeus with an inscription on its thigh, see Pausanias 5.27.12; further, Cicero, *Verrine Orations* 4.43.

78. For prodigies of heavenly armies in pagan battles or times of political crisis, see Pliny, *Hist. nat.* 2.58.148; Josephus, *Jewish War* 6.288; Tacitus, *Hist.* 5.13; as well as the excursus on prodigies in Aune, *Revelation*, 2:416-19. For armies dressed in luxurious clothing for the *adventus* of Antiochus IV, see Polybius 30.25.

79. For red as imperial military costume, see Herodian 2.8.6; Mommsen, *Römisches Staatsrecht,* 1:433.

80. For the Roman *adventus* ceremony modeled on Roman triumphs, see S. MacCormack, "Change and Continuity in Late Antiquity: The Ceremony of Adventus," *Historia* 21 (1972): 721–52; and Alföldi, *Monarchische Repräsentation,* 93–100. For white horses associated with apotheosis, see the comments of Aune, *Revelation,* 3:1051, in which he cites texts. See also P. J. Alexander, "Letters and Speeches of the Emperor Hadrian," *Harvard Studies in Classical Philology* 49 (1938): 141–77, as well as the commentary (143) of *PGiess 3* (117 C.E.), a text celebrating the deification of Trajan and his proclamation from a chariot of white horses of Hadrian as his successor.

81. Booth, *Rhetoric of Irony,* 240–41.

82. For full bibliography of studies and commentary, see Aune, *Revelation,* 3:1133–90.

83. Thus, for example, Edith MacEwan Humphrey, *The Ladies and the Cities: Transformation and Apocalyptic Identity in "Joseph and Asenath," 4 Ezra, the Apocalypse, and the "Shepherd of Hermas,"* Journal for the Study of the Pseudepigrapha: Supplement Series 17 (Sheffield: Sheffield Academic Press, 1995), 103–11; Robert H. Gundry, "The New Jerusalem: People as Place, Not Place for People," *Novum Testamentum* 29 (1987): 254–64; W. Thüsing, "Die Vision des 'Neuen Jerusalem' (Apk 21, 1–22, 5) als Verheissung und Gottesverkündigung," *TTZ* (1968): 17–34.

84. See Klaus Wengst, "Babylon the Great and the New Jerusalem: The Visionary View of Political Reality in the Revelation of John," in *Politics and Theopolitics in the Bible and Postbiblical Literature,* ed. Henning Graf Reventlow, Yair Hoffman, and Benjamin Uffenheimer, JSOTSup 171 (Sheffield: JSOT Press, 1994), 189–202; idem, *Pax Romana,* 129–31; Dieter Georgi, "Die Visionen vom himmlischen Jerusalem im Apok 21 und 22," in *Kirche: Festschrift Günther Bornkamm,* ed. Dieter Luhrmann and Georg Strecker (Tübingen: Mohr, 1980), 351–72; J. Comblin, *Théologie de la Ville* (Louvain and Paris: Éditions universitaires, 1968), esp. 191–230; and Unyong Sim, *Das himmlische Jerusalem in Apk. 21,1–22,5 im Kontext biblisch-jüdischen Tradition und antiken Stadtbaus,* Bochumer Altertumswissenschaftlichen Colloquium 25 (Trier, Germany: Wissentschaft- lichen Verlag, 1996), 50–61.

85. Wengst, *Pax Romana,* 131.

86. Lucian, *Vera historia* 2.11–13 (Harmon, LCL).

87. H. Rabe, *Scholia in Lucianum* (Stuttgart: Teubner, 1971), 21 (Schol. 14 on *Ver. hist.* 2.11).

88. For a general survey of ancient civic ideals, see Mason Hammond, *The City in the Ancient World,* Harvard Studies in Urban History (Cambridge:

Harvard University Press, 1972), especially the annotated bibliography of contemporary studies (468–529).

89. For the relation of ethics, aesthetics, and utopian urban thinking in antiquity, see Alexander Demandt, *Der Idealstaat: Die politischen Theorien der Antike*, 3d ed. (Cologne: Böhlau Verlag, 2000).

90. Dio Chrysostom, *Orat.* 32.37 (cited by Royalty, *Streets of Heaven*, 217–18).

91. Aristotle, *Pol.* 1253a.3; 1278b.19.

92. Ibid., 1284b.6–7.

93. Thus Zeno in Plutarch, *Alex. fort. virt.* 1.6, 2.329b (Babbitt, LCL); *Stoic. rep.* 2, 2.1033b; Chryssipus in Joannes von Arnim, *Stoicorum veterum fragmenta*, 4 vols. (Leipzig: Teubner, 1921–24), 3.174, 26ff.; for commentary, see Hermann Strathmann, *TWNT* 6:520–21, s.v. *"polis."*

94. See Horace's *Carmen saeculare* for a depiction of Rome as a divinely constituted political utopia. See also Cicero, *De natura deorum* 3.2.5; Ovid, *Fasti* 4.759–60. For fuller discussion with references, see Lidia Storoni Mazzolani, *The Idea of the City in Roman Thought: From Walled City to Spiritual Commonwealth*, trans. S. O'Donnell (London: Hollis & Carter, 1970).

95. For suspicion of emperors, see Cicero's comments on Alexander the Great's abuses of power in *Resp.* 3.9.15; *De offic.* 1.26.90.

96. Thus, *Res gestae divi Augusti* 1.1; 6.34.

97. For further discussion of Virgil's and his contemporaries' political ideology, see Douglas Little, "Politics in Augustan Poetry," *ANRW* 2/30.1 (1982): 255–370; for the ending of the *Aeneid*, see pp. 271–73.

98. For Alexander as vice-regent of Jupiter, see Fears, *Divine Election*, 57–60.

99. For *Roma quadrata*, see Dionysius of Halicarnassus, *Ant. rom.* 2.65.3; Plutarch, *Romulus* 9.4; and the discussion of W. Müller, *Die heilige Stadt: Roma quadrata, himmlisches Jerusalem, und die Mythe vom Weltnabel* (Stuttgart: Kohlhammer, 1961), 9–52.

100. Thus, Georgi, "Visionen," 364, 369; Comblin, *Théologie de la Ville*, 206.

101. See also Horace, *Carmina* 4.5.1. For utopias, see PW 14.2.628–32, s.v. *"Makaron nesos"*; Homer, *Od.* 4.561–68; 6.43–46; Hesiod, *Op.* 168–74; *Theog.* 215, 230–37; Aune, *Revelation*, 3:1191–94.

102. For loyalties, elites, and competition among Asia Minor cities in the early empire, see Friesen, *Twice Neokoros*; Magie, *Roman Rule in Asia Minor*.

103. Bertram Stubenrauch, "Endzeit statt Weltuntergang: Christliche Eschatologie Heute," in *Jüngste Tage: Die Gegenwart der Apokalyptik*, ed. Michael N. Ebertz and Reinhold Zwick (Freiberg, Germany: Herder, 1999), 360–78.

104. Emmanuel Lévinas, "A Man-God?" in *Entre nous: On Thinking-of-the-Other*, trans. Michael B. Smith and Barbara Harshav (New York: Columbia University Press, 1998), 56.

7. Remembering Apocalypse

1. John Howard Yoder, *The Politics of Jesus* (Grand Rapids: Eerdmans, 1972), 248.

2. Jacques Ellul, *The Subversion of Christianity,* trans. Geoffrey W. Bromiley (Grand Rapids: Eerdmans, 1986), 113–36.

3. Smaro Kamboureli, *In the Second Person* (Edmonton, Alberta: Longspoon Press, 1985), 8.

4. For "house of being," see Martin Heidegger, *On the Way to Language,* trans. Peter Hertz (New York: Harper & Row, 1971), 22.

5. Richard Rorty, *Contingency, Irony, and Solidarity* (Cambridge: Cambridge University Press, 1994), 186. Emphasis mine.

6. Ibid., 195.

7. Dietrich Bonhoeffer, *Widerstand und Ergebung: Briefe und Aufzeichnungen aus der Haft,* ed. Christian Gemmels, Eberhard Bethge, and Renate Bethge, Dietrich Bonhoeffer Werke 8 (Gütersloh: Chr. Kaiser, 1998), 541.

8. Thus ibid., 357: "christliche aber antiklerikale Weltlichkeit."

9. Ibid., 226: "Wir leben im Vorletzten und glauben das Letzte . . ." ("We live in the Penultimate and believe the Ultimate . . ."); also, Dietrich Bonhoeffer, *Ethik,* ed. Ilse Tödt et al., Dietrich Bonhoeffer Werke 6 (Gütersloh: Chr. Kaiser, 1998), 137–217.

10. For the Christian Church as "Mundhaus," see Martin Luther (*WA* 10.1.2, 48, line 5; ET = John Nicholas Lenker, ed. and trans., *Sermons of Martin Luther,* vol. 1: *Sermons on the Gospel Texts for Advent, Christmas, and Epiphany* [Grand Rapids: Baker Book House, 1988], 64), in which Luther, preaching on Matt. 21:1–9, commenting on the meaning of the place-name "Bethphage" (v. 1), writes, "Therefore the church is a mouth-house, not a pen-house, for since Christ's advent that Gospel is preached orally, which was before hidden in written books."

11. Douglas John Hall, *Confessing the Faith: Christian Theology in a North American Context* (Minneapolis: Fortress Press, 1996), 201–342.

12. "On the open road to Galilee" is how Elisabeth Schüssler Fiorenza describes the living out of God's *basileia* (kingdom/realm/commonweal/dominion) initiated in God's raising of Jesus from the dead, as announced first to Jesus' female disciples in Mark 16:1-8 and Matt. 28:1-10 (*Jesus; Miriam's Child, Sophia's Prophet: Critical Issues in Feminist Christology* [New York: Continuum, 1995], 187–90). Schüssler Fiorenza argues compellingly that these stories reflect a tradition in which Jesus does not ascend to heaven, but remains alive in the midst of communities who live out God's commonweal. "Galilee" here means the daily, routine, this-worldly, and politically charged realities that define our lives.

13. Julia Esquivel, *Threatened with Resurrection,* trans. Anne Woehrle (Elgin, Ill.: Brethren Press, 1994), 63–65. Excerpted from "They Have Threatened Us with Resurrection," by Julia Esquivel. From *Threatened with Resurrection,* © 1982, 1994 Brethren Press, Elgin, Illinois. Used by permission.

14. Emmanuel Lévinas, "A Man-God?" in *Entre nous: On Thinking-of-the-Other,* trans. Michael B. Smith and Barbara Harshav (New York: Columbia University Press, 1998), 55, translation revised.

Index of Names and Subjects